BACKSTORY

The Many Lives of
Granville Johnson

 FriesenPress

One Printers Way
Altona, MB R0G 0B0
Canada

www.friesenpress.com

ISBN
978-1-03-918412-1 (Hardcover)
978-1-03-918411-4 (Paperback)
978-1-03-918413-8 (eBook)

1. BIOGRAPHY & AUTOBIOGRAPHY, PERSONAL MEMOIRS

Distributed to the trade by The Ingram Book Company

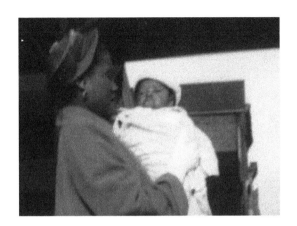

Ines Andrea . . . Granville Johnson

I knew of death long before life graced my world.
-Granville Johnson

My muse, without whose support
Backstory would never have been told.

Granville Johnson, Age Three

Introduction

· · · · ·

I AM A survivor of long-term sexual and physical abuse. Survival is the theme of this novel.

I was born and raised in the mean streets of Chicago's Westside Black ghetto. I am a two-tour Vietnam veteran (1967 through 1968).

I served as a combat medical corpsman, and I died during the 1968 Tet Offensive from a traumatic brain injury.

I have lived with vascular dementia since 2011—a long-term effect of traumatic brain injury. I also live with Converted Disorder, a brain disorder, as a result of repeated trauma throughout my life.

Backstory is my autobiography. I have fictionalized parts of it, and changed names, dates, locales, timelines, and characters for dramatic effect. There are spaces within my story, as there are spaces within my remaining life memories.

Warning: My story is esoteric. My story is unreservedly violent. My story is erotic, at times sexually explicit. Through first-hand experience, incestual rape, non-consensual and consensual seduction, of a minor is portrayed, depicting the point of view of the aggressor as well as that of the victim and its aftermath. For only by sharing the unvarnished truth of those experiences, and others, can I share with you, the reader, the depth of the wisdom gleaned through the living of them.

My story is a good read. It is not an easy read.

There is much within these vignettes to be explored in thought and emotion. What have been told here, in a sense, are the highlights and lowlights of what my dementia-fogged awareness has afforded my memory within my current consciousness.

Fiction is the story, and within the story is a message about how the seeds of abuse are planted, fed, and grown over time. Yet here, I tell no lies and sugar-coat no truth. I express, as best I can, the core truths and reality of what has been my life as it unfolded.

Table of Contents

. . . . .

Prologue One

In the beginning,

I was evolving in my mother's womb, seven months on, when my
father died.

Rage, fear, terror, hate, sorrow, horror, grief, comprehension, gave way
to resolve, determination, acceptance.

Throughout, in Hell, I roiled, kicked, twisted in the fluid wind.

Dragon's breath, hurricane boiling within.

His essence of spirited, heart of love passed through. Mainline, undi-
luted, held thus stuck.

So, was he thoroughly misguided? I'm sure. Hindsight is great for that.

True to his honour, superstitious to the bone. Mistrusted doctor's lies.

Feared cameras would steal his soul.

When doctors finished carving the body. Cameras would finish the
left-over scraps. The Devil be damned, glad to claim the rest.

Father was honourable, true to his word and world. Walked his talk as
he talked his walk.

Steered clear of both when saving his life-force,

In danger of passing on, long before his time became mine. After his life,
and before my birth.

We met in Mom's womb-verse. We chatted father to son,

Dad's spirit cradled and cuddled his only living legacy, his bond, his son.

Stroked my eyes, soothed my troubled brow, amidst Mom's turbulent sea.

Whispered softly, deep within my fretful
slumbering . . . Honourable above all, honour above, all.

I am now the only one to carry his banner, yet his legacy lives on. The gift of truth is a heavy burden, carried by the wise.

Honour is a priceless dream. Its piper demands are without peer. The eternal price of honour is self-sacrifice for whoever's most dear.

Mom's love child, conceived in love with the love of her life. Born of life, born in death throes.

Life and death laced with self-sacrifice, karma's the choice.

Made to protect and preserve the love, sacrifice to live the life deserved.

Granville Johnson, Age Five

Stand for your mother . . .!

Stand for your sister . . .!

Stand for your brothers . . .!

Lay down for the cousin who raped you last night. He will rape once more tomorrow . . .

Again, you will lay . . . still . . . quiet . . . the pain somehow soothing . . .

The rage of invasion . . . the touch soft/hard . . . malignant reek.

To protect all of the above . . . gifted child did endure

Stillness endured . . . silence . . . the theft of body sans soul . . .

Price of self given to savage a non-life shackled by fear.

Predators within and without . . .

Smiles all about.

Trust be ruinous . . . faith tenuous . . . living death a certainty.

Tarnished . . . damaged beyond worth.

I have done terrible wrongs in fear, hate, and loathing.

Symphony orchestra of wrongdoing . . . slime and shame.

My demons kept time, the refrain and chorus . . . I, only I, the verse.

Shame eternal in memory forgotten . . . yet forgiven not.

Make right the wrong at what cost be your home. Your life and all around you abide still.

What price will I pay . . . What price will I pay?

"I Am an Honourable Man" (Excerpt) by Granville Johnson

Prologue Two

. . . . .

RAPE, WHETHER IT occurs once in your life or multiple times, as it did throughout Granville's adolescence and teenage years, becomes a defining event that perpetuates its insidious influence for the remaining years of breath and growth. All that you are, all you will ever become, is altered by that violation of body and soul.

Rape obliterates all sense of self. Rape destroys your consciousness, taints your personality, perverts any hopes and dreams that precede it.

Rape strips your ability to experience the fulfillment, intimacy, and joy of physical contact.

A hollow imitation of life remains; a forever hunger for wholeness that can never be sated. Life itself is perverted. The guilt of the damaged becomes unworthy of true affection or love.

Familiar rape exacerbates the horror, for it takes place in the home, where nature, nurture, and protection are a given. Betrayal by those claiming to love as family opens the door for strangers to repeat the rape and the rendering of hope and dreams, as they claim to love you only to devour your soul as they rape and rend your mind and body.

Rape of a juvenile by an older woman, often characterized by elaborate, subtle seduction as part of the grooming process, is frequently thought, by society, to be a coming-of-age experience for the male child and, therefore, less an invasion and perversion of the victim; rather, it is considered part of an early sexual education, a "Mrs. Robinson" experience.

Rape is rape. The sex and age of the participants is irrelevant. The effect, both in the short and long term, is the same: insidious and equally damaging.

Being a sexual object, an ever-ready sex toy to abuse and discard when the fun runs out, is all you can be worthy of.

Worthless . . . hopeless . . . without forgiveness; Granville's future obsesses in ever trying to rid himself of the sense of being "only good enough to be fucked and to suck . . . fucked 'n' suck . . . fucked 'n' suck!"

On the block, in the ghetto, the obscene betrayal of familiar rape was a common perversion in the desolation of the familiar bond, occurring in secret, in silence, and in loud cries for help unheard. Never spoken, seldom revealed for contemplation or intervention.

Yet abuse survivors can be drawn together, recognizing in each other the struggle to find and be themselves; their common ground; a sense of not being alone in this non-human land; their mutual bond; and a life preserver in a quicksand sea.

A sexual abuse survivor wears a badge of honour and courage in unending fear. Yet, living within that awareness of what was done to you does not define you, even though it may have been a watershed, life-changing experience that helped make you the beautiful human being— an example of true humanity—that you have become.

Granville Johnson, Grade One

CHAPTER ONE:
The Kid's Just Weird

· · · · ·

GRANVILLE WAS IN love. Well, as much as a first grader in elementary school could be; it was more like an intense, very intense, like. Emma was coal black of race and colour. A deep, dark round face with brilliant sparkling blue eyes and sunrise-white teeth that smiled through her thick, full-lipped expression each time, gracing Granville's presence from her desk next to his.

She liked him as well, and it often touched her heart when Granville would respond quickly to almost any question that their teacher would pose. Their hands would spring into the air simultaneously, punching the electric atmosphere above them, rockets to the moon, each wanting to be the first to be chosen.

Mrs. Roman would pick Emma more often than Granville. He believed she liked to see young girls excel, more so than boys, because she felt life presented them with more challenges. Thus, she supported Emma's obvious smarts at every opportunity. Emma was brilliant; so was Granville.

[[Author's Aside]]

Though it would be many years before he would look upon his intelligence as a boon.

Together, they enjoyed, even relished, their competition for the little golden stars Mrs. Roman would place alongside their names next to various subjects—math, English, spelling, et cetera—at the end of the day. Their marks were the "best" in class.

Emma and Granville would often sit, again, side by side, under the school's side entrance awning, to have lunch, sometimes trading for favourite lunch choices. Granville's mom made great PB&J sandwiches, which he would share and trade for the cookies or chips that Emma's lunch box often held.

They even would pool their after-school snack money to buy a Coke from the lunchroom vending machine, sipping with two straws, so much better than the lunch-box juices.

Emma was indeed beautiful; the love of his young life, his first love. She glowed, a Black child in a Black world that appreciated her youthful shine.

As a young boy, Granville was cute to some, and pretty—too pretty to be a man-child. Though tolerated generally within his world, Granville was thought to be too pretty, too smart, and too independent not to be set apart, as though suspect of nefarious ways, in a place where he did not belong. Like Emma, Granville was young, gifted, and Black. They were a matched set.

Where Emma fit the mold that the expectations of their society, their world, had prepared for her, Granville did not.

Granville could read with comprehension at two years old. He absorbed the language of the adults within his family, to the extent that he would mimic their speech with clear intonation and expression. As he grew, he would use this particular talent to mock their accents and colloquial slang. Granville's brothers thought he was much too smart for his own good.

Granville was a late baby: nine years after his sister, Laura, and ten years after his elder brother, Levi— siblings from a separate father. As such, Granville was the apple of his mother's eye. Her love child, conceived with the love of her life. The spitting image of his father, who had had the eternal misfortune to die, with little warning and less care, when Granville's mom was seven months pregnant. A life loss that was never forgiven, of a man she never forgot or forgave.

Granville, her living memoir, lived in that special place within a secret heart held by the woman who gave him, only him, of all her five children, her surname.

[[Author's Aside]]

There would be many decades that passed before Granville discovered and realized the significance of that gift.

...

Upon entering formal schooling, his propensity with language combined with his naivety, enabled him to adopt the speech of his teachers, who were generally white. Thus, Granville began to speak above his "station."

"Who taught this child to speak 'proper,' taking on airs of those damn white-assed teachers? Boy, you think you better than us? You trying to disrespect your elders?" That was the common refrain from extended family members around the dinner table or as they lounged in the living room.

Granville's mom understood the innocence of his youthful play with language and voracious appetite for all knowledge, as he loved and lived in books.

Nonetheless, it was a source of rancour that bubbled up in conversation between the adults and reinforced the idea that he was different.

"Yes, Gran,"—his familiar nickname that, to this day, only his family and several dear, life-long friends are allowed to use— "was a different child from his siblings," his mother would condescend in response to the continued barrage of familiar opinions. "He's just a weird kid" was the defining expectation and conclusion that he lived under.

Part 1: Big Buck Says "Hello"

Recess and school ground filled happy sounds bounding off the red brick edifice that was Granville's scholarly home away from home.

"Hey! Hey, too-pretty-assed boy! Hey, Emma! Why are you hanging with that little sissy?" The hulking shadow blocked all sunlight. The shade it brought was cold and menacing.

Big Buck—BB to his friends—was in grade three. He had been held back from moving on to grade four. Buck was big, very big, for his age and as mean to all around him as his father, Big Brutus, was to him. The son of a brutal drunk that played the "numbers" and never won. Buck's mother had escaped, as he put it, on Christmas Eve, boarding a south-bound sleeper coach, chasing a new life with a new man. A tear-stained note from his mom and a rage filled beating from his dad were Buck's only Christmas presents that morning.

Buck fancied Emma. He would crow to all who'd listen that Emma was his little Black girlfriend, a boast she simply ignored.

Now, once again, Emma ignored Buck's presence. His jovial greeting wrapped in a ham-hock putdown of her best friend and classmate drew no response from "his girl," his person of interest, or from his intended target, the wimp sitting next to her. The slight did not go unrecognized. No one ignored Big Buck.

"Thwack" was the sound of the blow to the back of Granville's head. "Thud" was the sound of his right temple striking the hard gravel surface of the playground's walkway. Loud was his scream of pain from the cold-cock attack.

Big Buck had just said "hello" in his characteristic manner. The bully bullied every kid smaller, and sometimes bigger, than himself. When he did lack in size compared to his opponent, he made up for it through sheer meanness and love of violence. He lived for the fight; the bigger, the tougher, the better.

It was his only way to assuage the true demon living deep in his gut: his father.

All the kids stopped whatever they were doing to watch Buck do his thing. It was live entertainment of the first order.

Bouncing off the ground in a tear-filled growl, Granville charged the beast, only to be struck and thrown head-over-heels to the ground once more in one smooth motion. A rainbow of blood marked Granville's air-borne descent on the back of his neck and upper back. Blood spatters surrounded his face, nearly blinding him, as he saw the hulk descending upon him; a huge foot aiming for his abdomen.

Screaming through the panic, he kicked upward with all the force he could muster, grazing Buck's knee to strike high on his inner thigh. It was enough to unbalance Buck's momentum, causing him to land askew. His knee gave with a loud pop. Mad with rage and fear, Granville doubled his small fists together and tried to crush the bully's snarling face.

Granville broke his nose.

Ham-hock hands grasped his throat as his fists continued a rapid-fire drumbeat about Buck's face and neck, seemingly unnoticed by Buck. Red starbursts filled his eyes; breath ceased. Stronger hands pulled the vice-grip from his windpipe and lifted him up and away from the fuming, mad dog who was cursing death threats. Promises of mayhem to come.

Mr. Jenkins sighed as he watched Buck approach the pair of primary students sitting apart from the harum-scarum hodgepodge of children during recess at Gladstone Elementary. His sense of foreboding was well-founded in the knowledge among the staff of Buck's propensity to create havoc wherever he went.

Buck had become the bane of any staffer unfortunate enough to have drawn playground duty when the troubled kid had felt the urge to create more trouble and grief for everyone around him. The boy had gathered a following among the others, many of whom he had recruited through combat. The rumour was, "Be my 'friend' or suffer the consequences."

To join Buck's little gang was to bathe in the glow of his badder-than-badass reputation. Buck's gang was growing on and off the school grounds despite efforts by the staff and the parents of other children to thwart his influence and its growth.

Jenkins was hungry for a smoke. The nicotine craving usually struck when anything triggered his anxiety. His premonition of coming events probably did just that. Still, brushing that aside, he gave the playground a brief visual scan and headed for the area behind the yard keeper's tool-shed. He was just enjoying the successful formation of the third of his smoke rings within rings floating aloft (a talent he was proud of) when he heard the sound. Children screaming, children running pell-mell toward the school's side entrance; gathering, chanting, "Fight! Fight! Fight!"

His gut knew immediately what the source of the chaos was and who was at the centre of it all. His somewhat somnolent day had suddenly taken a dark turn for the worse.

He could hear the principal's diatribe burning his ears and his pride when she eventually heard of another violent incident on his watch. Of course, it was his job to report whatever was happening.

He broke into a full stride run when he saw what looked like little Andrea, one of the brainy children in primary, sailing helter-skelter though the air. His landing could be heard clearly even from this considerable distance, as the crowd gasped.

Breathing heavily, Jenkins' heart skipped a beat as he barged through the crowd of children, now deathly silent, to see Andrea's limp body hanging in a death grip from a hangman's noose of Buck's hands.

Removing those hands took no small effort. Jenkins, who worked out regularly despite his smoking, was amazed at the power within this child's rage, in his lust for blood. He now realized how much everyone on the staff was underestimating the danger within this young boy.

Little Andrea's cough of re-breath was the sweetest sound the teacher had heard in a while, a long while.

Principal Adams had a migraine. It had started on the commute to school from her upper-north-side suburb and was threatening to burst into full bloom before mid-morning. Having arranged the afternoon off, she was watching the clock, trying not to count down the minutes. "Knew I should have resisted that second cup of coffee with sweetener, and the double-chocolate donut with sprinkles. High blood pressure is hell!" Adams had a serious sugar jones.

Her phone rang, startling the principal out of her regrets for a habit that had controlled her life since her university years. Now, well into middle age, the dreaded mid-life crisis had cost her a second marriage, her health, and quality of life.

This high-pressure position in this ghetto school, these ghetto kids, this damn Nigger-burdened dead-end posting; it was perfectly suited for the only female principal in the district, a bitter recipe destined for failure.

The board, not wanting to get their everything-white pristine hands dirty dealing with all this Nigger shit, were more than happy to let her carry the weight. "Tow that barge, lift that bale, sho' goin' to Heaven, doin yo' time in Hell!"

"You've been called to the schoolyard, ma'am. There's been an incident. Jenkins is there and wants an ambulance called!" the school nurse blurted, two octaves too loud, into her right ear,

"What?" Adams's migraine had found rocket fuel and ballooned into a white-hot burst between her ears. Adams groaned under the heat of the onslaught.

"Are you all right, ma'am?"

"Hell no, I'm not all right! What the hell happened out there? Who was involved? No, let me guess. It wasn't that damn Buck, that little bastard, was it?"

"Yes, ma'am, it was him, and the little Andrea boy."

"Oh my God! That poor kid! Is he badly hurt?"

"Head injury, possible concussion, temporary loss of consciousness, abrasions."

"And Buck?"

"A broken nose and a badly dislocated knee."

"Well, I'll be damned! The little guy must have put up quite a fight?"

"Yes, ma'am. Should I call that ambulance?"

"Of course, can't be too cautious with a concussion, and the knee may need to be reset."

"Yes."

"And tell that idiot Jenkins I want to see him in my office, ASAP!"

"Right away, ma'am. Are you still planning to book off this afternoon?"

"Contact and inform the parents that I will be in my office if and when they arrive to see to their children, available to discuss the incident at their convenience."

"Yes, ma'am."

Adams knew that Buck's father needed no invitation to show up in her office breathing hellfire and determined to burn the place down with her in it. She knew the drill and would be sternly professional while he would be cursing her up, down, and sideways. He had no trouble in expressing his hatred of white people and the power he felt they wielded with impunity over Black people.

The same was doubly true if said whitey happened to be a woman. All out to emasculate and destroy Black people in general and Black men in particular. His boy was a bully, yes, true enough when truth be told, even a "little asshole," and he said so without batting an eye. Yet we clearly made him that way and his boy was just defending himself against a system determined to grind him into dust rather than to educate, which, of course, is our job to do!

A lose-lose situation all around.

Ines Andrea

Part 2: Ines Andrea

Granville's mother was at work when she got the call. By temperament a worrier, she was immediately concerned that something very bad had befallen her young son. Small of size, quick of mind, and big of mouth, he tended to draw trouble when it could otherwise easily be avoided. He was a perfect target for the school and neighbourhood bullies.

Being precocious was a problem that had set all kinds of pitfalls in his path forward. Protecting him from all dangers small and large had become her full-time maternal focus. The thought that he had been badly hurt in a place and time beyond her ability to defend him troubled her deeply.

It wasn't his fault that he was, well, different; this world around them just didn't have a place for him, at least not yet anyway. Deep in her heart-of-hearts she knew he was destined for some kind of greatness, that is if she could manage to keep him alive and well long enough for him to grow into his future, whatever that might be.

Shrugging with a heart-deep sigh, she went into the yard office to arrange to book the afternoon off.

Ines Andrea did a man's job at the B&O Railway yard. She was a coach cleaner; the only woman working on the crew. Considering her an exception to the rule was an egregious understatement when describing Ines. Her physical strength, which was considerable for a woman of her size, was clearly superseded by her round-featured visage, honey-brown complexion, near-hourglass physique, and jet- black-eyed beauty. In her time and culture, her exceptional physical appearance, presented as a "velvet glove," belied the tempered-steel spine within that was her strength of character.

The lady was a brickhouse in every aspect. The type of enviable woman memorialized by the legendary R&B group The Commodores.

Her yard boss, Mr. D'trinaire, was a good man as men went in her world. He tended to "look out" for Ines. He knew that, as a single mom, she was rearing five children on her own for all intents and purposes.

Admittedly, that was no small or insignificant task in any man's world.

His mother had been a single mom and "made me what and who I am today." He often recited this well-worn phrase to his wife, Harriet, who ceased listening years ago. She despised her pompous late mother-in-law, turning over in her still-warm grave, just as she sometimes hated the woman's arrogant, self-important son.

A quiet knock came at his office door that D'trinaire knew well.

"Come in, Ines."

Her form through the frosted half-glass office door, even in coveralls and heavy yard coat, was unmistakable. The yard boss, like all the other men in the yard, practically drooled when Ines walked by. She was so unlike his forever-whining, prim 'n' proper, bone-thin wife. Not Harriet, she certainly was not like Harriet.

The Black woman just didn't look or carry herself like an overworked single mother of five, with two children well under four years of age. No matter how many hard shifts she put in with the most menial and disgusting jobs that were her assignment (the jobs that were understood to be beneath the men), she walked with a ramrod down her back, head high, shoulders thrown back, fire hose slung-wrapped across her chest and waist, sometimes pushing a tool cart almost as big as she was, eyes straight ahead. All the way forward, all the time.

Ines exuded strength, a no-nonsense woman.

"Good day, Mr. D'trinaire, I just received a call from my son's elementary school. There was an incident in the playground during recess. My Granville, he's in grade one, has been beaten up by one of the older boys, the school bully, in fact. I'm told that he is okay, though an ambulance has been called. I will be bringing him home after I speak with the principal concerning what occurred and why he had to fight. My son is a lightning rod for trouble, but I know he never would pick a fight, not even on his worst day."

"Ines, sorry to hear that. You take the rest of the day off. Though you know that the line of VIP sleeper coach cars will be arriving at sixteen hundred hours for turn-around in the morning, at seven hundred hours. Think you could finish the remainder of your shift with the evening crew to get those cars done right 'n' proper?

"We need this job done just right to impress some power people that we hope will make a regular practice of traveling with the B&O. After all, you are the best CC we have. I'll even sign off on time- 'n'-a-half for your trouble. Of course, we will expect you to work your regular shift with your day crew tomorrow. Sound good?"

The carrot and the stick thought Ines. *Yes, the half-day off with time-'n'- a-half for the extra shift sounds good. Heaven knows we could sure make good use of that bit o' bonus come pay day. Still, it means working with that evening crew of closet-drunk slackers, and doing a double shift back-to-back come morning. I'll have to make arrangements with Sara to cover for me overnight and get the kids off to school. She won't mind.*

If I say no, I reject your offer and your "good" graces, the only thing keeping the other cock-hounds at bay. You will have your pound of flesh; so, I can have this important time with my son.

"That sounds fine, sir."

...

"Mom, I didn't say anything!"

"Are you sure?"

"Yes, Emma and I were sitting having a snack. She was teasing me about her having more gold stars last week than me. I said that this was Monday and I bet her Friday lunch money that I would outdo her this week. Anyway, Mrs. Roman always picks her first cause she's a girl. Mrs. Roman likes girls."

"Then what happened?"

"Then Big Buck came over and asked Emma, 'Why you hanging with that little sissy?'"

"That's what he said?"

"Yeah."

"Did you answer back?"

"Neither of us answered. We ignored him."

"Then?"

"Then, he hit me hard on the back of my head. I never saw it coming, couldn't duck. Mom, I didn't start that fight with Buck. I'm scared of him—everybody is!"

"I know, son. I just had to be sure. I know you wouldn't go out of your way to fight with anyone. We'll get you home and patched up. That dark bruise on your temple's giving you a black raccoon-mask shadow across your eyes and those welts around your throat could use a bit of TLC. Does it hurt?"

"A little, when I swallow."

"I'm off for the day, but I will have to work the evening shift to make up for it. I'm getting time- 'n'-a-half for that bit of inconvenience, though. How does popcorn and your choice of cartoons sound to you?"

"Sounds great, Mom."

Granville Johnson, Grade Two

CHAPTER TWO:
1714 West 14th Street

· · · · ·

1714 WEST 14TH Street was the red brick 'castle' that Granville called the family home. It was within walking distance of the trainyard and just across the street from Uncle Jake's gas station on the corner. Home was a two-story walk-up with a landing midway up the interior stairwell where Granville often played with his action figures. He loved his home, surrounded by family and all the love a young boy could imagine. It made him feel special.

Uncle Jake and Aunt Sara lived on the first floor. Because Uncle Jake's business was one of the few successful Black-owned businesses in the neighbourhood, their apartment was very well decorated. Aunt Sara took great care to keep it nice, with flowers throughout, sometimes plastic— "Never die or lose colour, just need a bit of dusting now and then."

Decorator dishes that never held food were displayed in the arbour that graced the dining room. A large, cozy couch and recliner chair in the living room were covered in thick plastic that crinkled when sat upon, to prevent stains and spills by little boys that would cuddle there with a favourite snack, usually a heavily layered PB&J sandwich that they would make themselves. Granville would be careful to lick all the oozing, gooey goo that sometimes escaped between his fingers and the twin slices of Wonder Bread with each enthusiastic bite.

Granville's home was set apart from others on the street by its locale. It was situated next to, and on the west side of, the elevated train tracks. The house, situated on a double city lot, had a large (by neighbourhood standards) side yard that ran the length of the building to the north, where a bush-laden, decaying fence defined the alleyway at the rear of the extended lot. There was also a second tall wooden two-story home. It had an outdoor staircase to the second floor, where Granville's cousin, Selene, lived with her mom, Joan, and her little sister, Felice.

On the east side of both homes and spanning the length of their double lot, in an otherwise vacant area, stood the concrete and steel structure that supported the elevated commuter train tracks. The arrangement afforded an unusual, even rare, high point to the overall topography of the compact urban ghetto street. Within Granville's adjacent side yard stood several oak trees; tall, broad, and overreaching, they covered both lots with thick, sky-painting branches perfect for climbing.

Granville loved to climb.

He became extremely adept at moving among the waving boughs. Ines often referred to him to other family members and friends as her little monkey-boy. Granville's favourite TV character was Tarzan, the Ape Man.

In his youthful teen years to come, he would climb one series of branches that reached much higher than the others. Their tops would extend through the crossbeams of the elevated tracks. Feeling daring, he would climb to the top to poke his head over the outward edge of the trestlework to see the oncoming train rushing towards him.

He would hold that position just long enough for the engineer to see him, then duck, retreating down the tree as fast as he could to safety. When his mother caught him at it, she called the city to have the tree given a long-overdue trim. He was grounded, literally, for two weeks.

Granville tended to play alone, being precocious and the middle child of a too-old pair of teenage siblings and overshadowed by a second pair of siblings just out of diapers. Plus, Selene and Felice were fun in some girly games. The rough and tumble of outdoor play, tree climbing (Tarzan), and pretend sword-fight adventures (pirates): like the difference between Barbie dolls and He-Man action figures, the play often was too much of one, not enough of the other. His familiar playmate options were slim to none.

Thus, he learned and reveled in the quiet joy of being content alone, yet not lonely. Granville lived in books.

He became a voracious consumer of anything printed. Flyers, cereal boxes, magazines, comic books, his mother's mail, story books *(with and without pictures)*, and absolutely anything that had to do with dinosaurs. They roamed freely in his imagination.

The great tyrant-lizard, Tyrannosaurus (Late Cretaceous) was his favourite, followed closely by the three-horned armoured Triceratops (Jurassic), and the mammoth arm-lizard, Brachiosaurus (Jurassic).

Though he understood the gruesome threesome did not share the same era, he often had them waging two- and three-way battles, defending against attacks by the ever-present super-predator, T. rex, in his world.

The larger-than-life beasts, fighting for their lives, were a dynamic violent trio that ruled their world; kind-of-like the insanely inept geniuses of the black-and-white TV situation comedy, *The Three Stooges*: Moe, Larry, and Curly Joe, only better, much better.

Part 1: Snowball

Snowball lived on the second floor back porch, which was completely enclosed, as per the architectural style of most homes in the West Chicago neighbourhood. A very large, pure white Alaskan Malamute with mis-matched eyes—one sky blue, the other midnight black—that tended to freeze the blood in your veins when he bared his teeth with a low, lion-like rumbling growl in displeasure with your presence.

Snowball was not a guard dog; he was a family pet and Granville's best friend.

They, boy and dog, would lounge together on the porch, basking in the endless stories with which Granville would enrapture his audience of one.

Sometimes he would even act out all the requisite characters and roles, good, bad, even ugly—as in gross, like puking on his new shirt and bowtie that Mom had bought for the school class pictures the week before. It had happened on Sunday in the middle of the pastor's sermon, too many sugar snacks after Sunday school. Mom was not pleased.

Snowball barked and howled, something he seldom did, when Granville danced for him like his mom sometimes did when the spirit would take her and she would begin to shout, "Praise Jesus, praise Jesus!" Head bowed, hands shaking high in the air, spinning, hopping, and shaking her voluminous hips, back 'n' forth, side to side. Sweating, flinging every which way, Mom would prance and dance, shrieking her joyful release from the ongoing daily trials and tribulations of a Black woman's life in a man's world, to praise her Lord, "My Lord, help me Jesus, my Lord, help me!"

Soon the ushers would arrive, four big strong men, to each take hold of an arm or leg and lift her high above their heads, still writhing, ushering her to the back of the church to the time-out room, expressly set aside, designated for this purpose, to let the rapture pass and rest for the spirit's vessel, in his name.

Now Granville, as like Mom, is writhing on the porch floor like a stepped-on garden snake, howling at the top of his young lungs in unison with his dearest friend, Snowball.

Granville was nine when his beloved friend died in his sleep.

Snowball was fifteen. The faithful dog had been relegated to the back porch to make room for the newborn. It broke the big dog's heart to be set aside and eventually shunned by the adults as a result of their blossoming preoccupation with the squirming, crying, colic-stricken new life-form.

Snowball's love for the too-human baby was never in question, and was deeply expressed in his heartfelt, protective fascination with the young toddler, who grew quickly into an eager playmate for the big white "Polar Bear"—sometimes play-bed, fur-pony, and/or nap-pillow dog.

[[Author's Aside]]

Granville cried inconsolable tears that drained his eyes and filled his broken heart with pain without end for weeks. He knew that he would never forget or stop loving Snowball. All of that proved to be true enough through the years. Yet, he was alone, in his home and world, once more.

Part 2: Laura Meets Man

Laura, Granville's older, singular sister, was in love. The object and focus of her teenage attraction and affection was a very big man, a mountain-tall of a man, named Hoarse. A name that was difficult to remember, and for some, just as hard to pronounce properly. The solution to both linguistic and recollection problems was solved by using his obvious attribute as a source of identification. He was called "Man," as if his size and muscular stature, which filled doorframes when he walked through them, was the defining feature of all men of note. When the "mountain" spoke, his deep yet soft voice filled the room and drew all attention to him. Thus, there was never any confusion or misunderstanding when Hoarse's nickname entered conversation in the neighbourhood.

Everyone knew Man on sight, if not by reputation. His being drop-dead gorgeous eye-candy did not hurt.

Man was a master mechanic in Jake's garage. He was a wizard with engines of all kinds, the bigger the better. He also had strong appetites, namely for big convertibles, the biggest of them all being the Cadillac, and young women with which to share his outstanding traffic-stopping ride.

Man's convertible Caddy was pink and was, indeed, a "Freeway of Love . . . in a Pink Cadillac," memorialized by Aretha Franklin's 1968 monster hit and road song.

Laura tended to hang out at the garage, often offering to tend the till when Jake and Man were busy in the shop. Sometimes she would pump gas, wash cars, and clean up around the shop with Granville, who loved having his big sister around to help even though he was well aware that she spent most of her time watching Man making engine magic.

Man was a ladies' man. He loved women, all shapes and sizes, as long as they were young. Man was a womanizer of the first order. They came to him, usually unbidden. When they arrived, they were easy to have, easy to use, easy to forget in the ongoing parade of females young, old, and all ages in between. All would vie for his attention with all they had to offer.

Laura was gorgeous in her own right: tall for her age; small, round, perky breasts; curvy hips; reed thin, in the fashion of the time. Big brown, honeydew eyes (her mother's gift) that could bore deep down to the pit of a man's soul before he knew what hit him. The kind of young woman-child, more than a little eager to be the hot young lady that she would become. When it came to Man, she knew she could 'give him something he could feel, from the top of his process-permed hairstyle to the soles of his wing-tip spats.

The teenager simply could not help the intensity of her blossoming womanhood. Her panties moistened every time Man pulled up to park his signature mobile in front of her house, usually to have a few beers with her Uncle Jake downstairs and discuss the latest developments with their "Numbers" lottery operation in the backroom.

It was in that dim-lit backroom, late one night after closing, that Laura and Man made sweet, intense, fevered love on the big plush-filled couch that lined one wall of the gambling den. She rode him long. She rode him hard. She rode the big man like a rodeo queen mounted on a massive Brahma Bull going for the record of a lifetime.

When it was all said and done, and Ines was informed of Laura's change of life-flow and the inevitable source of new life within her daughter, she only had one thing to say to Man: "You fucked her. You marry her."

[[Author's Aside]]

Man and Laura were married in front of the county clerk when his child bride was sixteen years old. Ines, her heartbroken mother, was not present.

Granville Johnson, Grade Three

Part 3: Red Shoes

Red shoes, red shoes
Never have the blues in red shoes
Buckled down tight, sandal light, red shoes girl shoes will pass, feet are fast, Red shoes, Momma's love will last, Red shoes
Red shoes, why red shoes?
The laces are straps with buckles. Mom tried dyeing them brown. Dark brown, like her loving gazes
Proud tears washing her phrases
Still they're red shoes, girl's shoes! Red shoes
Goin' to school in red shoes? Laughter goes round.
Dogging my steps, that pants can't hide. Second-hand love, first-hand pride.
Momma tried; red shoes will abide. Momma's love will last, Red shoes, red shoes run light and fast
Momma's child does the best he can.

Momma's boy becomes Momma's man. Nobody can catch my red shoes!
Momma knows, I love to run, red shoes, red shoes . . .

-Granville Johnson

...

Buck's gang had chased him for blocks. His crew was not done with the
punk that had humiliated their fearless leader. Buck had been expelled
for his part in the big fight. Kids had talked about it for weeks. It had
become a schoolyard legend, often repeated and embellished by those
that stood witness. Some even dared to laugh at him behind his back.
Buck's thirst for vengeance knew no bounds. Once the gang had discovered where the young punk lived, the hunt and steeplechase was on.

Granville was fast and knew well how to take advantage of all the
alleys and hidden passages between buildings and backyards to outwit
and out maneuver his pursuers. At last, he was in the home stretch, the
alley behind his home, when the rock hit him square between his shoulder blades. Down he went in dust, scraped knees, and bleeding palms.
Before he could rise, they were on him.

He rolled away from the rain of kicks and strikes, causing most to
miss their mark.

Once his feet were again able to find purchase, he saw his mother in
his mind: *Fight if you must. If you're outnumbered, run if you can, to fight
another day. But remember, Gran, these are bullies, and bullies aren't known
for their smarts, otherwise they would have better things to do than pick on
younger, smaller kids in a gang. You are the smartest child I've ever known.
Use the brains our God gave you to reason with them. Outwit them, challenge
them. Why do they need to hurt you, one little kid? You fought back and beat
him at his own game. Why couldn't any of them fight back? Are they really
that afraid of him? Why? Sure, all of them together could beat you; would
that make them tougher than the little kid that dared to fight the bully?*

Granville stopped in his tracks and turned to face them, and like
hounds confused by their prey's refusal to continue the chase, the pack
froze, looking quickly at each other, questioning the sudden change, the
void left by the lack of fear in the eyes of their prey. Now what? They

found themselves listening to Granville's barrage of questions with uncomfortable recognition that the truth was hard to hear. Yet it was still the truth.

Agreement blossomed among them. The tallest, named Zack, finally broke the heavy silence, in a voice so deep and soft that Granville wasn't sure he had heard him: "Come on, guys, let's go. Leave the weird punk alone. Buck can deal with his own shit. We've got better things to do."

Granville watched their backs receding toward the mouth of the alleyway. The metallic taste of adrenalin-driven fear began to subside deep down his throat. His heartbeat began to slow, the tears poised on the cleft of his eyes. He would cry if he could, but not today. He smiled at Mom's advice. It had taught him a vital lesson. Face your fear head on and you might, just might, live to face another day. Then again, you might not, but either way, you'll be true to yourself and live with honour. Much easier to be yourself than somebody else.

[[Author's Aside]]

Alas, this would not be Granville's last experience with the terror of being prey. His fate required that his gifts to the world, which were yet to unfold, would manifest through the recurrent role of outlier, perpetually set apart within society—wisdom gained and grown through obstacles to be overcome as he faced a world that more often viewed him as sport, not to be taken seriously. Thus, sometimes he was a convenient target, game to be had, in open season.

Part 4: Joseph, David: Big Brother's Rescue

Young Joseph, five and in kindergarten, looking younger even than his age, and David, six and a tall first-grader, were dawdling, playing step-on-a-crack, taking their time in their perpetual curious distraction.

Granville, their impatient big brother, was eager to get to his job at the gas station. He really enjoyed helping around the place. Watching the men working on the cars bore a particular fascination for him.

Watching the big engines, especially the V8s, sometimes busted badly, reduced to a million parts, small and large, spread on the floor, bench, or table, then cleaned, repaired, replaced, and reassembled to once again purr and growl like a big jungle cat as they pulled the beasts that carried them out the shop doors to run with the herd.

He loved working on replica model airplanes, deriving a similar sense of satisfaction when he shaped, shaved, glued, and taped what had come in a box, bestowed with a striking photo of the plane in action, into a beautiful—usually hand-painted—model amidst his growing collection.

Granville did not want to be late, for he knew Tippy would be anxious for his after-school walk. He tried coaxing them to hurry, an effort they easily, deftly ignored. Sometimes, like today, they were the gruesome twosome, the bane of his existence.

"I have to pee, Gran," cried David.

"Me, too," echoed Joseph.

"Can't you hold it? We're three blocks from home. If you walk faster, we can be there in no time."

"No," they moaned in unison.

"Come on, Joseph. Hurry up, David! We have to get home before it's too late, Let's run, race you to the end of the block."

The three brothers ran together a short distance down the long, industrial block across the street from their mother's workplace. Granville was only slightly behind, hoping that this idea, this tactical strategic delay, just might work. Then, full stop, with a sad whimper and a deep groan, nature unloaded in the trousers of both young boys.

All three stood stock still, frozen by the reeking problem filling their pants as the liquid stain ran down their legs. Granville never cursed, thought it was a sad, stupid habit of stupid people. Granville wasn't a stupid person, yet today, he cursed.

"Oh no! Damn! Damn! Damn it all! Now what?"

The boys began to cry; big brother sprang into action. While trying his best to sound calm and reassuring, so as not to make a bad situation worse, if that were possible, he pulled them into a dark alcove between two buildings, providing some cover from the traffic on the street.

Fortunately, there were no homes on this block, just the sprawling B&O complex and railyard.

Sparse shrubbery and crab grass had grown up through the cracks in the pavement. It grew everywhere in the ghetto.

"It's okay, no one can see us. We can fix this. Take off your pants. It'll be all right. Dave, can you be lookout? Watch the street, while I help Joseph with his jeans."

David was happy to follow his brother's direction, anything to avoid having to be pants-less in the street. Even at his age, his embarrassment was palpable.

Granville eased his little brother's jeans down each leg and off. The warm cloud of youthful urine filled his nose, though not altogether unpleasant. Next came the well-loaded underwear. Handling the garment with great care, Granville was able to draw it down Joseph's short legs without contact with its contents. This pungent aroma was sharp and made his eyes water.

Granville discarded them with a toss; they landed further back in the dark recesses of the alcove. *Rat food! Now the hard part*, thought Granville, eyeing the brown, gritty shit. "Shit . . .! So much fun!" The source of his exasperation clung to Joseph's body. Stripping the coarse leaves from a shrub growing along the crumbling, brown-brick column, he began to gently wipe his brother's behind as best he could.

Then, crumpling a sheet of notebook paper from his tote, he rubbed it between his fists until the paper was soft enough to use as toilet paper for the cleft between the firm round cheeks. Joseph waited, holding still throughout the process, grateful for his big brother's love and care.

"There, let's get these back on. Hold on to me and lift your leg, exactly, that's better. We'll be home in a bit and there's a warm, sudsy bubble bath waiting for you guys."

The boys switched places and Granville repeated the process. David was easier with less mess, though his underpants were also forfeit. Both stood before their attendant, feet slightly apart in their piss-damp pants, with relaxed, dry-eyed grins of gratitude shining brightly.

"Now, where were we? There's a race to win, remember? Last one home cleans the tub!"

Zoom! Three streaks of little boy exuberance flew down the street, strides barely touching the pavement as they laughed their way home. Granville was careful to let his brothers win.

Part 5: "What'd the Nigger Say?"

"What'd the Nigger say?"

"Didn't say much."

"I asked you, what did the fucking high 'n' mighty jungle-bunny say?"

"Sorry, boss, he said that his business was just that, his business.

There was no necessity for our association or protection. He'd built the station from a home-based garage business into one of the best stations on Chicago's West Side."

"That bastard, doesn't know what-the-fuck's good for him. Fuck the station! What about the numbers?"

"What numbers?"

"What?"

"We told him that sixty forty percent of a protected thriving enterprise was better than one hundred percent of a hole in the ground. Especially if you happen to be buried in it. He said that's his business, as in none of our fucking business. So, we could take our generous offer of a sixty-forty split and go to 'Whop hell in a handbasket!'"

"I'm going to tar 'n' feather his black ass, then we'll see whose business it is and what's what!"

Fat Rico, ever-present sweat rolling down the side of his puffed cheeks to form a pool around the collar of his fifty-dollar Italian double-knit shirt under his two-thousand-dollar shiny sharkskin three-piece suit, sat chewing on his cigar butt, like a cow chewing its cud. He was overdressed for the weather, as usual. Despite Chicago's summer heat, the boss loved to show off his wealth and taste in his extravagant dress code. "Burn it. Burn the fucking shithole to the ground. We'll make him an example: a message for the rest to heed, or else."

He had been hoping that the move into the ghetto slum could be accomplished without fanfare. A big splash was sometimes bad for business. Still, it was clear that this Nigger-bitch had to be dealt with,

removed altogether to prevent the cancer, this Nigga insurrection, from spreading.

He'd contacted the boy twice earlier, being pleasant, a phone chat at first, after sending one of his crew to the station for a brake job on one of his limos. The service was excellent, the charge reasonable, but still it was clear that the rumours of the back-of-shop Numbers racket was a not-too-well-kept secret. They had gotten a bit sloppy in how they ran things in that regard.

The next call was more business-like, after reintroducing himself, suggesting that they should meet to discuss the possibility of investment in the Nigger's station and, of course, other avenues of mutual interest. The boy hadn't heard him right and seemed to ignore what was being offered; of course, "Not interested," was unacceptable. So, he had sent two of his best lieutenants to negotiate in person.

"Enough of this shit!" barked Rico. "Who the fuck does he think he is? Hit it on collection day when the coffers are full. Be sure to make it look like it was an accident, gasoline spill at the pumps should do nicely. Shit happens, and these people are always careless. That Black bitch must burn, no witnesses, of course."

"Right, boss," and with marching orders in mind, they left the boss's office in eager anticipation to make that happen. Burning Niggers was more fun than hanging or shooting them, even though sometimes it was like shooting fish in a fucking barrel. They shared a dark chuckle over smokes outside.

Part 6: Whistling Joe's Demise

Alfred, Granville's young neighbour, was playing marbles with his cousin Michael. Alfred was winning, and if he aimed this bumper shot just right, he would be in a perfect position to take Mike's cat's-eye. The thought warmed the cockles of Alfred's greedy heart. His joy of winning was only overshadowed by Michael's hatred of losing at anything, especially if he lost to Alfred.

The two were closer than blood brothers yet competed against each other in everything. For each, to be outdone was to be undone. Bragging rights meant time to crow, while the sore loser ate crow to the other's delight.

The shadow crossed the chalk-drawn circle on the small patch of smooth pavement of the sidewalk that served as their game board just as Alfred let his large, clear bubble marble loose, fired straight and true, never to reach its target, and neither boy noticed.

The shadow had transformed in an instant from a man walking casually, almost strutting in his celebratory gait, dreaming of spending the thick wad of Numbers winnings he carried in his vest pocket, whistling, "I won at last, good God almighty, I won at last!" into a large sedan screeching to a halt at the curb, brakes grinding, gravel spraying both boys, the car door opening with a rush of cool conditioned air. Then there were two men in a desperate foot chase, one running for his life, the other determined to end it.

The piercing boom of the shot came so quickly, like a too-close lightning bolt, thunderclap. It was over before they knew it had actually happened, yet it left their ears ringing.

A man face down, a grapefruit-sized gaping gash across the top of his head, back to front, oozing life; the shooter, a big man-mountain of muscle, with a quick 360-degree cat-like glance for witnesses to be erased, if need be, ignored the two little Niggers playing in the street. They were of no consequence.

Shouldering his gun, which looked as big as a cannon to Michael and Alfred, he calmly returned to the black sedan as it picked him up and was driven away.

Shock gave way to a giddy sense of horror. Precious marbles quickly gathered in near panic, a fevered haste, the boys ran.

Part 7: Just Business . . .

Tippy, a tall, muscular Doberman pinscher, was a guard dog, whose job was night watchman. He had become Granville's dog when the boy helped around Uncle Jake's station, delivering lunch, cleaning the washroom, sweeping the office, loading the pop machine, taking out the garbage, and his favourite job, feeding and walking Tippy.

Granville watched his uncle with the two white men talking in the back of the shop where Jake's friends liked to hang out and talk shop. They were standing outside of a room that was absolutely off limits to Granville.

"Uncle Jake, you want me to clean-up that big storeroom in the back after I take out the trash? I looked in when the door was open, really smells bad. Ashtrays are all full and . . ."

"Boy, I told you once before not to go near that room. It's off limits to you, Gran, period. What's in there is none of your never-mind. Don't want to catch you in there again. Now why don't you take the dog outdoors for a walk? He needs some exercise. Been cooped up all day."

Granville's hungry curiosity could not be denied. He watched the three men intently, his presence hidden behind Tippy's bulk. In the quiet of the near-empty shop, he could just make out snippets of the conversation.

Uncle Jake was sort of friendly at first but became really angry when the other men kept insisting to see what was in Granville's "no-go-zone."

The two men looked scary when they stormed out of the garage shop, passing close to Tippy's doghouse in the corner by the office near the door. Tippy bared his teeth and growled as they went by. One of them noticed and hesitated, reaching into his coat pocket for something, his expression menacing. Granville cowered down, hugging Tippy's neck to quiet him.

Uncle Jake shouted, "You can leave now! Your business is done here."

"So's yours, fuckin' Nigger!" was the near instant reply, thrown over the shoulder by one of the retreating mobsters.

Part 8: Wild 'n' Idle in Idlewild

Jake, Granville's uncle and resident hero, was worried. The Mob boss's lackeys had just left with an all-too-clear warning, thickly disguised as an invitation to do business, the Mob's business, on the Mob's terms, which amounted to fiscal slavery.

"The word is out, Sara. Since Whistling Joe was shot by the Mob for daring to win last month, people have become fearful of even being seen anywhere near the station, let alone doing business with us, period."

"Shit!"

"Now the bastards are regularly driving by slowly. Looks like they trying to photograph our customers, or maybe their licence plates. They've got the cops stopping people when they leave, giving out tickets for rolling stops at the stop sign on the corner. Checking registration, asking about the nature of their business with us, as if they are planning to raid us.

"I'm sure that is the case. That city ordinance inspector's six citations and threats to close us down! People know what's going down. The intimidation tactics are working. No gas fill-ups, no brake work, no engine tune-ups, no shop work. Not even a tire repair, nothing. The Numbers? It's dried up. No one wants to play the Numbers and risk Joe's fate if they were to win."

"Baby, but . . ."

"No buts, Sugar, not one goddamn, Jesus-shit-on-a-shingle repair!"

Sara shuddered as she received the report of what had gone on in the shop, knowing what this would mean for her and her family.

Association with the Mob bastards would be a slow death on the killing ground. Hell on earth as the honky assholes bled them dry while making them their house niggas! They'd have to pay for the privilege to kowtow under those fuckers just to keep breathing!

"Shit on that! Hell no! No fuckin' way!"

Jake smiled. His heart swelled with pride, "Damn, I love you when you're pissed off!" His firebrand wife was the love of his life. What she lacked in size, she made up for in an abundance of attitude. "I tell no lies, *and* I don't sugar-coat the truth," was one of her favourite sayings whenever questioned about the weight of her words, on the ears, hearts, and egos of others.

Sara was "as straight a person as one singular direct line; A to B, in all she sees, no stops in between."

She and Jake had been together since high school, giving all their best selves to this marriage for thirty-odd childless years. The business was their child.

"What are we going to do?" Sara asked, snapping her head to the right, spitting through clenched teeth straight down the kitchen sink drain from an improbable angle. Jake was not impressed; he'd seen it before.

She'd dreamed of children, a burden she carried in her heart-of-hearts. Its presence had soured her through the years. Jake, watching her sometimes, worried for that weight she carried on her heart. The excitement and joy of the day they opened the gas station was second only to that of her wedding day.

Jake, staring deep into his mug of strong, dark-roast java, as if he were reading their future in tea leaves, said, "We can sell and leave this all behind us. We could move into our summer cabin in Idlewild and live there full-time until we decide where we want to go from there."

Jake had been mulling over this alternative possibility for some time. The Mob's bear trap had them between the rock and the hard place. Yet their dreams were not irrevocably tied to this place, as the criminals believed. Jake felt there were other options if they dared to explore a new community altogether.

"Sara, the station is our baby, yes, but it is not our child. It doesn't replace the one we couldn't have. We could build another shop and or station in Michigan, where the Mob is less active or connected."

"Our roots run deep in this community. We worked hard for many years to create this place, where a Black owned and operated business could not just survive but dare to thrive." Sara watched and waited for Jake to complete his train of thought.

"Sara, it's not the business they want. It's the Numbers! Yeah, yeah, I get that."

"So, give them the racket, Jake. Run the shop legit."

"They will not stop there. They'll make us maintain the shop as a front for the gambling. It was never meant to be that way. The gambling, as you remember, began as a sporting sideline, something to provide a bit of cash flow, a back-up, in case of emergencies. Now the damn cart is before the horse, and it's all fucked up."

"We are mercy-fucked with it!"

"Will you at least consider the alternative?"

"Country life among the cows? Moo?"

"Better than city life among the greased pigs, drowning in honky-hog shit. Oink, oink!"

"I'll never look at a platter of bacon the same way again."

"Ha, ha! Ha!" They both laughed together until their sides hurt and snot ran down and off their upper lips, tossed helter-skelter with each guffaw.

"Jake, I want to adopt."

Jake stopped laughing, stunned.

"We can afford it now, said so yourself."

"Sara."

"Live in the country."

"But . . ."

"Michigan's a small-town lifestyle: lots of green, quiet area, quiet time, probably pretty good small schools, small class sizes, lots of opportunity for quality instruction, few nosy neighbours, fresh air, give her and us a different life. It'll be the perfect environment to raise a little girl."

"Girl?"

"Yes, girl, a sweet little girl for you to spoil."

"You mean, like I spoiled you?"

"I said little girl, not a girlfriend. You dirty old man!"

"Okay! If we fuckin' do this, we adopt, lose the station, and its issues . . . then it's country life, wild 'n' idle in Idlewild, to raise our child!"

"Knew you'd see it my way." Sara knew how to make Heaven spring forth from the mouth of Hell, straight at the heart of life, and he so loved her, within their lifesaving turns of fate created. Her self-assured grin was in full bloom.

"Is there any other?"

Part 9: Tippy! Tippy! Tippy . . . !

Granville was getting ready for bed when he got permission from his mom to go say goodnight to Tippy while the Doberman was on duty and making his rounds. It wasn't his usual practice, but somehow tonight felt different; he had missed his usual walk with the guard dog after school thanks to Joseph and David, and Uncle Jake had decided not to open the station today.

"Just not enough business to make it worth my while, so I decided to reduce our operation hours. You can walk and feed him tomorrow when we will be open for the weekend's month-end business."

"Tippy, here, boy! Where are you?" Walking the fence perimeter several times, he finally spied him seemingly asleep in the lee of the lean-to that served as his outdoor doghouse when on duty. The big black Doberman was almost invisible, hidden by the structure's night shadow.

He was prone to lie waiting for someone to try the fence. Then he would charge, a huge, vicious blackness, deathly white teeth gleaming in the station's streetlights, barking and growling in attack mode until the intruder retreated with a healthy change of plan.

He would always respond to Granville's call. Tonight, he did not.

Granville threw a small stone that bounced off the blacktop near Tippy's nose. He did not stir. Granville tried a second stone with the same result.

Finally, he walked back across the street and down the block towards home, very concerned.

He just couldn't imagine what it could be. He would tell Uncle Jake tomorrow.

...

Sara and Jake waited in the quiet reception office. They had arrived almost an hour early to the orphanage, such was Sara's fear of being somehow late and creating unnecessary issues to complicate this oh-so-difficult experience. The bench seat was well padded and provided a more or less comfortable place for expectant parents to practice their patience. As if that virtue had not been thoroughly tested in the long months of form-filling and interviewing leading up to this moment.

The child placement agency had gone over their lives with a fine-tooth comb. No stone escaped being overturned and examined. The Numbers lottery was easier than they feared it would be to hide. Simply because the Mob's harassment of their business had effectively shut it down. The big back room had reverted to shop storage, its original intent. Unfortunately, this had not deterred the continued intimidation and aggression.

"There are silver linings in even the worst storm clouds; though this has been more like a tornado."

Part 10: "Hope Resides Here"

The room was drab, with tired pictures on tired walls, and wallpaper like a curse for your eyes. The lower outer walls were graced with dark oak from a bygone era, the forties, perhaps, when that heavy wood was cheap to build with. The faded forest scene above the banister, a lime green that used to be a tone of ochre, spoke of old dreams; autumn gone sour.

Life and dreams were born and died in this place regularly, not necessarily in that order.

A placard on the wall above the door read, "Hope Resides Here: You're Welcome to Dream."

That phrase stirred Sara's heartstrings, yet its tone was calming, clear as soft, mellow notes on an ancient harp. She was eager for this to be done.

Eager for her baby, her Dawn. Six years old, a beautiful child, with a sharp mind, strong will, and a dash of attitude rolled into a darling little girl. Sara, and Jake, perhaps, to a lesser extent, knew that Dawn, their eminent daughter, was the perfect choice, and her name (which clinched it) was indicative of the new life and direction she would bring to their world. Their "hope" indeed resided in the child's big hazel eyes.

Dawn, living up to her namesake, was an early riser. She usually met the sunrise with happy, expectant urgency for what the day would bring.

Her world had taken a dark turn with her parents' death. Dawn, almost from the beginning, with her first faltering phrases had said the words all parents await with bated breath.

"Dada" being clearly understood in her speech, hot on the heels of "Mama." It was somewhat a source of resentment for her mom. Like or love it, Dawn was her daddy's girl. Fortunately, her father was exceptional in his own right, in that he doted on his daughter and his wife in near equal measure. His wife loved that about him, and in doing so, forgave her daughter for her adoration of her father.

Dawn loved these mornings because she would get to have breakfast with her mom and her dad when he would get home from his night shift. He was an assistant shift manager of a large shipping conglomerate and, as such, worked primarily alternating hours between the evening and night shift with occasional day shifts as schedules warranted. Fortunately, he was flexible by nature and had adapted to the demands of a round-the-clock pattern of sleep deprivation. Coming off the night shift meant he would be available for breakfast with family and to kiss his wife before she left for work as head nurse (also rotating shifts) at the hospital emergency ward.

The dawn of the worst day in Dawn's young life began with breakfast, then a routine change. Dad had to drive Mom to work because her car was in the shop for a long-overdue brake job and had been held over-night, waiting for parts. Both cars tended to be maintenance-delayed due to each owner's erratic schedule.

Dawn's dad was tired, having worked a double shift (evening and night) covering for a sick associate. Breakfast was fun. Dad was giddy and playful to offset the grogginess of sleep loss. In the car, his radio was louder than usual, reporting the news of a house fire on the South side.

An entire family had died in the blaze. Mom asked him twice to turn it down or, better yet, off because he seemed unfocussed.

"Dawn does not have to hear about that. It will give her nightmares."

"What?"

"Please pay attention to what you're doing." Their red traffic light turned green.

Starting up, startled and offended, prickly from the night's exhaustion, shrugging his broad shoulders, while ignoring the traffic noise, he blurted, "It's just the news, honey, and anyway, these things happen; it's just li—"

The screaming horns and blaring sirens struck their hearing and awareness, just before the fire engine ladder-truck hit them broadside, passenger side, in the centre of the intersection. The T-bone collision nearly bent the car in two opposing directions.

Dawn's lung-bursting stratospheric cry was drowned out by the screech of overheated brakes and screaming tires of multiple collisions as the two vehicles spun into oncoming traffic.

...

[[Author's Aside]]

Dawn's life, as she knew it, ended with her conscious awareness at that precise moment. She never would be able to recall anything about the crash other than the cacophony of sound, then abrupt crushing silence that seemed to go on forever. When she awoke in her mother's hospital, weeks later, Mom and Dad were no more.

All had been erased from her mind. Only the subconscious would replay it in fitful recurrent nightmares that would haunt her into her adult life.

Part 11: ". . . You're Welcome to Dream"

The inner office door, a dark oak lower half that was the base for the upper portion—which held a framed, frosted, stained-glass window with a polished, silver-lead outlined image of two parents walking a garden path swinging their joyful young child between them, as an embodiment of the orphanage's policies toward family—opened softly. Sara's heart skipped a beat, just as she felt the need to question and challenge the delay.

"Mr. and Mrs. Watkins, please do come in. We apologize for the delay. The faxed approval from the state board has only momentarily arrived. We are happy to inform you that your application and subsequent submissions have been approved. Dawn has been told the good news and is gathering her things and saying her farewells as we speak. You will be taking her to her new home today."

Relief and quiet joy flooded Sara's forever-sad eyes. Hot, happy tears cascaded down her cheeks, and glistening white teeth filled her smile. A quiet, soft "thank you" framed her expressions; she dabbed the moisture with a soft tissue quickly removed from her purse. Jake's heart swelled at the thought of the end to her pain and his longing. Now they would live the life of their dreams, so long denied.

Dawn walked in, head held high, hugging a huge stuffed panda bear almost as tall as she. Nodding her recognition of her new mom and dad, she quietly slipped into the chair between them, her legs swinging back 'n' forth—the only sign of the ill ease she felt. She had met and enjoyed this couple each time they visited her room. She wanted ever-so-much to be away from this place.

She longed to have a home again, a house, a family, that would love her like her mom and dad loved her. Looking toward her right, first at her new mom, she unwound her small hand from the belly of her "going to her new home" present to hold Sara's outstretched palm, which closed gently around it.

Sara bent toward her, close, to plant a whisper-soft kiss upon her forehead. "We're going home, baby, our new home, with you, our daughter."

Dawn turned to look past her panda to see her new dad's tear-filled smile. His glistening cheeks and kind, hopeful expression melted the remaining knot of uncertainty in the pit of Dawn's stomach. She knew then that, sheltered between these two strong, caring people, she had found a new home. Feeling safe at last, she was happy to be Daddy's girl once more.

...

Part 12: "...Did They Know Each Other?"

Granville, playing on the landing of the entrance staircase, heard Uncle Jake and Aunt Sara's car pull up and park in front of the house. He waited quietly to get a look at his new cousin. He had wondered what she would be like. Months had turned into almost a year of interest-fueled expectation.

Aunt Sara had grown weary of his ever-present curiosity that met her with a barrage of questions at every opportunity. Finally, she had thrown up her hands, almost dropping the dinner plate she was drying. "Gran, Dawn will be here maybe next week, when and if the approval comes through. Then we'll bring her home. I promise to let you know the minute we know. I showed you her picture, we weren't supposed to even share that with anyone."

"Why, Aunt Sara?"

"None of your business! Please, no more questions, okay?"

Granville promised himself that he would respect Dawn's space and give her time to get used to her new home and family. Still, a new face in the family opened his world to a wealth of possibilities in sharing. He could teach her checkers, maybe even chess someday, when she was ready, of course.

He could read to her and teach her about dinosaurs. She would join him and his brothers on their walk to and from school. He would introduce her to his friend Emma; watch out for her during recess and lunch on the playground.

He knew from her picture that she was very pretty and smart, according to Uncle Jake, who didn't mind answering his questions as they sat in the office during slow periods at the pump.

He knew, of course, that her parents were killed in a big car crash-up with a fire truck. He saw an old news article, on Uncle Jake's desk, which he had read while having a snack in the office; minding the till while Uncle Jake was serving the customers.

Granville held his breath when he saw the front door open. A deep sigh released a happy, heartfelt, "Hi Dawn! I'm Gran, we're cousins. I live upstairs. Aunt Sara and Uncle Jake told me all about you. We'll be going to the same school. We—my little brothers and I, they're about the same age as you—we walk every day. We can go together. I'll introduce you to my best friend. Her name is Emma. She sits next to me in class and is really smart, like you. I like to play here a lot with my toy soldiers and my tanks. Maybe sometime, if you want, we could play together. Do you know how to play checkers? Wow, that's a huge panda bear! What's his name?"

Sara, Jake, and Dawn waited patiently for the rush of enthusiasm to subside. Dawn was mesmerized by it all. Like walking beneath a cool, refreshing waterfall after a long trek through a vast desert, his words welcomed her into her new world where the fear of loss was washed away.

Granville, Joseph, David, and Dawn were playing war on the landing. The space was a bit small to hold the four of them and the battlefield, so David and Joseph, the Germans, were on the step below the landing, while Granville and Dawn, the Americans, held the high ground above the contested battleground on the plain below.

They had been at it for about an hour when the Germans mounted a final assault on the Americans' entrenched positions, only to be decimated in an artillery barrage.

"Follow me," shouted Major David, going over the top of the trench, leading an all-out charge.

"Look out!" screamed Captain Joseph.

"Aww, I'm hit," cried David as he fell into the barbed-wire American barrier.

"Die, you German swine!" roared Colonel Dawn, throwing three hand grenades in rapid succession at the advancing German charge.

"Lousy, stupid Yanks!" yelled Joseph over the rain of shells and machine-gun fire racking the German trench line.

"Hold on, I'm coming," cried Joseph, sprinting through the no-man's-land hellfire to aid his commanding officer.

"Sir, we are ordered to retreat," cried Captain Joseph, fiercely shouting into his fallen colonel's ear.

"We've got them on the run, men," cried Captain Granville in convivial celebration at the retreating German troops.

Later that afternoon, the victors, Granville and Dawn, were walking through Jake's station. Granville was showing her his job responsibilities when they passed the empty doghouse that still stood guard near the office door.

"Whose doghouse is that?"

"It was Tippy's, Uncle Jake's dog,"

"Jake's, I mean, Dad's dog?" Dawn still had trouble calling Jake "Dad," though her love for the big man was undeniable. Unconsciously, "Dad" was still a tongue-twister in her heart.

("Don't worry about 'Dad,' Dawn, 'Jake' will do until you feel otherwise. It will take time. And we have lots of time, the rest of our lives, in fact.")

"Where's Tippy? Dad never said anything about him."

"He died," replied Granville, in a soft, regretful near whisper.

"How?"

"He was poisoned by the Mob. Uncle Jake doesn't like to talk about it."

"Did you see it?" Pain flashed in her eyes; she reeled in the horror, heartfelt, at the thought of his loss.

"He was the station's guard dog and patrolled inside the fence every night. He was my dog, too, after Snowball died, when I was eight years old. I used to feed and walk Tippy every day after school.

"One day, I was late and missed my chance. That night, I came over to say goodnight and he was dead. I thought that he was sleeping, but Uncle Jake discovered him the next day. We buried him in the backyard next to Snowball."

"Show me."

The two soon stood in front of the two large mounds under the big maple tree behind the house. Each was marked by a triangular stone with an engraved oval face. Snowball and Tippy lay side-by-side in the shade of the big tree, both partially covered by a thick layer of fall leaves.

"Did they know each other?"

"No, but they do now. Snowball has a running buddy, play date chase games 'tween Tippy black and Snowball white, running the alley together."

"Yeah, I guess so."

Part 13: "BEDwetter . . .!"

Granville awoke with a start, frantically checking his sheets. Sure enough, they were once again piss-stained, fresh, still warm. He started to cry at the horror of it all.

He'd had that dream again, he had gotten out of bed and was standing in the bathroom over the commode, needing to pee. Relieved that he had got to the room and inside before the urge embarrassed him, he relaxed his retention, and the flow began. It was feeling the hot wetness running down his thighs, buttocks, and legs that startled him awake to the clear evidence that his dreams had betrayed him once more.

Bitter tears of self-hatred scoured his cheeks. Hearing his brothers' derisive laughter, "BEDwetter, bedwetter, Gran's a bedwetter!" was heartbreaking and utterly humiliating.

Ever since he had become a target, prey for the local gangs, cornered and beaten more than once, the dream had begun. He didn't know why, or how to stop it from happening. He had become fearful; of sleeping, of going to school, of seeing his brothers, who slept in the top bunk bed, while he was in the lower.

Hastily, he stripped the bedsheets and bundled them together with his soggy pajamas, under the bed. He lay back down on the new, plastic-covered mattress Mom had purchased and covered after his had been soiled beyond saving. The cold, crinkly surface clung to his skin, almost as uncomfortable as his shame. The blanket was still somewhat damp and smelled of his loathing. His sleep was fretful at best.

He knew that he was not a toddler needing diapers. Yet at this moment, he feared that something was deeply, terribly wrong with him, to do this despicable thing over-and-over again.

He had not yet connected the two painful realities in his life, being hunted prey and wetting his bed, as the repetitive trauma of one being the likely expression of the other.

[[Author's Aside]]

The causality of the twin process would come later in life,
after years of professional help.

Part 14: "Said . . . BURN it!"

"Said, BURN it!"

"Yeah, boss, you also said, 'Sit on it for a while. I want to let the other Niggers know there's a new sheriff in town, and they'd best get in line or get dead!'"

"How long has it been?"

"Almost a year, boss."

"That long, eh? Been busy?"

"No, sir, taken over the Numbers, going great guns, Niggers switched like rats deserting a sinking ship. No complaints, not even about the sparse winnings."

"And?"

"Black bitch's business's dead-in-the-water, pretty much closed up shop."

"Time to finish the job. Don't want any coon to get the idea that we're letting that uppity bastard slide by. Might get the impression that we're getting soft. Time to light his fire!"

Jake sat at his desk in the station office, pondering his future. Dawn was a godsend to his family. Sara was radiating a joy he had not seen in her eyes since their honeymoon. The station was basically done. The sales and services had tanked months ago. His stubbornness was the only thing that kept the lights on. Even at that, reduced hours were the best he could conceivably manage.

Tippy's death had pretty much been the last straw in his broken back. "FUCK! Fuck! Fuck! They've won! If they still want this deadbeat business, they're welcome to it. My family's my life, and this business, this community, no longer has any part in it. I'm done. We're outta here!"

Jake had just finished closing the shop, gathering his important papers in the office, before shutting down the remaining pump station for the last time. The fuel truck was scheduled to siphon the last of the gas and diesel the next day.

He knew that he should have done this months ago, but part of him just wouldn't let this dream die. He was in the restroom cleaning up. He decided to put on the clean shirt that always hung there in case of emergencies, fuel spills and the like. Again, a symbolic way of washing his hands of the business and this future now past. Thus, this hand-washing farewell to this life took a bit longer than usual.

The long, black sedan pulled into the station and parked next to the furthest pump from the office. The whisper-quiet engine made no discernible sound. The disconnected hose alarm gave no warning.

The passenger door opened, and a dark figure dressed all in black stepped out, careful to remain in the shadows. Deftly, he cut the pump hose at the point of exit, above the little white globe that informed the customer that gas was in the hose and flowing into the customer's vehicle.

The device was meant to assuage any concerns of whether all was operating properly.

The valve ball fell to the ground, breaking the clear globe that was its rightful place, along with the hose length. The emancipated ball, still floating, followed the shallow steam of fluid as it was released from the hose's gaping mouth on the ground toward the curb, where the sedan's purring engine waited.

Fat Rico was slumped in the limo's back seat. His window facing the sidewalk next to the station pump area was partially rolled down so he could witness the imminent conflagration in all its horrific details without being seen or photographed. Normally, Rico did not bother himself with these paltry business details, which he left to his boys to carry out. This was different. He had been told that the bastard had held out beyond all common sense.

That bullheadedness must be repaid in kind. The message had to be clearly understood. Resistance was not only futile, it was also deadly. No exceptions, nothing personal intended, just business. Still, he could not deny his growing excitement at what was about to transpire.

His lieutenant stood casually smoking a cigarette, leaning against the sedan trunk, watching the gas began to pool in a low area on the sidewalk. There was no sense of hurry in his demeanour. He was known, as a "made" man, for his patient cunning.

Jake exited the restroom to be greeted by the sickly-sweet fumes of spilled gas wafting on the evening breeze. His heart tore at his throat as he saw the spill, the car, the monster now grinning within the limo's back seat.

Breaking into a panic-spurred sprint toward the damaged pump, the last image that seared his eyes was the tossed cigarette in the air, arcing its path toward him. The air exploded around him. Instinctively, he held a breath, only to have it expelled in a rush of searing, excruciating pain, beyond comprehension.

"Sara, I love—" A gurgling scream, melting eyes, exploding tongue sealed his voice, above searing lungs filled with flame. Skin melted in droplets before he collapsed to hands and knees, then face, as his desperate momentum carried this husk of life forward to lay in a heap, still thrashing towards the eventual surcease that could only be death.

Jake, as a human being, was no more.

Fat Rico smiled to himself. "Not half-bad for a Nigger! Okay, I've seen enough, let's get out of here,"

Part 15: Eulogy for a Hero

Sara sat in silence in her darkened bedroom. Her acrid tears of rage and sorrow continued to cascade down her hard-lined countenance.

"Baby! Baby, I love you so, how can we do this without you? Dawn hasn't stopped crying since your funeral. It tore my heart out when she tried to jump into the grave after they lowered you down, screaming, 'Daddy! Daddy! Wait for me! I want to come too! Please, Daddy! Please!' Kicking, crying, and screaming the whole time.

"It's been a week now and she still won't eat more than nibbling at a morsel now and then on her plate. Jake, I'm scared! Wanting a child, for you, all our life together, to finally have her, this glorious girl-child, only to lose you! What can I do now? Alone and lost without you, Jake. Oh my God, Jake!"

Her fear-fuelled tears flowed thick and hot till all was done and only the dry heaves between broken sobs of a wounded heart bled into the pit of her soul, filling the river of pain that flooded her mind and spirit.

Dawn slept fitfully. She had night terrors of being madly chased, falling down a bottomless black pit, falling, flailing, never landing, in a gut-tight ball of panic of the unseen horror reaching up from below to swallow her whole. Blazing fire eyes, grime-dripping jaws filled with glistening, blood-red, jagged, broken black teeth.

She would awaken cuddled in her mother's warm embrace and the soothing lullaby she sang to quiet her dearest human's fears of the bitter past and the uncertain future once more.

Sara, months later, requested and received a leave of absence from her position at the hospital, Cook County General. Her workaholic years on the emergency ward had built many months of unused leave time. She and Dawn had devoted themselves to pursuing the dream of a new life in a new place.

What was left of the station had sold quickly.

"God-damn sure the Mob bought it through some sham lawyer lackey on their payroll for pennies on the dollar. The same fuckin' bastards that burnt it down and killed my Jake! An accidental fire . . . my skinny Black ass!" Sara furtively glanced at her daughter, sitting at the breakfast table in front of a cold bowl of porridge, the child's rapt expression hanging on her mother's every utterance.

"Fortunately, Jake, your dad, ever watchful for his beloved family, bought into an excellent commercial business insurance policy. Fire being the ever-present danger for a gas station, bless his soul, never minded paying for extra fire coverage in the premiums.

"Here I berated him all those years about how it was an unnecessary waste of money that we could make good use of elsewhere. Now it's that insurance policy, that extra coverage, that saved our bacon and is paying for our new life.

"Don't you worry, my child. Idlewild's our new home, our new life. Jake did not mean to, but he paid for our chance at a new life with his life. We will honour your dad's sacrifice with our joy for how he gave all, to give all to us."

"I miss him so much, Mom,"

"So do I, daughter mine, so do I."

"Will we go wild in Idlewild?"

"We certainly will, Dawn. We absolutely will."

CHAPTER THREE:
Aftermath, Split Ends

· · · · ·

INES LOOKED THE apartment over carefully. It was an above-ground basement suite, not at all to her liking: two bedrooms, both small; hers would be the smaller of the two. The boys would have to share the larger room. Side entrance directly into kitchen, honey beige linoleum flooring throughout, tiny bathroom, not much bigger than a closet. Three shadowed windows, one in each room, let in little air with virtually no light. An overwhelming sense of chilling coldness was pervasive.

The entranceway skidded along a high grey/sandy/reddish brick wall, bordering a windowless, shoulder-wide walkway. Grocery bags would have to be carried with your body at a diagonal angle to the flat surfaces of the walls on either side; at times, only a slow sidestep shuffle could be managed carrying weight with both hands-on deck.

As a counter to the external darkness, the interior presented a different picture. The kitchen, bathroom, and bedrooms were painted a cheery light beige to white with light brown natural maple trim.

Ines's heart was heavy with this decision. 1714 W 14th Street had been the family home for many years. All five of her children were born there.

"Well?" said the impatient landlady.

"I'll take it."

"Rent due on the first of each month, no extensions, no cheques. First and last month's rent due in advance. Damage deposit will be returned after inspection, providing there have been no issues or complaints."

"There won't be any," said Ines, quiet, yet firm.

"If there happen to develop any problems that cannot be resolved satisfactorily, you will be given thirty days' notice, and any damages or clean-up beyond the reasonable wear and tear will forfeit the deposit."

"Thank you."

Jake's death—in her mind, his murder—was the death knell for their extended family home. Ines had known that it was the end of their "family community" lifestyle, even before the landlord's lawyers appeared to inform them that their lease had been revoked. No explanation or apologies offered, expected, or requested.

As shit floats and water runs downhill, what had to be done was clear to everyone. It was time to get the hell out of dodge before they came for the rest of us. There was a new sheriff in town and killing Black people was just profitable business, plain 'n' simple, thought Ines.

...

[[Author's Aside]]

There were few choices for a single mother with young children that would allow her children to remain in the same school district and school. Simply put, she had to, pretty much, take what she could get. This place afforded her continued access, being within walking distance to her work and the children's school.

...

"Ines, do you have a sitter yet?"

"No, having a very hard time, Sara."

"Same here. Jake left such a huge hole in our lives."

"Didn't realize how much I depended upon him for support, especially with Gran."

"Oh, God, yes, his broad shoulders and big, kind heart carried us all. Dawn has never been the same. Perhaps she never will."

Ines sat silent, staring into her cup of tea, long gone cold, as if mining its depths for wisdom. The look of her reminded Sara of her Jake and she felt her heartache begin to beat deep within her chest, now a familiar, near-constant reminder of his absence.

"I have been using a sitter with Dawn when I needed someone to cover for me. Her name is Ellie Mae. She's pretty good. Doesn't drink, smoke, or party, no boyfriends here while on duty, and Dawn seems to like her, though not overly much. Dawn is pretty picky about the people that she might, emphasize *might*, feel comfortable enough to be allowed in her presence. She is as finicky with people as she is with her food."

"Too many disappointments at an early age."

"Yes, I suppose so."

Once again, Dawn was falling, tumbling, flailing uselessly down a pitch-black, rancid pit without sides or bottom, rushing so fast that breath eluded her in brief, thin, hot gasps that singed her throat. Panic blossomed in her heart and mind. Suffocating, heat burning her eyes, throat, skin, blistering to flame burst in earnest. Everywhere was searing pain.

Demonic necromancer, essence of evil, roared upward toward her, its eye sockets and vacant nose-orifice sprouting greenish bile-coloured snakes, slithering across its skull. Its gaping mouth swallowing the rushing horizon. The horror smiled grimly . . . jagged, broken, blood-drenched teeth dripping thick slime, it called her name.

"Dawn, yes . . . Dawn! Never be free . . . come, child, come, child . . . so hungry, hungry . . . so happy to feast! Come, child . . . come, child . . . so tender to eat! Come, child . . . come, child . . . waiting for me . . . bring your sweet meat . . . hold now, child . . . hold fast to feast!"

Sobbing in her fitful sleep, then to slowly awaken, once more, held close, soft song sung within her mother's embrace. Sara's lullaby, sans words, hummed in her ear, being rocked in love's lap, kissed on forehead, cheeks, and brow, drove all fear away, to feel loved, forever loved, once more.

Granville was crying. He had been crying through day's light . . . through sunset . . . through full moon rise and set to suit the darkness within, perfect counterpoint to the darkness without, hope lost without faith in the day or the night. Granville cried. Chest heaves gave way to silent breath-catches, the deep gut ache that touched nothing, gave nothing, to bait the hope of dreams.

Dead and gone yet received no surcease from the hideous torment within.

They were gone, all gone. Snowball, Tippy, Uncle Jake, the family home. All dead. "Why?" screamed the distraught little boy at the four silent walls of his dark, predawn room.

"Life is sometimes that way. You must lose what you hold most dear to discover the true riches you have inside," said Ines from the shadowed doorway.

"I don't care!"

"That is also part of it. To not care about something is how we learn how to truly care about others and to honour, appreciate and protect that which is special and important to us. These are hard lessons, son. Life is often a cruel, even indifferent, teacher. The lessons must be learned all the same."

Uncle Jake's funeral had been very hard on young Granville. The need to rage aloud over the injustice of it all had shaken him to the core. Seeing Dawn try to throw herself into the open grave after Uncle Jake's casket, kicking and screaming, to be held back only by Aunt Sara's strong arms, had almost broken him.

Known as the family cry-baby, he forced back his river of tears by biting his lower lip till it bled. Big boys don't cry!

The floodgates had opened as soon as he was alone in his room after dinner, which he'd had no appetite to eat.

"Big boys, and sometimes men, do cry, Gran, when there is something or someone worth the tears. Death both small and large has been dogging our family's heels this last little while. I am crying for my brother-in-law, and I cried for Snowball and Tippy. I loved them both. I am crying for the pain my young son must endure. Still, endure we must.

"The sensitive amongst us have a greater burden. They must shed their tears wisely. Gran, my sensitive son, your task is to save those tears for the times, places, things, and people that warrant them. They are a precious gift, not to be wasted on TV commercials, say."

"I don't cry at commercials!"

"Son, you cry at Cracker Jack commercials."

"My favourite is Wheaties. Breakfast of champions."

"Be that as it may . . . To cry easily can be seen by some as a weakness, yet the tears only mean that you feel deeply and are comfortable enough in yourself to express your feelings openly. That's a sign of strength that few people have. So those without that self-confidence feel the need to attack that strength when they see it in others by claiming to cry openly is a weakness.

"Gran, cry when you will, cry when you must; just be aware that those tears have a weight, so to speak, that you must be willing to carry. So, you can be ready to defend yourself if need be."

"Thanks, Mom, I will. I think I'm cried out. I'm going to sleep now."

"Good. Goodnight, son."

"Goodnight, Mom."

"Sweet dreams."

Part 1: Ellie Mae, Johnny Dollar . . . A Quiet Place

Ellie Mae was beside herself; couldn't eat, hardly sleep, lying in bed for it seemed like hours, dreaming, fantasizing, planning, and scheming about Johnny Dollar. She had met him at the graduation dance at Roosevelt High School. He was a graduating senior, she just a sophomore. He was experienced, ready to go to junior college in the fall. She, very inexperienced, happened to be a virgin, in fact. She was eager, oh so eager, to explore the world and all it had to offer. He had become her key and the roadmap toward that wondrous new reality just outside her reach and waiting for her to come calling.

This unexplored world was the magic lamp in her dreams. Johnny was the genie held tightly, cruelly inside. Her love was the three wishes that would set him free. Of course, one of her wishes would be that he should have his freedom. A gift that only she could give. In gratitude, naturally, he would love and cherish her forever. Away they would fly to all the exotic places of her dreams.

She was very bright and self-aware, the eldest child and only girl of what had become a staunch Jehovah's Witness family.

It being against church doctrine and practice, her family would never sanction or support her secret dream of attending university and medical school to become a psychiatrist or perhaps a neurosurgeon; then to devote herself to finding a cure for Alzheimer's, the invisible, terminal disease that had killed her beloved grandparents. She was not at all interested in becoming one of the religion's so called 144,000 anointed.

Since her parents had converted to what, in her understanding, was a cult of false beliefs, a doctrine that separated her family and enslaved the children to a way of life that had become a universe of have not, do not, cannot, or be disassociated, disfellowshipped and thereby damned.

She felt that being of the world, or "worldly," as some of the Witnesses called those who did not believe as the cult members did, basically boiled down to "my God is better than your God, and I can call him by his 'true' name."

The Witness God, created and worshipped in its likeness to man rather than the other way around. According to the Witnesses, their church, or the JW Governing Body, was the only visible channel by which their God communicates with humankind. In that regard, there was much commonality with Catholicism and the Roman Catholic popes, also thought to be God's conduits on earth.

Yet the Catholic Church was thought, by the JWs, to be a vehicle of and ruled by Satan. To disobey or disrespect the dictums of the JW Governing Body was tantamount to denying God, with true death, or death without resurrection, being the resultant penalty. The pope's dictums were to be followed under the penalty of heresy, something that would warrant being burned alive on a stake not all that long ago.

The juxtaposition and hypocrisy were not lost on Ellie Mae.

She loved and respected her parents but had grown to detest what they had become. It all had become a huge heartache, a burden in Ellie Mae's life that she craved only to be free of.

[[Author's Aside]]

She was rapidly becoming a budding agnostic in training.

"Johnny! Johnny Dollar!"

"Lady! Lady, lady, why must you hollah? Ain't nobody seen your Johnny Dollar! I can't get no sleep on this noisy street. I've got to move. I've got to move. I've got to find me a quiet place."

Johnny sang his heart out to the lyrics to his favourite song, "A Quiet Place" by Garnet Mimms. It was a soul hit in the ghetto. The karaoke contest was the highlight of his grad dance. Besides being universally popular as an anthem for life in his West Chicago ghetto, it had special significance.

Coincidentally, his name was Johnny Dollar. Thus, this song of the ghetto was a song about him.

The song gave voice to his dreams, and those of many like him, to find a place; almost any place, where peace of mind and spirit was congruent with the environment, supported by the resident society, within the ghetto and without.

Johnny attended Chicago Technical College, a junior college, which channeled his appetite for adventure toward the technical side of helicopter maintenance and advanced flight techniques. Johnny had always dreamed of flight. The dream had led him to enlist in the Army Air Corps shortly after graduation and train as a helicopter pilot.

[[Author's Aside]]

He then flew Hueys in the early stages of the war in Vietnam, when it was still called a "police action," which in turn led him to his fate, to be shot out of the sky while flying a medevac mission in the Mekong Delta swamp outside of Saigon. He would die a hero.

...

Ellie-Mae groaned under his weight, welcoming every pound of him, every inch, filling her with heat unknown in her short life. Johnny, partially perched on both elbows while stroking deep into the girl's tight vagina. He had so wanted, throughout their brief courtship, to have her exactly where she was now, open and greeting his each thrust with her own counter-push. He felt like she was swallowing him whole.

Momentum building, tempo increasing, heat mounting, Ellie Mae's firm breasts bouncing, keeping time with each stroke.

Johnny almost upright, arms outstretched, resting tight against Ellie Mae's shoulders. Eyes shut tight, her head clasped firmly within the vice grip of his huge palms; the girl's legs, locked around her big lover's thrusting hips, above his tight, full, round ass, riding him, grinding up against him, for all she was worth. Their breath, in unison, screamed lust for each other, for the moment shared. No matter how fleeting that moment might be . . . now . . . right here . . . right now was all that mattered to their lust and love and everything in between!

"Yesss! Yes, yes! Fuck! Fuck . . . YES!"

...

Granville watched it all silently from the crack between the door and the door frame that was left open by Ellie-Mae to, "Listen for the kids, just in case they might wake up."

A necessary trip to the bathroom had become an opportunity to observe his sitter and her boyfriend having sex. At least that was how it had begun for him. Now, it had become an irregular, secretive, and somewhat scary part of her presence in their lives.

Since he had become a bed-wetter, sleep tread lightly in his slumber.

The inadvertent sounds of the teenagers' copulation, combined with the inevitable bladder-born pressure, was more than enough to rouse him from his precious sleep. The fear of being discovered was nearly overpowering, initially. Yet with repeated observations, his curiosity held his attention despite his fear.

He now understood the giddy nervousness that Ellie Mae would exhibit around bedtime, hurrying through dinner and their baths, as if bedtime could not come fast enough. Yes, now he knew what he had never thought he would have known or cared to know . . . and he was afraid . . . very afraid.

What would his mom do when she found out? He knew he had to tell her.

Granville Johnson, Fourth Grade

[[Author's Aside]]

Fourth grade was a tumultuous year in Granville's world. His life, through influences that were far beyond his preteen control and understanding, seemed to cascade, like a landslide of stress filled with the debris of times past, raining down upon the quicksand of his consciousness. One thing did lead to another, which in turn led to further redirections, none of which he could have seen coming. Yet it all was only the beginning of a new life in an old world lived within a devil's brew of fear and anticipation.

Part 2: Puberty: Sexual Abuse and Circumcision

[[Author's Aside]]

Puberty: Sexual Abuse and Circumcision

Growth spurts can happen at any time in the life cycle of a young boy.

BACKSTORY: THE MANY LIVES OF GRANVILLE JOHNSON

Granville's preteen growth spurt began after fourth grade. All of Granville's extremities extended dramatically. In the picture above, he is wearing the same shirt that he wore in the grade three class photo.

Over the year, that shirt had not shrunk.

He remained one of the shortest kids in the class, yet everything—arms, hands, legs, feet, penis—grew longer. His torso remained unchanged.

The overnight stretch was so abrupt that his clothes could not keep up; hence, the spring class photo.

For the most part, adjustments were made as needed.

The exception to that growing comfort zone was Granville's penis.

The cap enclosing the head did not grow to the necessary size to accommodate erection. Consequently, mornings when he would awaken with an erection from needing to pee, the expansion would become intensely painful and only subsided upon softening.

Puberty combined with the psychological response to the onset of repeated overt visual stimulation and sexual abuse, beginning at age nine, created a hyper-sexualized consciousness.

Translation: reoccurring, vivid wet dreams bringing searing penile pain from an erection in the middle of the night.

Eventual relief required circumcision at age eleven.

Relief from the physical torment was near immediate. He healed quickly.

However, the psychological torment of the ongoing sexual and physical abuse intensified.

Ellie Mae stood across from Ms. Andrea. The girl's hands twitched and squeezed each other as if the right and the left were battling for supremacy, or perhaps just looking for a safe place to hide. That was exactly how she felt.

Her thoughts spoke loudly. *Just say it. I know that I . . . we shouldn't have betrayed your trust . . . by what we did in your home while I was on duty and responsible for the kids and everything that happened on my watch. So, fire me already. I told you, honestly, what Johnny and I were doing. We were making love, as lovers do, or have you forgotten what it's like to love and be loved by someone like Johnny? I did not mean to or try to have him here. It just happened.*

"Are you pregnant?"

"No . . . I don't know . . . maybe. Yes, I suppose so!"

"Does he know? How far along are you?"

"Yes. I wrote and told him. Two months?"

"When did it start?" *Don't you dare lie girl! I'll know the truth!*

"When did what start?" *Oh God! Please have mercy! We met three months ago. Just before you hired me to watch your kids. I'm so sorry, Ines! I love him!*

"Your parents. What did they say?" *Not having any of it I imagine.*

"I am disowned. I have to move out after my baby's birth. Mom was able to persuade Dad to let me stay home until then. We have friends in their Witness congregation who understand that anyone can make a mistake. I can stay with one of them until I can find a place of my own."

Ines vented her exasperation, "I can't work without someone to look after the kids. They really like you and you have been good for them. If you promise there'll be no more of this bullshit going on, you can stay until I can find someone else. I'm very sorry, Ellie-Mae, that things have turned out this way."

"So am I. This is my mistake, my baby, and my life. Johnny and I are going to build a life together. Johnny's going to send money to help out. It's so very difficult now. But it will be so much better when we are together. He is such a good man, kind, loving, and he loves me and our child, as much as I love him, maybe more. I by no means saw this coming; yet I have no regrets. We are planning on getting married when he completes his tour in Vietnam."

"Good, I'm glad that both of you have committed to doing right by your baby and for each other. It is a hard road you've chosen but it is not the end of your dreams. A post-secondary education is still within your future. Just will take longer to achieve in that your child comes first in everything and in every way. If you can love and support each as you grow through all the changes, all the unforeseen experiences, it will take a while to get where you want to go, yet you will get there together."

[[Author's Aside]]

Several months later, Ellie-Mae would be informed of Johnny's fate and would know, in her grief and horror, that she would be facing this new life alone with their child.

Part 3: The Fall of Ms. Chambers

Granville was in a piss-poor mood. Once again, he had been hassled in the school yard by the remnants of Buck's gang. It was another fight, another loss in a war he could not win. They were like pack dogs, always sniffing, hunting, digging for an opportunity, to exert their malice, to disprove the cowardice that hounded their heels, as it did Buck's.

Granville was just a means to an end, something to do when the boredom of the uninterested, under-educated reared its ugly head to become, once more, the invisible enemy they all dreaded.

Gladstone Elementary was a tall, three-story red-brick structure.

In Gladstone Elementary, the students traversed the wide stairways, which had a landing halfway between each floor, in a line, walking up and down in single file. Boys would be on one side, the girls on the other. Neither were allowed to climb or descend by using the central area.

On this day, Buck's gang lined up behind Granville. Within a distance between the ground floor and the first landing, several had hop-skipped through the line to be just behind him.

Then the hassling began anew, though careful not to be seen by the teacher monitoring the ascent from the top of the staircase. To escape more bruising, Granville moved to the middle area between the two lines of children slowly climbing in relative silence.

Ms. Chambers saw him walking up. The lines turned the corners on the landing and began to approach her floor. Eyeing the young boy in the middle of the stairway, she told him to get back in line.

Granville continued to climb, acutely aware of the gang watching and waiting for him to be forced to join them, an opportunity for further abuse, and the girls also watching in obvious disinterest, except for Emma, who watched intently.

Granville focused on the teacher at the top of the stairway leading to the third floor. He knew of Ms. Chambers; besides being the fifth-grade teacher, she was also the vice-principal. She often spoke at the school assemblies when Mrs. Adams was not available.

Ms. Chambers was also the only Black teacher in the school, a fact that she was never allowed to forget during breaks in the staff room, where she always had to be on guard for staff politics laced with racist innuendo.

Vice-Principal Chambers was a "by the book" disciplinarian. "Stern and stubborn" was how some teachers who respected her would describe her to others. Those who did not respect her, and perhaps envied her position that they felt she did not deserve, would add the word "stupid" in whispers behind her back.

Chambers respected the children in her charge more than she respected most teachers on her staff. Still, she felt driven in her position, feeling that she forever had something to prove.

Granville did not move to either side as he continued to climb toward the teacher, veering to his right as if to move around her left side—the side of the staircase lined with the boys.

The vice-principal, a tall, statuesque woman, reached with her left-hand palm out to stop the boy who lithely dodged her by stepping back down a step. Reaching a second time with the right hand, she was able to briefly grasp Granville's jacket lapel. Once again, he ducked into a crouch, away from the teacher's grasp, by pulling hard, further toward her left side, still two steps below her.

The combined effect of her precarious position above, and Granville's evasions below in his determination not to be dissuaded from going to his class, thus avoiding the gang, caused Ms. Chambers to pivot awkwardly off balance.

"AHHHHH!"

Spinning, her momentum catapulted her down three steps to land painfully on her right hip, shoulder, and back of her head, sprawled across several stairs, unconscious.

Silence.

All the children stopped, staring, frozen in disbelief, seeing what had just happened.

Granville turned, glanced briefly at the teacher's sprawled body, and ran down the stairs two at a time, out the big front double doors, and most of the way home as fast as he could, bitter tears of fear and frustration stinging his eyes.

Ines received a call at work once more. Her time off was once again bartered with the yard boss, this time to replace the evening crew chief, who was out sick, for the next two nights. She was very grateful that she could trust Ellie Mae to sit for her through the double shift. The girl was very thankful for any extra hours she could work.

Ines and the soon-to-be mother had come to an understanding that benefitted both women. They needed each other and that was enough to rebuild trust.

The principal waited patiently for Ines to relax and take in the rather stressful situation before she began.

"Ms. Andrea, according to the eyewitnesses, Granville managed to push or perhaps trip Ms. Chambers, causing her to fall, when she was attempting to make him walk in line with the rest of the boys. Apparently, it was not purposeful and there were extenuating circumstances. He was trying to evade a group of kids from Buck's little gang of gangsters that were following him up the stairs.

"I'm told that he and the gang had been fighting again behind the gardener's toolshed, just before the bell rang. Ms. Chambers was not aware of what had transpired in the schoolyard, having not been on duty there.

"I'm sure if she had been on yard duty at the time, the fight which precipitated this unfortunate consequence would have never happened.

If, and I do mean if, there had been a fight witnessed by her, I would be considering the suspension of those boys, not your son."

"How is Ms. Chambers?"

"She has a sprained ankle, a badly bruised hip, which is being x-rayed, and a concussion, also being x-rayed. If all goes well, she will be back to work in a week or two. It's up to her as to when she wishes to return to her class and duty."

When Ines first arrived, on the way to Mrs. Adams's office, the first people she went to see were David and Joseph, reading picture books in the school library. They were overjoyed to see their mom, having been assured by their teacher that she would meet them there to take them home. The teacher had left them in the care of the young librarian, a very pleasant recent teacher's college grad, one of the more kid-friendly adults employed at the school.

"There're my beautiful boys. Have you been good for Miss Jones?"

"Yes, Mama, we're reading about dinosaurs."

"Ms. Andrea, they have been wonderful little scientists, hunting for dinosaur burial grounds."

"When we grow up, we're gonna find lots of dinosaur bones . . . huge ones!"

"I'm sure you will."

"Can they stay here a bit longer? I have a meeting with the principal. I shouldn't be long."

Ines felt she knew what this long-winded woman was getting at and wished she would just get on with it. Apparently, though, she had much more to get off her rather flat chest.

"Granville is a valued honours student. He had been performing at the top of his class since first grade, with no disciplinary issues whatsoever. Due to his exemplary record, and with the understanding that he has been an unfortunate target for the bullies, I have decided to suspend him for just one week, effective immediately."

"This is Monday."

"Exactly! He may return next Monday."

"And the young bastards that have been bullying my son?"

"They're suspended for two weeks for fighting and bullying."

...

Carefully searching his mother's demeanour for clues to her mood, Granville asked, "Is Ms. Chambers all right?"

"She had a bad fall and will be recovering at home for a couple weeks, but she's okay."

"Mom, I'm sorry."

"I know what happened, Gran. The principal told me all about it, the fight, the stairway, the accident. I know it was an accident, that you didn't mean for Ms. Chambers to fall. These things sometimes happen. It has been a rough year for you, son."

"I didn't mean to run away . . . the gang."

"No harm done, you had good reason to be upset and afraid, it was pretty scary stuff . . . the vice-principal, sprawled out on the stairs and everyone watching."

"I almost peed my pants."

"I bet."

"Mom, I don't want to go there anymore."

"Go where?"

"My school. Gladstone. I hate that place."

"I know you do, son."

"Can I go to a different school?"

"Gladstone is the school in our district. To change schools, we'd have to move out of the district or attend a private school, and I can't afford to send you and your brothers to a private school."

"Then let's move to a different district."

"We've only been here less than a year. We were very lucky to have found this place."

"Mom, there must be a way."

"Okay. I will investigate it and see what I can find to help me figure all this out."

"Thanks, Mom."

"You're very welcome, son."

Part 4: From the Frying Pan into the Fire

The sermon at Christ's Shepherd Southern Baptist had been interesting if not informative, yet there was a bit of news in the new business section of the church flyer about a storefront satellite ministry that was being started in a building purchased by the church recently. The building had apartments to rent in the building that were soon to be available.

Members of the congregation would be given preferential consideration.

Ines could not help but reflect on the timeliness of this "did-not-see-it-coming" opportunity. It was as if God Himself were listening to her son's prayers, not to mention, her own.

"What do you think, Sara?"

"Sounds like somebody upstairs is looking out for you. I would jump on it in a heartbeat, if not for having committed to moving to Idlewild."

"The deacon says that it's in an all-white neighbourhood, no Black people living there, period. It's not a rich suburb, rather the working poor and some small businesses. Sometimes, they're more fearful and bigoted than the rich folks."

"Yeah, less to hold on to, more to lose."

"That does not bode well for any Black family moving in."

"The church will be there to provide support."

"Perhaps, but would that be enough? Given that it would be attended only on the weekend, we would be there seven days a week, living there full-time. We both know what can happen when a neighbourhood starts to change colours," said Ines.

"Right. Recipe for blockbusting. Are you up for that if it comes to it?"

"I don't know. Gran really needs to get the hell away from those young bullies in Gladstone. It's getting worse week in and week out. They just can't, or won't, protect him. Sara, I'm worried that I'll be called to that fucking school one day only to claim my boy in a box!"

"You got me there, Sis. I don't want to see you jailed for life for killing one of those little bastards. Just don't take your gun to school."

"Amen."

"Well, are you? Or ain't you?"

"It may be jumping from the frying pan right into the fire . . . still, Lord willing, there may very well be a solution we haven't discussed."

"Such as?"

"There's a Catholic elementary school very close to the church."

"A Catholic school?"

"Yes, Our Lady of Sorrows, within short walking distance. There's a private Catholic high school right next door to the elementary school."

"Trust an all-white neighbourhood to have two Catholic schools next door to each other right in the middle of it. Ines, those schools are all white, not public, and cost a very pretty pile of coin to attend."

"I had an interview with the head nun in Our Lady of Sorrows Elementary last week."

"You've been busy."

"Gave Ellie Mae some extra hours so I could sort all this mess out."

"And?"

"They have an honours program in the school that allows honour students, transferred in, to attend the honours program for reduced charge, and they are eager to let Black students attend, so eager, in fact, that David and Joseph will be allowed to attend for free as part of their outreach program catering to visible minorities, as the "holier-than-thou" Sister Superior put it."

"That is a superior offer. What's the catch?"

"I have to convert to Catholicism."

"What!"

"Exactly."

"You can't be serious!"

"Serious as last week's heart attack."

"Well, it is a way out, still, likely to be a fight, doubtful that the honky heaven of a low-mid-class cesspool is going to welcome you and your boys with open arms."

"Sometimes that hellfire underneath the pan you're being fried in is the only way."

"Sis, like my Dawn, your boys are special. I'd cut the balls off the Devil his-damn-self to give her what she needs. I know that, for a fact, you would do no less. Don't forget your gun."

"Amen, already packed."

CHAPTER FOUR:
3148 West Harrison Street

· · · · ·

Part 1: Summer in the City

[[Author's Aside]]

It was summertime in the city.

Chicago's "season of the hawk," when the bitterly cold wind off Lake Michigan is blowing snow and sleet sideways, cutting through you like a thousand tiny razorblades, bringing merciless pain to any exposed skin, eyes, nose, and throat; from October through March, this is otherwise known as winter.

Summer in that same city cooks its inhabitants in August monster heatwaves that can and will kill the unprepared. The same moist, lake-fed air boils the skin, being so humid that sweat can't evaporate; thus, the body's cooling system does not operate. Sweltering shade brings no surcease.

The nights only magnify the stifling discomfort. The mind cries out at the senselessness of the heat without sun to feed it; yet the pavement and red brick buildings, having roasted all day, release their pent-up fire to fry in the breezeless night. All sleep, in sopping, clinging sheets, becomes fruitless, even fatal.

Garfield Park, the community park near Granville's soon-to-be new home, was a favourite gathering place for a multitude of families from several neighbourhoods that surrounded it.

Thus, it was one of the few public locations where the population enjoying its benefits was very much a mixture of races, and societal and cultural orientations. It truly was a representation of the melting pot montage that American society, right or wrong, is known for. This was never truer than in the community pool that was in its centre.

The pool was full of children of all ages, shapes, sizes, and colours. The shallow end held so many bodies bobbing up and down, in and out, shoulder to shoulder in its three feet of depth that, from above, it was difficult to see the water.

The sight reminded one of an over-populated, swarming anthill, engrossed in feeding time over discarded morsels at a family picnic.

Due to this very same mass of young cavorting bodies, the pool's water was heavily treated with many chemicals to counter-act the effect of the propensity for little boys and girls to use the surrounding liquid depth as a convenient alternative to going into the changing room to use the facilities. Human urine was an ever-present issue for the community health authorities.

The deep end was ten feet deep under two diving boards: low, three feet above the water, and high, a ten-foot tower next to it, above the sparsely populated area of the pool allocated to the more experienced swimmers.

The lifeguards, all white, were bored. They watched the teeming scene in the shallow end sporadically. Most of their focus on the throng was directed toward the young teen female bodies of budding womanhood wrapped in various styles of bikinis, especially if the girls were somewhat endowed in a way that suited their taste or interest. There certainly were many examples of female flesh to choose from.

Now and again, a lovely body would take flight from the high board to slice the liquid surface below in near perfect form, barely making a splash upon entry.

Those moments were retold repeatedly, embellished dramatically in the sharing amongst themselves after the day spent on the podium languished to its end. Not much else ever broke the tedium.

Granville knew how to swim. Ines had spent the early days of last summer giving him swimming lessons. She, herself, was an excellent swimmer and was determined to pass that lifesaving skill on to each of her children. David had taken to the water like he was born there; played and swam like a dolphin. Joseph was a bit more timid, though he did catch on very quickly, following his brothers' lead.

Granville had grown tired of the rough and tumble of the shallow end and had taken advantage of his mother's preoccupation with the boys. She had taken them to the women change room to dress, then have snacks, while he, being the oldest, was allowed to swim on his own while they changed. It was so nice to be free of his little brothers being underfoot, with him on duty full time. He had been wanting to try something he had never done before.

He dove into the pool at the five-foot marker, heading for the deep end in long, easy strokes and strong kicks. As he reached the far wall, he treaded water, looking straight up at the base of the ten-foot support tower for the high diving board directly over his head.

At that moment, he saw her. The girl dove, bouncing once, twice to travel high above the board, arms stretched out, making flight wings in the air on either side; then, at the peak of her upward trajectory, she bent at the waist, beginning her descent, arms to come together, hands forming an arrowhead, followed by her lower body straight as a missile into the water directly in front of him with a whoosh. He felt the underwater current part by her near silent passage, pushing him against the wall of the pool.

He had to try it.

The grade seven boys, members of the Harrison High School swim team, were playing tag. The game started as an antidote to the boredom of being in a pool so crowded that they were prevented from swimming laps, which was their preferred pastime on a hot Saturday afternoon. The game soon burst out of the sea of children to land on the pool side, where they continued the chase and dodged onto, over, and off the bleachers that functioned as a viewing area, mostly populated by observant parents. The chase hardly abated as they frantically covered ground, slipping, sliding, running in evasive maneuvers to avoid being tagged.

Granville watched the progress with interest from his high perch atop the ten-foot diving board tower. He marveled that, though he was not all that high above the pool surface, everyone below seemed so small.

Refocusing on his purpose for being there, he approached the board itself. A long plank stretching through the open sky toward the horizon, looking as long as forever. Stepping gingerly away from the safety railing, the big toe of both feet now touching the rough surface of the springboard, he felt his resolve ebbing, his fear blossoming within his chest as the awareness of his rapidly beating heart filled his ears. Nevertheless, sliding one foot in front of the other, determination gathering courage, he approached the leading edge of the springy board.

Hesitation became the order of the day. He studied himself, breathing deeply, eyes closing slowly, tightly, in preparation for the feat at hand.

Dive . . . no, jump . . . Is the landing below clear? Can I do this? Is Mom watching from the bleachers? Did someone just call me? Thought for sure I heard someone calling me. Just a bunch of kids shouting. Ignore, forget it, focus. Breathe. You can do this. Mom will be so proud, thought Granville.

"Granville! Granville. Gran. Gran . . .!" Ines shouted, waving both of her arms toward her diminutive son high atop the last place on Earth he should be. She knew that he had never done such a thing before, and wondered what in the hell had got into him to think this was a good idea.

The pool noise suddenly felt deafening, swallowing her screamed warnings, reducing them to insignificance as she watched in horror, the helter-skelter approach of the racing group of boys that, just a moment ago, had almost trampled anyone in their path as they ran through the observation bleachers.

The lifeguards, standing on their perches, were now voicing their alarm at the out-of-control teenage stampede, mindless of its surroundings, all lost in the fleeting, sheer heat of their chase of each other, obstacles—human or otherwise—be damned. The boys were charging toward the inevitable fence at the poolside surrounding the high dive tower and the end of ground level real-estate.

There was only the tower, at that moment being the tenuous perch of one little, unaware, almost oblivious boy-child, as an exit for the lead boys to escape their pursuers.

They climbed with ferocious speed to burst over the top of the ladder like a human geyser, hardly breaking their momentum.

Granville heard his name, clearly, from his mother's explosive final clarion call, just as he felt the tower shake from the onslaught of stampeding bodies. Suddenly, his eyes flashed open, he knew of the danger and turned to retrace his oh-so-careful approach back toward the platform edge as fast as he could.

Too late, much too late; he was struck, pushed, and partially carried by two of the biggest of the herd back toward that open sky and horizon he had so wondrously admired, back-paddling on air, he tumbled, head-over-tails, in total panic, completely disoriented, screaming; frantically, he tried to see where he was. In that split-second desperate search, he found the water's surface, crashing hard into it, flushed face first, with his eyes and mouth open wide.

The lifeguards did their job. The one on the stand closest to the shower of flailing bodies knifed through the turbulent waters just as the teenage heads broke the surface. He came up shouldering Granville's limp form.

Ines's heart skipped several beats as she choked on her bile that blossomed in her throat.

Granville did not become fully awake until he was at the emergency ward at Cook County General. Ines was there and so were David and Joseph.

"Mom?"

"Are you okay?"

"M...m...my throat hurts. What happened? Where are we?" "We're at the emergency ward at Cook County General. You fell off

the high diving board at the swimming pool."

"I did? I don't...I remember."

"I think you were about to jump when this rampaging bunch of young teenagers charged up the tower and knocked you off the board. Gran, why were you up there in the first place?"

"Yeah. I saw this girl dive off and I wanted to try."

"Was this the first time you thought of doing that?"

"No Mom."

"You should have asked me first. Gran, you could have really hurt yourself. You scared me half to death."

"Sorry, Mom. I wanted to surprise you with how good I can swim and dive."

"You've only just learned to dive off the low board. I guess you've learned that the high board is a whole different animal that requires many, many hours of supervised practice to learn how to fall from that height without hurting yourself. But then I guess you've learned that on your own the hard way."

"It really hurt, Mom. The water was hard; it burned bad."

"You swallowed a fair amount of it. Thought they'd have to pump Lake Michigan out of your belly, waiting to see a fish jump out."

"Ha, ha, ow! It hurts, Mom, don't make me laugh."

"Then I guess I better not tickle you."

"Mom, no!"

The hospital curtain parted, affording Granville a brief reprieve from Ines's threatened tension-breaking tickle assault.

"Ms. Andrea, you have a very tough youngster in your son. He has a mild concussion; there has been some infiltration into his sinuses and the area behind his eyes on the left side due to impact with the water, which filled his orifice. I believe he will be all right. You should observe him over the next few days. Watch for low fever, light sensitivity, headaches. In any rate, all of it should pass quickly with no protracted damage. Community pool water is nasty stuff when it gets in places where it shouldn't be."

The young doctor smiled and turned to Granville. "You're very fortunate, young man, that you did not strike the pool's edge or any of the others that were with you. Things could have turned out very differently. Watch out for and beware of heights in the future, or next time you may not have a future."

"Yes, sir."

[[Author's Aside]]

Granville never mastered his high-dive technique. Throughout the rest of his life, he never tried again, yet has been forever fascinated by the majesty of others. Still, as a young boy he had dreamed of flight.

Part 2: "Call It Dumb Luck . . ."

The room was pitch-black, dark as a grave, white hot, stifling air heavy with the lack of circulation, yet the window was open as wide as the frame would allow. The breeze, what little that happened to have travelled into the darkened enclosure, carried virtually no relief due to the thick, heavy curtains drawn down to block any possibility of light penetrating the gloom. The bedroom door was shut tight against what errant reflective light might ricochet from window to ceiling to wall, down the short hall to slip-slide 'neath that door and light the half-inch gap between it and the floor, to be blocked by a thick towel stuffed within.

On the bed was a young boy-child, fitful in his sleep, fearful in his vivid dreamscape that only magnified his evident discomfort. Rivers of sweat poured from every pore, pooling in every crevice; every bend harboured its own tiny rivulet flowing over the small frame to pool atop the sweat-saturated sheet, never to be absorbed.

Granville shivered, cold to the core amidst the unbearable heat. The fever seemed to periodically break, only to reassert itself; a Phoenix rising once more from the ashes of its own flame to burn a new, higher, yet brighter in this black nebula, hostile stranger, home of eternal night.

Weeks had passed since this hell began. It had begun slowly, faintly, almost imperceptibly, beneath notice. A slight headache, a runny nose, the occasional blurred vision. Nothing that a mother or an active summertime child paid much attention to. Fleeting pain, a nosebleed after assertion, a spotty appetite progressed to disorientation, acute light sensitivity, mounting pressure, and migraines.

Then came the fever-demon and Granville's mind imploded upon itself.

Ines and Granville sat in the quiet waiting area. Granville sat blinded from the light by a thick blindfold. He wore a winter jacket and flannel pants; still he shivered. His mother could see the sometimes-concerned stares sparked by his out-of-season garb when most around him sported T-shirts, sandals, and shorts.

Ines simply ignored them all, having much more concerning matters on her mind. They had been given a number and told to wait their turn with the others in the emergency ward. Eventually, their turn did arrive, and a duty nurse took Granville's temperature while Ines filled out the forms listing her son's history and complaints.

They were quickly ushered into a cubicle where he was told to undress. The duty doctor arrived to examine Granville, who was suffering under the thin sheet. All was quiet until the young resident removed the blindfold and Granville screamed, a blood curdling siren cry that stopped all activity throughout the busy room.

The doctor jumped back several feet away from the crying child, certain that he had somehow mortally wounded the boy. Ines instantly took his place at her son's side replacing the blindfold, shutting out the offending light.

"How long has he been like this?"

"I don't know, maybe a week or more, I'm not sure. I would have brought him in sooner, but I couldn't get time off from work."

The nurse was summoned, and a call went out. Ines and her son were moved to a darkened room outfitted with light-stands and examination lights of varying types and sizes. Granville was covered with a blanket to help with the shivering. Ines was asked to wait in the hall just outside the room.

Ines saw them approach, a rather tall, imperious-looking, grey-haired white doctor striding down the hall toward her, followed by a gaggle of much-too-young-looking doctors and nurses. The leader, apparently very much an authority, stopped briefly to speak with the resident that had tried unsuccessfully to examine Granville.

Flashing a soft, seemingly sincere smile, he stopped to speak with Ines. "Ms. Andrea, I am the chief of staff and head diagnostician. I understand that your son is experiencing an extremely painful issue. We are here to find out what's the cause of the problem and do all we can to relieve his pain and deal with the source. It may take some tests to get to the bottom of it all. So, I may not have an answer to your concerns today, though I promise to get to the bottom of it. We will probably want to admit him for observation and to run those tests. Can I have your permission to admit him today?"

"Yes."

"Thank you very much, Ms. Andrea. This preliminary examination shouldn't take too long. If you care to wait in the lounge or cafeteria, I or one of my residents will inform you as to our progress, and let you know what we have found and where we intend to go from here."

"Thank you. I'll wait."

Ines, not used to this type of consideration from medical professionals, was very surprised and somewhat relieved by his manner and forthright sharing of information regarding Granville.

In the cafeteria, she treated herself to coffee and a muffin.

Granville whimpered when the specialist focussed a small light indirectly into each eye in order to see into the eye socket and tissue located behind the eyeball, but other than that, he was quiet, cooperative, and kept still as possible.

The chief of staff gave notes to his watching associates on what he observed through his examination.

"I want all of you to take note, for what you are observing in this unfortunate, yet fortunate, young lad is a miracle of nature. It appears, though it must be confirmed by CT scan; that he is the walking dead."

Granville's heart skipped and his throat constricted involuntarily at the pronouncement of his own evident demise.

"This boy's sinus cavity is completely compromised by a massive infection, an infection that has begun to attack his nerves at the back of both eyes and is even in the process of compromising his frontal lobe via his small and large veins. By rights, he should have succumbed to this infestation weeks ago. I believe the virulence of this condition can be attributed to the toxic combination of concentrated human urine and chemicals, chlorine being one of many, used to treat the water in the community pool. No doubt occupied by a rather large number of young children playing, pissing, and defecating in the water."

One young face looked up while the rest were furiously noting what was being said. "In your opinion, sir, why do you think he's still alive?"

"Call it dumb luck, or someone upstairs really likes him, probably has something really special planned for his future, and is making damn sure he is around to fulfil that particular fate."

"Then you believe in manifest destiny or fate?"

"Of course, I do." To Granville: "Son, I really hope you are up to it . . . for now, let's get you fixed up."

Granville sat in the high-back cushioned chair. He was belted in to ensure there would be as little movement as possible. A thick, cushioned strap also held his forehead in a rigged position facing the ceiling. He was any-thing but comfortable, yet he held the position. There were cotton pads over both eyes, blocking out the soft glare given off by the examination lights close by. This room had become familiar to him, after his discharge from the hospital, having returned to it once a week since the course of antibiotics had finished.

The process, the cure, he was about to undergo was, in some ways in his opinion, far worse than the disease. He had survived the massive infection of his sinuses and other areas. The question now was, would he survive the aftermath?

Apparently, the formerly infected areas had to be drained of the sepsis that had formed in his sinuses and ocular cavities. This could not be done in a formal operation, under anesthesia, due to the nature and location of the material. Nor could a powerful local anesthetic be applied.

The alternative amounted to medieval torture: a small prick from a local anesthetic applied far up and through the top of his left nostril was only the beginning. This was followed by a long drill bit, which was forced, while turning clockwise too slowly and extremely painfully for Granville, upward, ever upward, through tissue, cartilage, and bone, to reach an area adjacent to his frontal lobe. The progress of the drill was watched very closely by the doctors, assisted by several technicians, as though they were mining for gold in a silver mine. Through that unnatural tunnel, once formed, a powerful suction was applied to draw out the offending material without damaging the adjacent nerves or blood vessels.

Granville, fully awake and aware, would cry through a cascading waterfall of tears, a low, siren-like moan and groan that was virtually continuously rising and falling as the various facets of pain crawled along in succession throughout the procedure.

The boy suffered repeatedly, as the process was duplicated as necessary for many weeks. Eventually, his CT scan results showed that the region was clear.

The by-product of it all was that some inadvertent nerve damage had occurred, perhaps caused by the infection and the sepsis left in its wake.

Granville's left eye had developed a will of its own, no longer under his control. The resultant double/triple vision was exacerbated by the loss of 20/20 vision, which had been reduced to a proficiency closer to 20/10.

One eye being that wayward and generally blurred was a constant irritant, to say the least.

Rehab constituted once-again weekly trips to the ear, nose, and throat clinic for more work in a darkened room. Granville would sit staring into an ocular remediation device. He would be presented with two disparate yet identical images, one for each eye, left and right, to focus on independently.

The goal was to bring those images together as one in the centre area between the original independent opposing images. With practice, while enduring much pain, he was able to develop a level of proficiency. He would arrive at the clinic in the morning in good spirits and with high hopes, only to depart for home that afternoon in abject pain and with a migraine headache that would last the rest of the day.

[[Author's Aside]]

Thus, he was assigned by capricious fate to wear corrective lenses for the rest of his life and never would realize his dream of flight. Piloting an aircraft through

*the wild blue yonder would remain a forever dream, yet the possibility that died
on that high-dive board lives on, within his imagination, into his present day.*

Part 3: Blockbusting

Blockbusters . . . first Black family on the white block . . . in the hood.
First Black family on the white block. . . in the hood. . .
The gangs were white. . . to fight. . . mostly daytime. . . to night. . .
"I Am an Honourable Man" (Excerpt) by Granville Johnson

[[Author's Aside]]

*3148 West Harrison Street no longer exists as a residence. The address now
supports a giant, sky-scratching billboard and is straddled by the Chicago Police
Department HQ on the corner of Harrison Street and Kedzie Avenue
on Chicago's urban West side.*

...

In Granville's youthful time, it was the address of a Southern Baptist
storefront church, a satellite ministry of its parent church, Christ's
Shepherd Southern Baptist. The church purchased the building, located
in an all-white working-class neighbourhood, wishing to expand its
influence in the far West side of the city.

The sale of the building, for abstruse purposes, likely was done to
squeeze every remaining ounce of real-estate profit from the rapidly
declining neighbourhood through the process of reverse gentrification;
otherwise known as blockbusting.

The establishment of a Black-owned building and church in the area
was tantamount to inserting a long, slow-burn fuse into a powder keg.

Once the building was sold and Black church members appeared on
the street front at the church every weekend, the residents would strin-
gently object to no avail. In their horrified frustration, the slow-burn
fuse to the powder keg would be lit.

When Black families moved into the building above the church to take up residence, those same realtors would appear on the doorstep of the white-owned homes and businesses to exhort and extort the white families to sell in a timely manner; before the value of their properties would plummet due to the presence of the Black people, drugs, crime, and abject poverty their presence would bring.

Once that process crawled to its self-evident conclusion, the powder keg would explode in peaceful-turned-violent demonstrations, street violence, gang wars, and localized race riots. Poor people, Black and white, fighting for land and a rightful place in the American dream.

The instigators, the realtors, would have bought cheap and sold high to absentee landlords. Owners that would purchase whole city blocks of homes and businesses, then rented the properties to the incoming Black and Brown families at exorbitant fees, without any intention of maintaining the properties in an expectable condition. Thus, the preordained outcome would be validated in ruined properties filled with broken lives. Blockbusting.

...

Part 4: "The Niggers Are Here . . . Shit!"

3148 West Harrison Street was a three-story building with two suites on each level, one that faced Harrison Street proper and a second suite that faced the alleyway behind the building parallel to the Kennedy Expressway.

The bridge over the expressway supported the entrance to the Kedzie Avenue elevated train station, for the elevated train travelling at above ground level below. It was in the middle of the expressway's eight traffic lanes, four lanes of traffic in each direction: east to west, a main traffic artery between the lakeside downtown proper to the east and Chicago's western environs.

The building's ground floor contained the Christ's Shepherd Southern Baptist Church Ministry, a storefront satellite Black church, small yet large in its attendance and support by the local Black and

Brown congregation. From its inception, it quickly became a gathering place for Sunday service, Bible study, and community missionary outreach activities.

Answering the outreach call of the church elders, Mr. Prince Williams and his wife, Mrs. Leena Williams, otherwise known as Great Uncle Prince and Great Aunt Leena by their great-nephew Granville, lived in the suite behind the church on the ground floor, which opened to the alleyway it faced. The large overhanging back-porch structure of the above floors afforded the couple a covered patio—a unique feature in the three-level walk-up that was the classic urban West Chicago architecture.

Granville's family lived on the second level directly above the church below. The family's front or living room was graced with a large bay window overhanging the church entrance below. Each short wall was filled with a nearly floor-to-ceiling window giving an excellent viewpoint of the sidewalk below.

Directly above Granville's home on the top floor, front apartment, lived his oldest brother Levi with his wife Beatrice; they had recently moved back to the family enclave from Elgin, Illinois.

Thus, the Andrea family had gathered once more in an extended family configuration, as leaves falling from the denuded branch, scattered by an errant breeze, may convene in a new place, a new relationship, yet reflecting resilience and a defiant closeness in the face of hardship.

Led by Ines and her children, being the first to arrive, the extended family, by no stretch of anyone's quibbling imagination, was welcomed as a new addition to the block. They were treated as the first cancerous tumour to rupture in their midst. The early malignant sign of a terminal disease that must be isolated, ostracized, alienated, extinguished, removed before it metastasized throughout their community.

"The Niggers are here . . . shit!" was a common refrain among the despondent homeowners.

The small business owners, on the block around the church, across the street, opposite the church, and in the intersection of Harrison Street and Kedzie Avenue, did not share the same need to be hostile toward the new residents. Just the opposite was expressed, a tacit sort of acceptance was the norm among them. Increased population brought enhanced sales, expanded market, and greater demand for services that superseded concerns of race and ethnicity. The almighty American dollar was welcomed and respected by all members of the country's ethnic minorities.

Despite the hyper-poisoned atmosphere among the neighbourhood's white residents, after a time, mostly due to power of youthful personality, Granville was able to secure part-time, after-school, and weekend employment in the butcher shop next door to the church. With his newfound earnings, he was able to feed a pleasant Sunday addiction to the chocolate eclairs sold in the bakery just across the street from his home. His family made very good use of the dry cleaners only a half a block away.

...

[[Author's Aside]]

Granville, born on Labour Day after his mother had spent twenty-six hours trying to evict her traumatized fetus from her womb and into new life, having suffered through his father's untimely death during her seventh month of pregnancy. He had come out kicking and screaming into weeks of colic to redirect and sometimes rule her future life unlike any of her other four children. As he grew into the significance of his role in her life, he never tired of the irony of his birth on "Labour Day," her day of labour; yet that his birthday always signalled the end of summer and harrowed the start of the new school year, also was a bit of an ironic bitter-sweet fate-accompli in his life.

...

Part 5: Greased Lightning

The swing was huge, much taller than Granville had ever seen in any playground, including back at Gladstone Elementary. Loving the exhilarating feeling of suspension at the apex of each upward climb before the descent that felt like a deep dive to a hard snap at the bottom as the chains reached their limit, his eyes closed tight, savouring the thrill, with the impetus of a hard pump to begin the climb once more, higher still.

This summer Saturday afternoon was made for this limitless flight-like sense of pure fun unleashed. He was alone in the playground that belonged to his future alma-mater, to begin in the fall one week after his birthday, on Labour Day.

"Hey, Nigger! What the fuck do you think you're doing? Your kind of jungle bunnies don't belong here!"

Granville's eyes snapped open to see four angry white faces, two on each side of his flight path, scowling at him as he flew past them, once, twice, then brought to an abrupt halt as two of them grabbed the chains attached to his seat, catapulting him up out of his perch, through the air, and onto the pebble covered ground below.

Literally running on air, Granville's cat-like reflexes came to the fore as he twisted in midair to land facing the interlopers. He didn't need any further indictment to face the apparent danger; four white kids, two of which were much bigger and probably older, were a threat not to be taken lightly. Still, he was sorely pissed off at their rude interruption of his perfect day.

"Go fuck yourself, honky assholes!" was his somewhat fear-laced, yet furious retort as his red shoes gained traction, spitting pebbles in his wake. Granville took flight.

Sister Mary Joseph had watched the young Black boy on the swing from her stairwell in the nun's rectory across the street from the playground. Initially, she was concerned by the height that the boy was able to attain with the momentum he had mastered in his desire to push the swing's apex height as high as the long chains attached to the seat would allow him to soar skyward. Seeing him approach the weightless freedom of simulated flight reminded her of the joy inherent in that release from gravity's grip.

Watching him delayed her progress toward joining the other nuns in afternoon prayers in the chapel, long enough to note the small group of boys who were hurrying toward the playground gate, obviously focused on the same scene of quiet joy that she was witnessing. Hearing their shout, the loud utterance of that racial slur dripping hatred, at the top of their lungs, confirmed her concerns about their intentions toward the boy.

She instinctively decided that an active intervention of this unfolding danger was more an expression of her Lord's presence in this world than passive prayer now. After all, one of that advancing group, intent on menace, was to be in her seventh-grade class. The recognition was appalling; she knew that he knew better. Hastily, she made it to the front door and flung it open just as the group was passing through the playground gate across from the rectory's entrance in hot pursuit of the quickly disappearing Black figure, who was already up the handicap access ramp leading to the footbridge.

...

"Robert! Robert Franklin!"

The group almost tripped each other up as Robert, who was the leader, skidded to a halt, recognizing Sister Mary Joseph's voice.

"Yes, Sister?" *Oh, fuck! It had to be her!*

"Young man, what do you think you're doing chasing that boy?"

"We . . ." *Think fast, the Nigger's getting away!*

She could see the wheels of the lie working hard in a vain attempt to justify his behaviour in this situation to his teacher for the coming school session.

"I thought he was trying to steal something."

"It would be pretty difficult to steal that playground swing while he was enjoying the same equipment that is there for the enjoyment of anyone in the community, no matter what colour they are or what race they may belong to.

"Unfortunately for you, I know you're lying, because I watched your little gang in action, and heard what you said. I am very ashamed of all of you. I know all your parents as well. I will be having a discussion with them about this incident ASAP when the school year resumes. Count on it! Now go about your business, and I don't ever want to hear that kind of language again. Do I make myself clear?"

"Yes, Sister Mary Joseph, ma'am." All was spoken in unison. "Shit!" they said quietly among themselves as they walked away, out of the nun's earshot, also in unison.

That went well, Sister Mary Joseph thought once inside and resuming her progress to the chapel. I must find out who that little boy is and whether his family lives nearby. Perhaps just across the bridge, he obviously was heading for safe harbour, probably home, like greased lightning.

...

Part 6: "Same Ol' Shit. . . Just a Different Colour"

Out the playground gate, racing toward the footbridge that spanned the freeway, Granville was a blur. The joy of near flight in a swing replaced by the heart thumping adrenalin rush of true foot speed. He was more than halfway across the bridge before he realized that he was no longer being chased. He slowed to an easy pace, looking over his shoulder occasionally, just to be sure he was indeed alone. Musing to himself as he pondered his new reality that, in fact, felt like more of the same.

Prey once more, unwelcome and hunted for what he was rather than who he happened to be. *Same ol' shit, just a different colour. Fuck. I'm tired of this crap! Why can't these people just leave me alone?*

Ines had dutifully warned him about what to expect in their new neighbourhood.

"Don't worry about it, Mom. I'll be okay. I can take care of myself."

"I know, Gran, you've had lots of practice; still, you will have to be even more careful. You don't know the neighbourhood like you did before. You can't count on the neighbours being friendly or even helpful if you get into trouble."

"You mean, when trouble finds me."

"Exactly, our home is your only safe harbour, so I don't want you to stray too far from home. The playground next to your new school is as far as you should wander; say, stay within a three-block radius. We are the only Black family here and some of the white people are threatened by having to share the air they breathe with Black folks."

"They can just stop breathing, then."

"Right, problem solved. Unfortunately, they will seek the same solution for us."

"I know, I know violence, no matter the cause, is not a solution. It only creates problems or makes them worse. No resolution can be achieved through violence."

"Yes, that's my boy. I have taught you well."

The next confrontation between Granville and the other school kids on his block occurred on that same footbridge he had raced across earlier. Once again returning from the playground, he had been cornered by the other kids in the middle of the span, cut off by two groups that coincidentally happened to be crossing the bridge from both ends at the same time.

"Nigger, your little black ass is mine, this time," was the last thing that was said before Granville charged the smaller group that had blocked his path toward home. Head down, he rushed the slight space between the three kids that were trying to grab him as he ducked, dodged, and bowled into the smallest of the group, knocking the boy flying against the high fence. Bouncing off the barrier, Granville rolled onto the bridge surface with the surprised boy underneath him, literally running him over.

Granville hardly felt the blows that were raining down upon him by the pursuing group that had managed to close the distance while he recovered from the impact.

All his experience with Big Buck and his gang had taught him that the best defence was a resolute offence. Granville became a human buzzsaw, a cornered ferret, surrounded by rats; he transformed into a ferocious entity, all teeth and claws. He fought as though he had nothing to lose and everything to gain, namely his freedom.

Gaining daylight, he moved into that split-second open space between them and beyond; suddenly he was gone, as if he had not been there at all.

Bobby and his gang froze, stunned at the little Nigger's fight as well as his flight.

"Fuck, he's fast!"

...

Part 7: Jekyll and Hyde

Bobby Franklin was a chameleon, a Jekyll and Hyde personality, a teacher's pet. Throughout his years at Our Lady of Sorrows, he had made it his business to move, in the class environment, within the teacher's blind- spot. Always on his best behaviour in class, utilizing the sister's ego or perceived self-interest to ascertain what she wanted to hear, what behaviours were rewarded, or what her expectations were.

Once his objectives were realized, Jekyll behaved flawlessly to meet those requirements. Outside of those performances, Hyde ruled. Jekyll played his teachers like finely tuned musical instruments; Hyde ruled his gang with an iron fist. Bobby was also a coward, who had no idea which persona was his true self; this made him fearful.

Somehow the nerve, the courage he saw in this little Nigger, enraged him. He would hunt the little black bastard until he killed him, once and for all.

"I almost got him today."

"Did he get away?"

"We had him pretty much pinned on the footbridge. One of the guys, Chris, got in my way, and was rolled over by him as he was trying to escape. We caught him again, but he's fucking fast."

"Watch your mouth!"

"Sorry, Mom."

"One more like that 'n' I'll give you something to be sorry for."

"Is Dad home?"

"Working an extra shift again."

"We goin' to move?"

"Hell no! The Niggers are. We're counting on you and your boys to help with that."

"We're working on it."

...

Part 8: "Where's My Place?"

"Gran, what's wrong, chased again?"

"Yeah, Mom, it's really getting old."

"I know, son. Let me see that eye." Ines sat her son down at the kitchen table while she carefully examined the bruised, darkening, slightly swollen eye socket and bloodshot red eye at its centre. She then went into the adjacent bathroom to return with a warm, wet facecloth and an icepack wrapped in a second cloth. She cleansed the area around the abused eye with the warm cloth, then placed the cloth-wrapped icepack over the eye, covering the area.

"Hold that in place, son. How's that? Better?"

"Yes, thanks, Mom. I'm so tired of this. Just want to have a life without always looking over my shoulder for the next."

"It won't always be this way. You will find your place, Gran."

"Where, Mom? Where is my place?"

"I don't have an answer to that question now, son, only to say that the key to your eventual success is to be true to yourself and not let others define you or your happiness. The world will learn to accept you as you are.

"You are a fighter and a survivor. The struggle is what defines you, not the lack of it, as difficult as it may be. Some people choose to follow whatever, and whoever tells them what to do and how they should be in this society.

"You think for yourself and live by your own inherent sense of what's right or wrong. Having the courage to be true to that choice is why others are threatened by you and what you stand for . . . the power and strength in being an individual, an outlier. Your place is to lead by that example. I know it is hard now; your enemies are many and the danger they represent is everywhere.

"Though you may stand alone, your courage is a beacon for others, also to believe in themselves. The world needs more people like you, my fighter, my survivor, my leader, my son. I am so proud of you."

Granville Johnson Grade Eight

Part 9: "Daredevil" Craig Montrose

Granville watched the boy from his second story back porch with curiosity and wonder. He was curious as to how the boy was racing helter-skelter down the incline parallel to the highway, and wondering how long it would take him to die or become gravely injured in the process of doing it. At any rate, it looked like a whole lot of fun in the trying.

The expressway underneath Granville's porch ran parallel to the alleyway along the length of the block and beyond. The eight-lane traffic thoroughfare sat at the bottom of a thirty-to-forty-five-degree grade. The slope, from the alleyway to the traffic lanes, was covered with grass. The green surface tended to be slippery, especially when wet.

The daredevil boy who Granville was admiring was riding what seemed to be a home-made toboggan constructed from a large cardboard box. The base appeared to be reinforced against the wear- 'n'-tear of the grass surface, while the sides were shaved or reduced to provide some protection while affording handle-like attachments for support. Steering seemed to be accomplished by the boy shifting his weight from side to side, aided by foot drag, which provided a type of braking when needed.

The boy, who appeared to be white, would start at the top of the incline on the flat area then run few paces to build momentum before jumping into his box-sled toboggan to glide down the incline on a diagonal to the slope, which carried him to the parallel shoulder of the roadway. There, he would allow the sled to lose speed and brake to a careful stop, accompanied by the blaring horns of passing vehicles.

Quite the daredevil! thought Granville, very much impressed.

It took more than a week before Granville found a discarded cardboard box, large and sturdy enough to suit his purposes, behind a heavy equipment store and truck repair shop some blocks away.

The curious, suspicious, and sometimes hostile looks he received as he pushed, carried, and dragged the box home left him with the impression of being a thief in a broad-daylight robbery. A daring criminal act indeed . . . *I'm stealing garbage. Arrest me already!*

He worked on the box sled on his great-uncle's unused patio. Fortunately, having witnessed the daredevil's sled and subsequent performance, he was able to incorporate several simple design improvements in his version: thickened base, wood reinforced runners, reinforced sides and handles, and an open back to make entrance easier on the fly, like a bob-sled design.

"Boy, where're you going to ride that sled? This is still fall; the winter snow is a long way off. Good job, though!" Great Uncle Prince was impressed; that meant a lot to Granville.

First trial: his new sled performed well, so much so that Granville developed enough speed that his brakes were insufficient, just stopping his sled a heartbeat short of the outer lane of the roadway. The woman that he almost hit looked like she might have a heart attack as she swerved to avoid colliding with the slightly out-of-control sled. When his heart quieted, he felt sorry for her.

Second trial: good start and slide, controlled speed and direction, easy glide to effective braking, daredevil ride!

Granville watched for the daredevil sledder every day, to no avail. A week passed with no sign, probably because it rained as only Chicago can rain, hard and dirty, cleaning the air, making it so much easier and pleasant to breathe afterwards. When the sun re-emerged, the washed air was sweet in the bright sunshine.

There he was zooming down the slope when Granville spotted him. Granville was down the steps and down the alley in a breathless rush to join in the fun. He started his sled after the other boy began his run. The design improvements paid off once again in greater speed and control.

Halfway down the slope, his sled caught the daredevil and followed him to the end of the slope's improvised sliding area, next to the roadway.

The surprise on the face of the daredevil was worth almost all of Granville's efforts to emulate him.

"Hi, I'm Granville."

"Hi, I'm Craig; nice sled!"

"Thanks. I've been watching you for a while, so thought I'd give it a shot."

"You built the sled?"

"Yep."

"Where d'you live?'

"On this street, 3148, second floor above the storefront church."

"Right, you're the new Black family that just moved in."

"Yeah, we're the first to . . ."

"No, my family was the first."

"You're Black?"

"Yeah, my family moved here from California for my mom's job. She's a city planner. We're all light skinned, though my dad's dark, like you. Mom says, blame it on Great Grandma, who did pass for white when she was young to get better jobs and stuff. We are Black. Period!"

"Were you hassled when you moved here?"

"No, most white people think we are white."

"But your dad."

"He's away a lot. He's a captain of a destroyer in the navy. I'm a sea cadet."

"So, you're going to enlist in the navy?"

"Absolutely! One day I'm going to captain my own ship, just like my dad."

"Cool!"

"Ready to go again?"

"Race ya to the bottom."

"Last one there buys treats at the bakery."

"You're on. Three counts: three, two, one, go!"

Experience matched improved technology. They tied and shared the prize.

[[Author's Aside]]

"Daredevil" Craig Montrose and Granville remained best friends from that moment onward, only to lose touch with each other after each in turn answered their country's call and went off to war.

...

Part 10: "That's a Lot of Gods . . ."

Granville visited Craig at his home often. It was only a block and a half from Granville's house, located two houses from the corner of West Flournoy Street and St. Albany Avenue. Craig's family lived on the first floor of a two-story walk-up. Craig's older sister was away at university and his mother usually at work. Thus, Craig was basically living as an only child with his own key to his house and freedom to come and go after finishing his homework, while his mother was at work. Like Granville and his brothers, he was a latchkey kid.

Craig and Granville were relaxing on Craig's front stoop, munching on their favourite treat, chocolate eclairs with vanilla cream filling purchased at the bakery after their sledding session.

"Do you go to that church downstairs below your place?"

"Yeah, sometimes. Mom goes, and I tag along to help with my little brothers. They get bored easily; then I take them upstairs to watch cartoons until Mom comes home."

"Do you like it?"

"Naw, not as much as the Baptist church we used to attend before we moved here. It was big and had a great choir that could really rock, really sing. The organist was hot once she got going.

"When Mom got the Spirit, she could really boogie! The ushers would have to carry her to the time-out room to cool down and relax. The treats in Sunday school were great. It was fun."

"Do you believe in God?"

"I don't know. Never thought about it much, until I started reading Mom's Catholic study stuff."

"Mom says there are as many gods as there are religions that worship them."

"That's a lot of gods."

"Exactly, every country has its gods; the same is true of every culture within those countries. Just depends on where you were born and how you're raised when it comes to who worships what."

"Yeah, and each claiming to be the one and only true God."

"Amen."

"My dad said that people created gods to give themselves something to believe in when people could no longer believe in themselves or each other."

"Sounds about right, Craig."

Part 11: ". . . I Got Your Back!"

"Hey, Nigger-lover! What the fuckin' shit that we have here! What you doin' hanging out with that little black bastard? We've been looking for you, punk!"

The two friends looked out at the group of six boys gathered across the intersection. Granville recognized Bobby Franklin immediately, and in that same instant, decided there would be no running this time. Craig and Granville then looked at each other and sighed.

Craig spoke first. "No Niggers here. Just two Black kids that're going to be very happy to kick your sorry honky asses six ways from Sunday, cock-sucking motherfuckers!"

"What the fuck!"

"Stay behind me, Gran! We goin' kick some honky ass, back-to-back."

"I got your back!"

Granville knew from their many conversations and sparring sessions that Craig was a dangerous person to threaten. He was not at all violent or ill-tempered; on the contrary, he was calm, cool, and self-assured in the most challenging of circumstances. He was well suited for a life at sea. His years in the sea cadet training program had included a thorough exposure to and development of self-defence techniques and strategies.

Tall, yet slim in stature, Craig's physical appearance was very deceptive. The boy was quick as a cat and strong as a rhino. His blocks were like hitting steel rods and his strikes were precise and penetrating.

Granville had the bruises to prove it. He had learned much from Craig in the time they had been inseparable. His seaworthy friend had been more than happy to have a practice buddy, euphemism for punching bag, in his new best friend.

Now, Granville was excited to have an opportunity to fight for real against his enemy, who he had yearned to hurt in the worst way.

The uneven numbers, two versus six, only presented more possibilities for the two boys to inflict well-deserved painful retribution on the young bigots.

Casually walking across the sidewalk from Craig's front steps, they met the gang in the middle of the street devoid of traffic or parked cars.

The boys quickly took position back-to-back facing the menace that surrounded them: stalking in a rough circle, feigning strikes, testing the boys' defensive posture, spitting insults as they went.

Granville, following Craig's example, held his position in stillness, conserving energy, studying their opponents, gauging the evident speed, skill, and potential effectiveness of the gang's collective physical threat.

Bobby was the first to lose patience and went for Granville, the smaller of the two, whom he clearly thought was the weaker, swinging hard at Granville's head to strike only air, then suddenly to find it very difficult to breathe. Painfully discovering that Granville's speed was also inherent in his hands, which had delivered a hard straight jab to Bobby's throat before he could recover from his swing. Choking, Bobby staggered back out of the fluctuating circle, watched by his startled gang members.

"Kill the Niggers!" was his croaked command.

The remaining five charged in masse, seeking to overrun and overwhelm with their numbers. The dodging, ducking, weaving, moving, lunging, spinning, charging death-dealing-dance was on. Craig became a machine piston engine of combined coordinated strikes and blocks; Granville went into buzzsaw mode, taking more blows than his battle buddy, yet striking just as effectively at anyone within reach.

Sweat, spit, and blood began to fly, cries of pain-laced frustration and rage filled the air as the boys lost touch with the world around them.

The ongoing melee drew a growing crowd of observers in passing, lining the sidewalk on either side, and at the windows, porches, and balconies of nearby residences. Cars stopped in the street as drivers and passengers watched from their vehicles.

All of them were white. Some cheered, others jeered, most waited in abject silence, unwilling witnesses to the battleground of racial animosity their neighbourhood had become.

None of the combatants noticed any of it. All of their attention was laser focussed on the task at hand.

"Get out of my way!" from the centre of the fight. "We are Black! You hear me? We're Black! This is our home! Get it through your thick skulls.

"We're not goin' anywhere! We're not afraid of you! You hear me, people?"

It was Craig's mother, Clarice, calling them all out as she pushed through the gathered throng to rush toward the sounds and stand with her bruised and battered son and his friend.

The arrival of the true adult in the room brought it all to a screeching halt. It was over as quickly as it had begun.

The crowd melted and quickly dispersed. Bobby's gang limped away to disappear within the midst of the traffic's restart.

Part 12: "It's All About Race . . . So, It's All About Colour

"That sounds pretty rough."

"Yes, Ines," said Clarice. "I could not believe my eyes or ears when I parked the car in our spot off the alley behind the house. All this racket going on in front, the screaming, yelling, calling our boys horrible names as some were chanting for their blood, 'Kill 'em, kill 'em, kill 'em!'"

"Damn!"

"I know part of it was because since we moved here, they believed that we were white, and I did nothing to change their fear-based bigoted, pseudo-acceptance. As far as I was concerned, it was none of their damn business in the first place. Secondly, it enabled us to live here without any problems. We kept to ourselves, and the neighbours seemed to respect that."

"Never questioned your husband's presence, his colour?"

"He has been away on an extended tour in the South China Sea. When he was home on leave before the start of his current posting, we were just moving in, coming, and going all the time. If they were watching us, and now I am sure they were, probably thought he was one of the crew moving us in."

"It's all about race, so it's all about colour. So essentially, in their eyes, you have been passing for white in their neighbourhood because you and your son are so light-skinned and did not announce your racial identity when you first moved in. Perhaps, in their eyes, you should have posted a sign on your door: *Heads up, people, Black people here,* or more like . . . *Niggers present. Crackers BEWARE!*"

"Ha ha!"

"I'm a city planner. I have known for a while that this area is slated for gentrification, and that generally leads to some local upheaval and unrest. It is an unfortunate by-product of the process."

"This is not gentrification; nothing about this is upscale. This is blockbusting!"

"Absolutely! That can, does and is happening and we're in the middle of the shit as a result of it. It's unscrupulous and unethical but, unfortunately, not yet illegal. It drives and thrives as the systemic racism within real estate agents' practices."

"My boys and I have absolutely jumped from the fryin' pan into the fire!"

"We lived on a military base in California and were very unhappy with all the regimentation and the elitist attitudes."

"Beats the hell out of this guerrilla warfare in the street."

"Got that right. So, what can we do about it?"

"Survive and protect our children."

"Lord Jesus, help us save our children!"

"Amen!"

Part 13: "This Is Fucking War!"

Word of the street fight spread through the white community like a wind-driven wildfire across a dry prairie pasture, burning everything in its path, consuming all life. Meetings were held, decisions were made, courses of action were planned.

The emergency, evident by the storefront Black church's presence at 3148, consisted of the unwelcome immigrants and the general belief that had been demonstrated as a threat, a clear and present danger.

"God-damn it, it's them or us! This is our home, our families. Our children can't walk the streets without being attacked by those little Black bastards. This is fucking war!"

"Ben, we can't go 'round killing folks, killing kids. . ."

"No, of course not, but we can make their lives here so uncomfortable that they will wish they were dead and get the hell out of our neighbourhood!"

"Aren't you forgetting an important word you just used? Like it or not, these people are our neighbours, and by the way, Bobby and his gang attacked them. I saw it all happen from my front window. Those two Black kids were minding their own business when Bobby, your son, arrived, calling names and spitting hate."

"Do you own your home?"

"Not yet, the bank does."

"When you pay off that mortgage, after you've invested thirty years of your life and the lives of your children that you want to send to college, do you think it will have half the value when it's sitting in the middle of a Black ghetto slum hellhole?"

"You all talked with the realtors. I know they visited everyone here. They weren't joking. They weren't lying, our hard-earned value in our homes will be virtually worthless, if we allow them to stay. The crime, prostitution, gangs."

"We already have gangs."

"Our kids like to hang together; there're no gangs here."

"Coulda' fooled me."

"Look, if you like to live with Niggers—"

"Enough with the hate!"

"Those who lay with pigs wake up with fleas and reeking of shit! You're welcome to move with them! We're staying put and those people will be encouraged to move on, or else!"

"Who's providing this encouragement? Who's going to make this happen?"

"I'll see to that myself!"

Part 14: "Tool or Weapon?"

"Gran, I have something for you, "called Uncle Prince from his patio rocking chair beneath his front window. Sometimes he would sit there to watch the traffic in the expressway, and on the bridge over it, along with the occasional passing alley traffic. It wasn't much of a view, yet he often said it was somehow soothing in its monotony.

Granville, hurriedly on his way to the playground, stopped short at the base of the rear stairwell. "What is it, Great-Uncle Prince?"

"Boy, must you always be in a hurry? I know it's all that youth flowing through you, grabbing life with both hands, hurrying for fear you may miss something."

"Yes, Great-Uncle?"

"Your mother told me about that street fight. How are you?"

"I'm okay."

"Looks like you picked up a few ugly bruises in the battle.""No problem, Craig was great."

"Your sea cadet friend?"

"Yeah, he really knows how to block and strike, kept most of them off me."

"He's the one you call 'Daredevil?'"

"The sea cadets taught him a lot about martial-art fighting techniques."

"He's teaching you?"

"Yeah, we spar all the time. What do you have for me, Great-Uncle?" Granville's youthful impatience was showing despite his reverence for his Great-Uncle Prince.

"It's in that box by the door."

Granville had not noticed the box, about the size of a milk carton crate, resting just between the screen door frame and the adjoining wall. He investigated the box to find a length of braided, thick white cotton twine, usually used as clothesline, forming a rope with a braided loop through the centre of a large machine-sized bolt-nut at one end, and a similar hollow loop at the other end resembling a hangman's noose and knot. The centre portion of braided rope between the looped ends was about sixteen inches long.

He examined it closely. "What is it? What's it for?"

"Put your hand through the noose so it's around your wrist and hold onto the knot. How's it feel?"

Granville did as he was told and instinctively began to pendulum swing the nut on the other end, back and forth, then in careful circles, eventually carving figure-eights in the air, to discover exactly what he imagined it was for. "Is it a weapon?"

"If needs be."

Granville's mounting excitement was palpable, "Feels great, Uncle Prince!"

"Gran, the purpose of a weapon is to maim or kill, be it offensively or in defence. I don't believe you need a weapon. For your purposes, this is a tool, meant to intimidate, threaten, subdue, all to discourage an aggressor, in defence, before the need to use it as a weapon becomes necessary. Do you understand?"

Granville nodded, keeping his keen eyes on the soaring tool.

"Good. Now make no mistake, this tool can hurt you as easily as it can hurt anyone else, maybe easier. You must practice getting the feel of it, practice till that rope is an extension of your arm and hand, until it feels like it is part of you.

"Your friend may not always be with you, or even here to watch your back. This is a back-up option that you may need one day.

"Now, when you are ready, I want you to store it someplace that it will not be misplaced or discovered by anyone, especially your little brothers. For now, you can keep it here. Ines may not approve, though we will share the secret with her when the time is right.

"I want you to practice here, and only here, where I can keep an eye on you. Okay, enough for today. We can practice more tomorrow, a bit of time each day to build up your arm strength and control.

"Now, be off with you."

"Thanks, Great-Uncle, you're the best!"

Granville arrived at the appointed meeting place with Craig later than planned. To his surprise, the grassy plain on the hilltop above the expressway was empty. His friend, nowhere to be seen.

"Hey, Granville!"

"Yeah, Craig, what's up?"

"Great news! A new sea cadet unit has been formed at the Naval Station Great Lakes. I've been accepted in the first Naval Sea Cadet

Corps unit: Sea Cadets 9-1-1. There are only forty-eight sea cadets and ten officers. I'll be in the senior cadet program and be attending a required mandatory two-week recruit training camp.

"I'm advancing from the US Navy League Cadet Corps (NLCC), that's for the ten- to thirteen-year-olds, into the US Naval Sea Cadet Corps (NSCC) for thirteen- to eighteen-year-olds. The NSCC is the full rigours military training, including advanced training sessions. It's much more difficult. The courses are taught at the Navy's Recruit Training Command.

"My training starts next week; after that, Mom is taking some holiday time off so we can meet Dad in San Diego, at my grandparents'. He'll be on leave for three weeks while his ship is in port for refit and upgrades. Cool, huh?"

"All right! How about school?"

"I'm in the eighth-grade honours class at John Marshall this year. Mom arranged with the principal a late start this year. I'll only miss about four or five weeks. Some of the courses I'll be studying in training have crossover with those at John Marshall. The sea cadet academic courses— math, physics, science, oceanography, and history—are harder than what they teach in John Marshall, so I might be able to transfer some credits."

"You are coming back? Going to miss you, Craig."

"Definitely returning for Mom's job. I'll miss you too. You can hold the fort without me."

"Sure thing," Granville was quietly glad that if push did come to shove with Craig away, he had a back-up plan, thanks to his beloved Great-Uncle Prince.

...

[[Author's Aside]]

Craig did return, a year later than planned. His mother's holiday time metamorphosed into a year-long leave of absence from her job. Craig spent his eighth grade studying in California—her solution, enacted by the need to save her child and reconnect with his big sister. The family enjoyed the year's respite from racial conflict; the peace of California sunshine never felt so good.

...

Part 15: Fury of the Sad and Angry Absentee Fathers

The time passed slowly for Granville. Living on an island within a sea of hostility was quite boring, though thankfully uneventful. He managed to keep to himself with his little brothers.

His little brothers were not so little anymore. Seeds of jealousy had been planted by the desperate influence of David's father, Mark, a sergeant major in a lifetime military career, with authority issues and an overinflated ego, and Joseph's father, Rain, a faithless, married man and classic alcoholic with co-dependency issues.

Each vied for Ines's attention, while undermining her influence on their sons at every opportunity, as part of a passive-aggressive vendetta towards her. A woman who refused to be manipulated or intimidated by either man.

Each man resented the strength within the mother of his child.

Mark and Rain felt their lives were haunted by the spectre of Ines's past love, Granville Howard, "love of her life." A living memory with which they could not compete. Granville, his namesake, another man's love-child who remained the subject of Ines's enduring affection.

David and Joseph, caught in the middle, became pawns in a struggle they could not recognize or understand. Poisoned by the ever-present, simmering hatred by each father towards Granville, the boys slowly turned against their big brother.

[[Author's Aside]]

Granville, fatherless with none except his mother to speak for him, represented an object of shared hostility as each man viewed the boy as a drain on the support payments they both were forced to pay—as little and infrequent as that was. This evil lived deep in the psyches of both Mark and Rain, the quiet, sometimes ugly fury of the sad and angry absentee fathers.

Granville's oldest brother, Levi Andrea, had moved into the third-floor flat above them, with his wife, Beatrice, and their new baby, Lars. The baby nephew that Granville never tired of holding, kissing, and cuddling. The youngest addition to the family treasures.

It was nice having his big brother's family close by. Levi had moved to Elgin, Illinois, to attend night courses in a school of architecture, along with his high school courses.

His return had reinvigorated the sense of extended family within Granville's world. A sense that helped him feel less alone, less click-bait, less a target for those who had made it their avowed purpose to do him harm.

[[Author's Aside]]

In retrospect, he would come to realize that this "boring" time of family introspective struggle would be dearly missed, as it was the quiet before the storm.

Part 16: Birth of an Urban Legend

They came bearing arms: bats, chains, bricks, knives, and a phalanx of angry adults and parents to back them up, cheer, and urge them on.

It was a Saturday afternoon, a hazy, lazy late summer, early fall sort of day. The sun was high in the cloudless city sky and what some would call "Indian summer" was thick within the close environs. All things considered, a nondescript setting for a confrontation that was to become the stuff of urban legends.

"Gran, come look at this!"

Granville had heard and been awakened by the noise audible in his bedroom at the back of the apartment where he had fallen into a nap, consuming an Encyclopedia Britannica article about his favourite topic: dinosaurs, in this case Tyrannosaurus Rex.

Ines had purchased an entire volume of the encyclopedia series along with yearly additional updates from a door-to-door salesman many weeks ago to feed her son's insatiable curiosity and appetite for knowledge. He read them incessantly. It was "The best birthday present ever!" for a bored preteen trying desperately to master life in a new, and in many ways, hostile community.

He hurried out of bed and into his slippers to join his mother in the living room bay window, his favourite place in the apartment.

David and Joseph were spending some quality time with Great-Uncle Prince and Great-Aunt Leena in their apartment, while filling up on milk and her eye-watering delicious apple pie, also Granville's favourite. Fortunately, they missed their mother's call.

Granville froze at his mother's side; deep within, a fear-near-terror blossomed.

The sidewalk and much of the street in front of his home was filled with angry white faces. The chant: "Niggas, this ain't your home . . . Niggas, go back where you came from," began low, with only the kids repeating their mantra, to rise in volume and malevolence as the adults picked up the evil refrain.

Granville giggled in a nervous, instinctive recollection of the nursery rhyme: the big, nasty wolf outside the last remaining home of the three little pigs. *"Come out, come out! I'll huff and I'll puff and blow your house down!"*

Ines watched, simmering rage filling her throat with adrenalin's metallic bitterness. She began to unconsciously murmur in a low, ferocious growl, "Shit. Fucking goddamn crackers!"

The sound she made had never been heard by her son before. He had heard her curse from pain or frustration, though never toward him and his brothers. This sound was different; he could hear and feel her fear lurking underneath her words.

No one is going to threaten my mother! No way, not when I can do something about it! thought Granville in grim, youthful determination.

Ines was so deeply disturbed and outraged, she was unaware as her one and only "named love-child" silently left her side.

His tool was still kept in the box where he had discovered it. With cat-like stealth, he withdrew the well-used rope, the wrist-noose now almost worn smooth from his many hours of boredom self-therapy, otherwise known as practice.

He had started with a practice rope, woven by himself, identical to his tool, except for a bean bag attached to the business end instead of the large bolt-nut of the same weight. He had to practice and become proficient before he was allowed to work with his tool.

"Don't want to lose any of that brilliant smile. Your mother would skin me alive. Leena would hold me down!"

For Granville, a very quick study, practice was dance-like, a duet between his body and the flashing bean-bag blur. Granville loved to dance . . . a silent meditation in motion.

Prince Williams, Granville's great-uncle, watched from his rocker at the window as the boy moved like a shadow toward the box. "Good, it's time!" His pride in the boy was palpable, yet he knew, despite his fear of the possible outcome, what must be done, period.

Granville, careful not to disturb his brothers' visit, paused at the staircase base, sensing his mentor's gaze, eyes met, a shared nod, then moving on, sprinting around the building, through the narrow walkway between the buildings, pausing in its shadow, seeing the mob, small and loud.

Bobby's gang was closest to the curb, looking nervous, pacing back 'n' forth and in small, uncertain circles, very out-of-place. Seemingly unsure of what to do next, in behind and across the street were the rest, in full determined support. "Niggas gotta go! Niggas gotta go!"

From that shadow, Granville began his wrist-spin, the nut making a soft whir beside his ear as he stepped into the bright sunlight next to his front door to face the mob alone.

Ines saw her son. It was at that moment, she realized what had happened, "Oh my God! No!" She went to get her gun.

...

Granville's jaws were hard set; noticing his tenseness, he recalled his mentor's voice: "Relax, Gran, the tool is your friend. It's a dance; intimidate, threaten, wound only if absolutely necessary for defence; bide your time, no need to rush to battle, let the others make the first move, conserve energy.

"Make your strikes count; no second chances!"

Granville waited, eyes flitting from face to face, noting the weapon each boy held and how he handled it. The closest boy had two different-sized red bricks he was almost juggling; the itch to throw was apparent. As if on cue, the larger of the two bricks was in the air, whistling toward his belly.

Granville side-stepped the missile, which bounced off the pavement behind him, showering his legs in cement chips, and shifted the arc of his whirring tool to a figure-eight-circular helicopter pattern as he walked into the gang-held space, closing the distance between himself and the rest.

A bat was swung low under the arc, aiming for his legs. Again, he shifted his stance to avoid it, while lowering the arc of the tool, clipping a white fist turned red from an open gash. "GAAAH!" The boy's scream electrified the crowd. "ROAAHH!" Granville heard their roar, saw their fear, their trepidation evaporating as they closed around him, staying just out of striking distance of the tool.

Suddenly realizing that their number and close proximity would overwhelm him, tool arm fully extended, he began to dance, spinning, moving in quick, small catch-steps, constantly changing the tool's flight pattern to an irregular shape of varying height and direction, much more difficult to judge.

All manner of weaponry was levelled upon him and thrown at him. Some struck home to bruise and bloody, leaving ragged trails that he was too busy, within an adrenalin haze, to take notice.

Eyes so tear-filled he could hardly see, yet never leaving his attackers. He became a human buzzsaw with bite, hungry for blood, eager to have this over with, too afraid to care whether he would survive. Thus, determined to beat them back and out of his life once and for all, or die in the effort.

Bobby's consternation was growing to a heated crescendo, as his gang was not having the effect he wanted in this fight. The punk, a nimble moving target, was just too hard to hit.

"BOBBY! Boy, what the fuck's wrong with you? Get that fuckin Nigga Jumbo!" Hearing his dad bellowing for results forced his hand and fuelled his desperation-driven onslaught at the Black boy's rear. The tire iron he was using barely brushed the Nigger's back before he had to duck under the arc of that flashing, singing roped bulwark.

"Ugh!" Granville felt more than saw Bobby's metal rod leaving a deep diagonal welt across and down his back, ricocheting off his spine, between his shoulder blades, underneath his blood-spattered, torn shirt.

He bit 'n' gritted his teeth hard at the contact, nipping his tongue, sprouting a stream of blood which began to flow down his throat. The taste, hot and salty, caused him to hesitate, stumble, while resisting the urge to swallow for fear of becoming sick.

Mouth filling with his lifeblood, Granville's rage redoubled against the unforeseen, hot duelling pain and discomfort.

"No more, Mr. Nice-Fucking-Guy!" Granville spun to face the source of that searing strike, facing Bobby through his red haze; several stutter-steps closed the distance.

Granville began a slow, deliberate shuffle toward Bobby, the flashing bulwark clearing his path as Bobby began to back-paddle with equal care. Within the fighting circle, there was little room to maneuver. The surrounding gang members moved away to clear a path for their leader, until the boy's back was pressed against and partially across the top of a car hood across the street.

With no evident possible escape, and the singing whir of Granville's tool bearing down toward his face, an unconscious, low, guttural whine began to emanate from deep in Bobby's throat that rose to quickly chime with the whirring weapon. "Help! Help, helllp meee . . .!" screamed the trapped, panicking gang leader.

Granville's snarling expression grinned through blood-drenched clenched teeth, and in blind red-rage, he went in for the strike.

CRACK, was the ear-splitting retort of Ines's 45-calibre handgun firing into the air. "Motherfuckers! Leave my son alone! I'll kill all a-you!" Pointing the gun with both hands at the mob, aiming at random from side-to-side.

In the immediate silence, white people were ducking for cover in the walkway, behind cars, in the bakery, the butcher shop, in building entrances, anywhere that would afford cover if not safety from being shot, by one enraged Black woman and mother that they, simply, had pushed too far.

For Granville, so intent on crushing Bobby's terror-stricken face, the sound only gave him space to realize what he was about to do and what that meant. Once again, he heard his great-uncle's words: "Gran, wound only if absolutely necessary in defence. Never with willful intent to do harm. People go to prison for that!"

Granville paused his advance and stopped his tool's spin long enough to lean over Bobby's prostrated form, holding the tool's large machine bolt-nut above his head; he spat a very large clot of blood and sputum directly into the boy's ashen face and bulging eyes.

"Ahhh!"

"Bitch. Fucking pussy!" hissed Granville, then turned and bolted for his front door and the safety of his mother's strong embrace.

It didn't take very long before the heavy knock on the front door signaled to Ines that the consequence of her son's rescue from the mob had come calling for retribution, perhaps incarceration if she didn't handle this just right. The situation was not unexpected for Granville as well.

"Gran, where's your six shooters?"

"My Colt .45 replica six shooters?"

"Yes, son. Get your cap guns; the ones with the loud caps that I won't let you shoot in the hall or on the porch."

"It's cause they're too loud!" Granville's eyes came alight with recognition and comprehension of her plan.

"Right! Be quick!"

The knock came again, louder, insistent. "POLICE!"

Hurry the fuck up, thought Officer Hal Cronus. He didn't like this call to this Nigger's house after a citizen call of shots fired. This neighbourhood was getting jumpy, heating up. Goddamn Niggers always brought trouble. *Like a fucking cancer!*

The door opened to a strong, erect Black woman, not tall, small in stature yet appearing tall. Standing ramrod straight, very fit, drop-dead gorgeous and clearly Black and beautiful. *Damn, she's one fine Niggra!* Hal was momentarily thrown completely off his game.

"Can I help you, officer?"

"We received an anonymous call about a gun fired at this residence. What's your name?"

"Ms. Ines Andrea. I don't own or have a gun . . . Officer Cronus, is it?"

"We have a number of witnesses that report otherwise," he said, noting that she'd had the presence of mind to read his nametag and probably memorized his badge number, in order to report this conversation later. This Niggra woman must be handled carefully.

Barely held in check while devouring her completely, the cop's eyes roamed her body, beginning with her breasts; crawling downward over her form, reaching her svelte waist, to caress her hips, to be startled like a deer caught in the headlights when suddenly confronted by little Granville's knowing eyes meeting his leer.

"The only things we have, that others might have seen, is this pair of six-shooter Peacemaker replica revolvers. My son's cap guns."

The boy, standing as straight as his mother, was also pretty, *too pretty for a boy-child and the spitting image of his mother*, and wearing a western gun-belt with a pair of six-shooters hanging off his small waist.

Hal couldn't suppress his surprise, "Is this the little Nigger that's causing all this shitstorm? What's your name, boy?"

"Granville."

"Granville? What kind of name is that?"

"My father's name. It's French; means 'big city.'"

"Okay, 'Big City,' let's see that cap pistol."

Granville, uncertain, not trusting, turned to his mother for direction, then a nod returned, a quick-draw, and the guns were in his hands, pointing, handle first, up toward Hal.

The smooth blur of that movement renewed Hal's uneasiness with the situation. *Shit! If that'd been a snake, it'd have bit me. Watch yourself, man, there's more here than meets the eye.*

Hal took one of the guns, noted the realistic weight and feel. He carefully examined the pistol, aware that from a distance, a mistake could have been made. "It fires caps?"

"Yes, they're loud. My mom won't let me shoot them in the house or in the hall, not even on the street. Have to shoot in the back-alley sometimes." He pointed his second revolver down the hallway away from the policeman. "They're really loud, see?" *CRACK* as the cap in the pistol exploded in the narrow hallway, reverberating off the walls' tight confinement.

Startled by the amplified burst of sound, Hal had to fight his instinctive urge to duck for cover. His ringing ears slowly quieted. "This is what you fired on the street? No other guns?"

"Yes, no other guns! I had to scare them off my son, who was just trying to defend himself."

"So, I heard." Hal was uncomfortably aware that this single-parent family had committed no crime other than being the wrong colour in the wrong place at the wrong time. Still, this situation was not going to end well, as it ran its course.

"Boy, you keep these guns in your holsters, not anywhere near the street, ever. You understand?"

"Yes, sir!" Showering Hal with an easy beaming smile, Granville knew that he and his mother were safe.

"You folks have a good day." Turning to leave, Hal felt relieved to be out of the presence of that stunning Black woman and her hellraising little boy. *Far too attractive for her own good. How do these fucking Niggers make such fine Niggras?*

...

Black to White . . .
White gone Black . . .
Right fuckin' on! Fight's a fight . . . no matter the colour. . .
We all bleed . . . blood red . . . for each other.

-I Am an Honourable Man (Excerpt) ... by Granville Johnson

The neighbourhood changed after that confrontation—not quickly and not overnight, as some seemed to recall and retell in the days that followed the "Showdown at 3148," as it was described and embellished in the retelling through the weeks, months, years of the story being told.

White families, all that could, fled, migrating further west and north, some as far as the suburbs. Black and Brown families moved in to take their place. A culture of multifaceted working-class poverty remained.

...

Part 17: The Catholic God

Granville looked at his reflection with bemused interest. The clothes his mother had brought home from her shopping trip were strange and all blue: navy blue pants and matching clip-on tie, light blue dress shirt, cobalt blue sweater, and new black dress shoes. The only thing about this image that he approved of were the new shoes.

So, this is my school uniform that I'll have to wear every day, thought the young boy, who embodied a fluid sense of style and loved to dress up. *Cool!*

He was overjoyed at finally escaping the deadly madness at Gladstone.

No matter what he did, no matter how well he did in his class, there was always someone determined to hurt him because he was doing so well.

It was as if there was an unwritten law of physics, that a boy child was preprogrammed to fail. If by some gift of fate, that child tended to succeed in his efforts, he became a freak of nature, to be treated as a pariah in society for once again performing above his station in life, and against the societal grain. Heaven help that boy child because no-one else was going to.

At first, the teachers used to help him avoid the gang. Eventually, they each grew tired of it, threw up their hands in exasperation, turned the other way, and just stopped caring.

After Ms. Chambers' fall, they weren't sure that he had caused it, yet many thought he had. Still, it was an accident. He was just trying to get to his class and avoid the bullies.

Fending off Bobby's little gang was just another unfortunate irritant in his life that seemed to go with the territory, life in his ghetto.

"Mom, this Catholic school, is it a public school for Catholic kids?"

"It's not a public school. It's a private school for Catholic children. Their parents pay the school to teach their children. The Catholic Church owns the school and pays all the teachers and school employees . . ."

"Are the teachers priests?"

"No, the teachers are Catholic nuns."

"We aren't Catholics, we're Baptists, aren't we?"

"That's true. I talked with the principal of the school, and she agreed to let us transfer into their honours program because you have done so well in your classes at Gladstone; being an honours student, they gave you an academic scholarship and enrolled you in the fifth-grade honours class. So, we just have to pay for your uniform, books, and supplies."

"I'm moving up into fifth grade?"

"Yes, Gran and I know you will do just fine. My boy is so smart. I'm so very proud of you."

"Do I have to be a Catholic?"

"No, son. I have decided to convert to Catholicism. I like the Catholic faith and some of what it teaches is a lot like the Baptist religion. I've started taking classes to learn more about it."

"Are you converting so we can attend the school?"

"Yes, it is the least I could do to give us this chance at a new life in a new place, as I promised I would find a way out of that dead-end school. It really is all right. I don't mind. It's a nice change."

...

Our Lady of Sorrows turned out to be exactly what fate chose to give Granville, a way of feeling that there truly was more to school than dodging bullies, while needing so badly to belong in the world he lived in, without standing out. Though Black students in this Catholic school could pretty much be counted using the fingers of both hands without running out of fingers.

The subjective effect of bullying by both Black and white kids had taken its toll on Granville's psyche—chronic bedwetting being only one of the by-products. The rigours of being not Black enough or being Black at all left him desperate for a place where living well, or living at all, did not require subjugation.

Somehow, many of his classmates were smart, very smart, and didn't mind running through their schoolwork with all cylinders firing at full capacity. Granville was no longer the exception to the rule, just par for the course; it was simply a given that excellence was a state of belonging. He was loving every second of it.

He blossomed in his gratitude for his surroundings. He didn't even mind the religion class, viewed as a historical interpretation that was filled with stories of ancient societies and cultures, not theological indoctrination, which it was in fact.

Schoolwork was a joy that released his passion for scholarly pursuits.

Granville, the ravenous, parched, bone-dry, lost-in-the-desert sponge was rapidly filling up to the brim and beyond with this rich brew swirling around and within him each day.

...

Curiosity, finally unleashed, became a fire warming the depths of his soul. In this heady heart heavy environment, Granville discovered the Catholic God.

Granville had no idea how ripe he was for all this new world had to offer. He only knew that the more he experienced, the more he wanted. It was not rocket science that his longing drew him into what he experienced as the core ritual at the heart and soul of these wonders to behold.

First came his mother's catechism classes in preparation for conversion and the literature to which she only paid a passing interest—just enough to answer the quiz following each lesson. Granville, having often gone over them with her in review, knew the answers by heart, enthralled with the poetry, promising a selfless, ascetic life and love.

Mass: the core ritual that seemed to emanate from all other aspects of his education. He found that he luxuriated in the gilded presence of the soaring cathedral, Our Lady of Sorrows Basilica. The quiet reverence, something so nice, somehow held the essence of a listening, attentive God presence worth investigating, and perhaps even worshipping.

There was no choir, no Black people to speak of, no music, no dance, no language (Latin) that he could understand, yet he found that he hungered to be a part of it.

...

The sometimes jovial, loud, bawdy atmosphere of the Christ's Shepherd Southern Baptist Church often felt more like participatory live entertainment and less like worship, to Granville's youthful awareness.

Amid it all, behind the scenes, there was clandestine messaging, maneuvering for sensual sexual favours and relationships that had little to nothing to do with God's worship that was supposed to be the initial core purpose of membership participation in the church congregation's ceremony.

It was the absence of all the "noise" that he had identified with God's worship; the enveloping stillness accented by the hundreds of flickering candles placed in small alcoves and at the feet of the many statues and tableaus depicting aspects of Christ's life. The Virgin Mary and the Holy Spirit spoke to Granville's quieting spirit.

These were white faces in a huge presence that once again identified his tokenism. True, he felt the old individualism in the pit of his stomach. Yet it was less painful because he did not expect or assume that he should belong, as was his birthright.

Instead, it became easier for him to accept his differences, his aloneness. It was obviously clear and self-evident for all to see, yet none to question, the pigment of his skin or the colour of his soul; for him, neither was of little consequence.

What mattered was that there seemed to be a place for him within these gilded walls, where he could be himself, without judgement, rancour, or suspicion.

during this time, he wondered about the nature and meaning of a recurrent dream: Granville would be afflicted with a deadly terminal disease (his guilt demanded suffering for the magic to occur), almost die, then recover somehow transformed into a Pegasus, a magnificent, pure white winged horse that would race across the landscape to then spread his massive wings and race among the clouds.

...

[[Author's Aside]]

Many years later, he would understand that among the Black society of his birth, he was and had been living a type of tokenism since his birth, an outlier; set apart, different by nature and nurture.

Oreo: Black on the outside, white on the inside . . .

He grew to despise the derisive nature of that metaphor, for it implied
that he was inherently separate from and at war with himself.
Where all was colour; when all was race, he was neither.

Granville's conversion to Catholicism was not surprising nor traumatic. Following his mother's lead, encouraged by his teachers and the nuns' approval, particularly Sister Mary Joseph, who found his bright-light intelligence refreshing and endearing, Granville applied for the coveted church role of assistant to the priests: altar boy, after his baptism, during his first year at Our Lady of Sorrows. The experience embodied the love and forgiveness of a renewed sense of self, empowered by the new direction. The responsibility of serving as acolyte to the ritualistic presence of "Jesus" in the sharing of the wafer (His body) and the wine (His blood) during communion, which took place during every Mass. The Mass itself being the construct created to be a vehicle for the communal sharing.

The new acolyte reveled in the opportunity to pray at the base of the altar. Prayer, prior to this time, existed as something that people did and aspired to, but did not really touch him personally.

Dressed in the long black tunic and spotless white over-blouse, clearly emulating that of the priest's elaborate ecclesiastical vestments, Granville relished in the quietude of soul-felt prayer.

The altar was hallowed ground; to be in its proximity, to touch it, was a wondrous experience for young Granville. He wanted to love God with all his heart, unreservedly, completely. His soul yearned for release. He felt this new love would not hurt or betray him with hidden alternative motives that only masked deeper true feelings of resentment, disgust, even hate.

...

Part 18: A Two-Edged Sword . . . Cuts Both Ways

He desperately hungered for the father he never had.

This hunger found an object, in a redirection toward a sense of clear entitlement and paternal influence through this presaged church presence. This newly discovered "God" sensitivity radiating through his inner awareness would grow, as a safe harbour, within the maelstrom of puberty, flowering amongst what would become a hyper-sexualized extended family dynamic.

As much as he loved his mother, her being the centre of his universe, he envied his younger brothers for the fathers they had, though he did not like either man. Their fathers, at least, appeared now and again to feign care for their sons, even though the expression was somewhat dysfunctional.

He endured a life of revolving male faces, a mélange of handsome men, some with children of their own, some without, either being attached to his mother or covetous of that role. This intermittent male presence, needing to compete with him for his mother's affection and attention, had been the main sense of maleness, in his world.

The conflicting influences—love of mother, hunger for father—were two trains on the same track racing toward the tunnel between them, on a collision course. Inevitable collateral damage was a certainty.

...

[[Author's Aside]]

Unfulfilled father hunger, coupled with unique physical attraction, would form both his blessing and his bane throughout his life.

The counterpoint to this religious fervour was his awareness of the "Blackening" neighbourhood around him. The evident poverty grew in prevalence as the racial cultural demographic altered and the dominant daily street life devolved to be more like the world his family left behind at 1714 W 14th Street: the broken sidewalks, boarded-up buildings, street trash blowing in the wind, Friday and Saturday public alcoholism and substance abuse, subsistence-level backyard businesses used mostly as gathering points for the poor and the forgotten.

With the disappearance of the white majority population, Bobby Franklin and his gang ceased to be a problem. The Black youth gangs were formed from the simmering discontent amongst their Black replacements.

The avowed leaders were generally recognized as the oldest, biggest, meanest, most violent, best connected, having the most money, or sometimes simply the smartest of the group.

The gangs garnered their members from the Black kids that lived primarily in a radius of the area where most kids lived. This area generally became their territory, to be defended from encroachment by anyone that didn't belong.

The gangs were the instigators, the judges, and the jury that dispensed "justice" for the crime of trespassing on their turf, in any way they saw fit. The "time" seldom fit the crime in the gang-world.

Granville's family home was located on a geographical racial divide. They lived on the edge of what was still an area where the kids, arriving from their suburban commute each weekday at the Kedzie Avenue elevated train station, traversed the expressway bridge, then walked north several blocks to Saint Philips Basilica High School. The remaining bastion of religious white majority culture, an island, in a growing sea of Blackness moving north.

The expressway also served as a border separating the North side, a predominately white neighbourhood surrounding Saint Philips BHS and Our Lady of Sorrows Elementary, from the South side, the predominately Black, mixed-race community of Harrison Street expanding south, west, and east.

...

Part 19: Sapphire: Black Fire Burns

Granville was thirsty. He had been chilling with Craig down on the expressway slope, just watching traffic and talking about girls, all afternoon. He was having a quick glass of milk when he heard the noise from the guest bedroom, which was located just off the kitchen.

He thought that Sapphire was awake. She had arrived from Mississippi a week earlier and was still adapting to the time change in Chicago. A distant cousin, and one fine coal-Black woman, big chest with hour-glass hips and waist, not much younger than his mom. Her soft southern drawl only enhanced her allure.

She had been the subject of Granville's puberty-driven wet dreams since her arrival; watching her breasts heave and bounce when she moved was almost more than he could handle on a hot early summer afternoon.

Craig liked skinny women, like his mom: small breasts and waist, broad shoulders, narrow hips, and long legs, the longer the better. "Nothin' like high steppin' ladies." It was a look he called athletic. Not so Granville; he was a breast, hips, and ass man, though he did like a small waist; made the rest look that much bigger. "Hourglass always goes to the head of my class."

Granville noticed that the door to the bedroom was slightly ajar and, flashing on a vivid memory—watching his babysitter Ellie Mae making love with her boyfriend Johnny Dollar—his heart began to beat hard in his chest. He knew that he should look away; this was definitely a no-go zone. Spying on a house guest, his cousin, was nothing but begging for huge trouble; still, he could not look away from her sterling figure. All he could do was watch, enraptured by the gleaming blackness of this voluptuous woman.

Sapphire saw her young cousin in her full-length dressing mirror. The reflection was just the right oblique angle that afforded her a clear view of him frozen in the bright kitchen light, fridge door left open, half-finished glass of milk in his hand, transfixed.

She really hoped he wouldn't drop that glass; he was so beside himself.

Still, she couldn't resist giving him a bit of a show. It had been a long time since a man, any man, looked at her that way. She felt the blush rise to her face and the heat fill her loins. After all, her young cousin was so, so pretty, so damn cute. *Why do you have to be thirteen goddamn years old? That trouser bulge says much about what you have to offer a girl, young boy. I'd love to make you a man!*

Sapphire began to slowly slide the translucent purple chiffon night-gown down her curvaceous body, slowly allowing the material to caress each peak and curve as it made its way softly toward the floor at her feet.

Then, naked except for a pink satin triangle hiding her pubis, her curly black pubic hairs framed the cloth on three sides, meeting at the apex of her full thighs, as if vying for freedom from the soft, stifling bondage.

Sapphire, her reflection framed by the mirror, slowly turned her back towards the door, allowing the lighted mirror to offer a frontal view while she gave her back and sumptuous round behind to his unfettered eyes.

Pausing to play with her hair, and suppressing a giggle, she softly wiggled her breasts side-to-side, then slowly bent at the waist to pick up the discarded gown. Watching him from that position, she spread wide and slightly bent her legs, to improve the view, juggling her exposed cheeks, just before retrieving the soft cloth.

Crash!

"Shit! Shit!"

"Gran, Gran! Did you drop one of my good goblets?" asked Ines, calling from her air-conditioned bedroom where she had been taking a nap, a respite from the June heat wave.

"No, ma'am, it was just one of the old glasses that Aunt Sara gave us when she moved. The ones she bought from a second-hand shop."

"Okay, make sure you clean up all that glass."

"Yes, Ma'am."

Granville looked up from the milk covered glass shards that littered the floor at his feet to see a closed bedroom door in the place of the vision that would haunt his dreams and fantasies for years to come.

Behind that door, Sapphire was almost splitting her sides, as every curve jiggled and bounced with suppressed silent laughter.

Part 20: Shoeshine Entrepreneur

Granville's sense of being a social outsider, an outlier, gave him a predisposition to venture into areas, places, activities that others would not consider for fear of the repercussions of being outside their avowed element or comfort zone. As an outlier throughout his life, he fostered the spirit and courage of the adventurer, daring to walk paths where others wouldn't dare to tread.

If I don't belong anywhere—and I don't, that has been made perfectly evident—why can't I belong everywhere if I choose to? What's to stop me?

Amos and Andy was one of Granville's favourite situational comedy TV shows. He watched it regularly and loved every second of it, never tired of even watching the reruns. One of the cast of characters was a shoeshine "boy" (man) who often shined Amos's shoes while imparting sage advice.

Watching that shoeshine "boy" gave Granville an idea.

Granville wanted to make some pocket change for himself. He had his heart set on a new pair of Converse All-Stars gym shoes and wanted to pay for them himself, instead of badgering his mother for an expense she couldn't afford. Using his baby-sitter income gained from watching his nephew Lars, he purchased a very compact but well-equipped portable shoeshine kit at the corner drugstore.

The kit came in a polished wooden box with attachments on each end for a shoulder strap, also part of the kit. There was a tool drawer with a handle at one end, and on the lid of the box was a shoe-sized footrest support for the customers to rest their shoes on while they was being shined. Granville felt that it all looked quite professional.

Now where to find the customers? He pondered this for some time. The customer would have to be sitting down. Since he did not have a shoe stand with seats, he would have to go where the potential customers were already sitting.

His initial search led to community barber shops, which did not bear fruit since all had shoeshine "boys" (men) working in them and were not interested in his offer to apprentice with them. "No place for a thirteen-year-old kid to be hanging out, getting underfoot, and on my nerves."

Thus, he realized he would have to go further to find what he needed. One weekend, on impulse, he boarded a westbound city bus that took him toward Pulaski Avenue, which bordered the Cicero business district, a decidedly white neighbourhood.

He walked until he found a cafe that seemed to cater to businessmen.

Shoring up his courage, keenly aware of the risk he was taking, he entered. "Hello, my name is Granville. Would anyone like his shoes shined?"

Conversation ceased, as suddenly all eyes were upon him. Granville waited about two of his hard-thumping heartbeats before turning to leave, when he heard from the back of the cafe near the restrooms, "How much do you charge?"

That question, he was prepared for. "By donation. After I finish, you decide what it's worth."

"Are you that good?"

"Been practicing on friends and family."

"Okay, I'm meeting an important client in thirty minutes. Can you give me a spit-shine in that time?"

"On the wingtips and a soft buff shine around the rest?"

"That'll do. Come over here and get to it. My meeting starts in twenty-five minutes."

Granville hurried over and set up quickly, dusted then brushed to refresh what polish existed in the leather. The toes, or wingtips, were the hardest portion of the shoe and would take most of his time to spit-shine.

Taking out his neutral polish and shine cloth, he spat on the cloth, tightly drawn over the balls of his index finger and the one on each side, rubbed the triangular tent-peg firmly on the polish block, and began rubbing the saliva-tinged polish into the tips of each shoe.

As he rapidly repeated this, a hard shine began to surface in about ten minutes. Two minutes more and his young face started to mirror in the shiny black wingtip loafers.

The shoes were not new, yet the leather quality was excellent and appeared to be in very good shape. Once the sheen was set, he applied a light coat of polish to the remaining area around each shoe, then snap-cloth buffed the heels, brushing the sides as a finishing touch, in eighteen minutes flat.

"Nice, here's twenty. Keep the change. Thanks." And the businessman hurried away.

Granville worked that room for the next two hours, earning one hundred dollars and a free meal.

Not one to shy away once discovering a good thing, the following weekend, Granville decided to take a walk, with his shoeshine kit and pocket change, west toward Garfield Park. He had not returned to the park since the diving board accident almost cost him his life. As it was, a year of painful medical treatments, the loss of 20/20 vision, and the dream of ever becoming a pilot had been very difficult time for him. Still, the park was the only green area within walking distance, with abundant flowers, trees, two small lakes, ponds, even a conservatory. It was a beautiful early summer day, not too hot, with a bit of breeze off Lake Michigan.

The park seemed to be quiet, very little vehicle or foot traffic. He decided to sit beside the duck pond and watch them swim, flock, and feed. The sun warming his face felt relaxing, a bit drowsy and hungry, as only a teen who travels by his appetite can feel. He took out the lunch he had prepared. His lunch bag contained a Coke, a ham and cheese sandwich, and a peanut butter and jam sandwich. Deciding to save the peanut butter and jam sandwich for dessert, he began eating his main course with relish. Leaning back on the park bench, closing his eyes as he chewed, only opening them to take bites.

Granville heard the approaching footsteps. Glancing down to assure himself that all was intact, he continued to chew, sightless.

"Nice-looking outfit. What is it? Must be lunch break in your park shoe-shine shop?" The chuckle in that pleasant female voice popped Granville's eyes open, instantly wide awake.

"It's my shoe-shine kit." Eyeing her five-inch-high, blood-red pumps, he asked, "Would you like your pumps shined? I see there're a couple of nicks at the ball and instep. My polish would fix that problem with a spit-shine."

"So, you know your women's shoes. Think you could match this colour?"

"I use neutral polish, works with all colours and types of leather."

"What's the charge?"

"Pay by donation. When I'm finished, you pay what you think the job is worth."

"Confident as well. Hmm, I'll bite. Don't you want to finish your lunch?"

"It'll still be there when I'm done." Granville quickly rewrapped his sandwich. "Please have a seat." He brushed off an area on the bench next to him.

Once she was seated, he moved to a kneeling position in front of her and placed his shine kit in position for her foot to rest on. Brushing off the street dust, he quickly examined the shoe, looking for imperfections in the leather that he would need to address.

The woman was the first female customer he'd had so far, and he noticed the difference in her attention right away. The men pretty much ignored him while he worked until toward the completion of the shine; then they would only pay attention to judge the results.

She watched him intently from the outset, tracking his hands, every movement. Her gaze was almost uncomfortable for the young boy, as if she was sizing him up for something else that he had no idea about.

"How old are you?"

"Fourteen," he lied.

"You're pretty small for fourteen."

"Yeah, I get that a lot. I can still get into the movies under twelve."

"Do you live around here?"

"Harrison and Kedzie."

"That's quite the walk; did you take the bus?"

"Nope, walked. I like to walk, and the park is not far for me."

"What's your name?"

"Granville."

"Granville. Interesting name. What does it mean?"

"Big city. it's French, after my father Granville Howard."

"Big name for such a little guy."

"Big things can come in small packages." A paraphrase of a saying he had read somewhere, yet long forgotten the source.

"That so? And what could those things be?"

"Diamonds, big value, small package; the brain, for instance, one of the smallest organs in the body, yet it controls everything you do, big as in being very important to everything else."

"Smart too."

"I read encyclopedias a lot. Mom bought me a set for my birthday." All during their conversation, Granville, aware of his position, kneeling beneath her lower legs and skirt line, had focused exclusively on her feet and the job at hand. Once the right shoe was ready with the base polish that would support the spit-shine, he glanced up at her face.

His eyes flitted past the shadow of her upper thighs meeting within her skirt, then onto the left shoe.

While he efficiently repeated the process on the left shoe; his mind replayed what his eyes had seen but refused to acknowledge. *She's not wearing panties. She not . . .* was the thought that ran through his mind like a gerbil running in a treadmill freewheel, around and around, chasing its tail, going nowhere fast.

Embarrassed beyond measure, Granville redoubled his focus on the shoes, while hoping that she had not noticed how his cheeks were suddenly on fire and his ear lobes burned.

Finishing each shoe in grateful silence, Granville was relieved that nothing had come of his unintentional indiscretion.

"Good job, you're talented. Good mind, great hands! Here's ten. By the way, did you like what you saw? Consider that peek a tip, for services rendered."

Granville froze, speechless, facing her frank expression, eyes wide, ears now burning in earnest.

"My name is Noelle. I'm a nursing student and I have an offer for you. I live in a large sorority house for female students attending University of Illinois Chicago. Our house is about four blocks from here. There's six of us staying there. You do such fine work; how would you like to shine all our shoes?"

"How many pair?"

"Probably a dozen or so. You'd be looking at five to ten dollars per pair."

"Today, now?"

"Tell you what, I've interrupted your lunch, and I'm sure you're still hungry."

"Yeah."

"Finish your lunch. Here's the address. If you're still interested, I'll go ahead and arrange things at that end. You can walk over when you're done. If you decide not to take me up on it, no harm, no foul, no hard feelings. Deal?"

"Deal."

Granville considered the offer as he finished his lunch. The thought, *never look a gift horse in the mouth*, came to mind as he did the math. Maybe eighty dollars, up to possibly a hundred and thirty, was more than he had earned to date on any of his outings. Mom had long since given her approval.

"Keep your head up, your eyes open, and at the first sign of trouble, get to a pay phone and call me."

Eventually the money was just too tempting to pass up. He thought of calling his mom to tell her what was happening, give her the address, just in case he needed back-up, but decided against it for fear she would not approve of his visiting a stranger's house, no matter the bait.

"Gran, kids disappear that way."

...

The house was not small, but well-proportioned for a sorority, housing six university students, each in their own wing, with a large common kitchen and spacious living room. A three-story concrete and river stone facade, it had a wide central stairway leading to a pair of dark wood double doors.

Big bay windows on both sides, a series of trio-windows going up each side and floor, gave an open view of well-appointed common rooms. Living room with a large fireplace on the right, perhaps a studio space with a baby grand piano on the left.

Granville had never seen a full-sized piano in a residential home before. He was impressed. He hesitated before approaching the building's front door; walking once around the block to think it over, he decided that it certainly did not look to be the home of potential kidnappers.

Noelle answered the bell. "Come in, Granville, we're glad you could make it. Let me introduce you to the gang, my housemates. This is Marie-Alice, Nicole, Elsbeth, Pilar, and Frieda." She pointed to each woman; like Noelle, all were beautiful, all were Black, six hues, from light cream to coal black with four shades in between. It wasn't an actual sorority, more like six women who had opted to live off campus in shared housing.

Very casually sexy would be an apt description of the six of them.

Standing side-by-side smiling serenely, Granville forgot all about his financial reward. To be welcomed like this by the gorgeous sextet warmed his heart better than the sunny day had caressing his face earlier during his luncheon in the park. He beamed back at them.

"Hello, nice to meet you." Granville's shyness made him drop his eyes to their shoes, all five-inch heels of varying styles and shapes. It was clear to him that they loved colours. Each contributed to the project, offering the high heels they presently wore, and their closeted pairs. The wear and tear on their high- and low-heeled shoes showed that they probably loved to dance.

"These are my best dance shoes. Sorry about the scuffing," said Marie-Alice.

"I want to see my face in the toes," smiled Nicole.

"Can you do two-tone spats?" asked Elsbeth, looking at him some-what unsure.

"Neutral polish, won't be a problem."

"These have a bit of gold strapping, please polish that as well," directed Pilar.

"Will do."

"These are suede, the leather looks tired. Can you refresh them?" asked Frieda.

"Yeah, I have a dry spray for suede. Once it dries, a soft brush, and they'll look like new."

Granville tried his most gentlemanly best to stay focused on the shoes. Still the beautiful humans in that household were all around him going about their business, attired in short-waist t-shirts over bathing suit bottoms, or long, clingy, soft nightshirts accentuating every gentle curve, no bra anywhere near those near-perfect, athletic torsos with legs that went on forever.

He found a new appreciation for Craig's taste in women. Lucky he wasn't here. He'd tripping over his tongue drool, probably fall flat on his face in the mess. *Wait till I tell him, that's one Black cat that'll be red in the face and green all over with envy.*

The ladies did not seem to mind his attention. Each graced him with soft, gentle, smile-filled expressions of renewed welcome each time their eyes met. They plied him with Coke as he shared stories of his time and life on 1714 W 14th Street, and the Mafia that set a gas station fire that cost him his favourite uncle. Then the blockbusting that he, his brothers, and mother endured and survived—the showdown at 3148 West Harrison Street.

"Well, Granville, you are quite the little shit-disturber," said Elsbeth.

"Amen to that, little man, where do you keep all that spit 'n' vinegar?" Noelle half spoke, half laughed at the question.

"I'm little, bullies have always underestimated me because of my size, and the way I look to them, much to their downfall.

"My mom is a superwoman, small but mighty. She works a hard man's job in the B&O railway yard. Only woman on the restoration crew working in the yard, a coach cleaner.

"She is as beautiful as all of you, and very powerful for her size. She can lift and carry her weight, and then some. Mom's rearing us to be like her: smart, honest, fair, and tough as nails when the needs be."

"I like your mom already," smiled Freida.

"Mom would like you, too, all of you."

"Does she know you're here with us?"

Granville dropped his gaze once more, finding the shoes he was working on, a safe place to park his eyes. "No, I was afraid she'd say no if I told, asked her, before I came."

"Time to make a phone call," Noelle declared.

"Hello, Mom! No, everything is okay. There's no problem. I'm calling from a customer's home, a sorority of six student nurses at the University of Illinois Chicago. They hired me to shine everyone's shoes. I met one, named Noelle, in the park and shined her shoes. She invited me home to their house to do everybody's, five or ten dollars a pair. Mom wants to talk with you, Noelle."

"Hello, Mrs. Andrea."

"It's Ms."

"Ms. Andrea, I am the culprit here. Your young entrepreneur truly impressed me, all of us, with his intelligence and candor. We apologize for not confirming that he had your permission before allowing him to come. Yes, ma'am, he'll be heading home very shortly. We all would like to invite you and your children over for dinner sometime. Thank you for understanding."

"Not quite finished with the job, Mom. Marie-Alice, one of the students, says she'll give me a ride home right after I'm done. Thanks, Mom, bye."

"Pretty-boy, you are quite a handful indeed, a tall drink of water in the desert," announced Pilar, yawning.

"Let's finish-up so we can get you home. We don't want your mom mad at us, period!"

...

Part 21: "What's Your Problem?"

"Boy, what is your problem?"

"I'm fine, Levi. What's your problem?"

"Mom told us about this shoe-shine business you've started, going all over hell's half acre, trying to be a shoe-shine boy."

"Pays a lot better than delivering papers, and I only work when and where I want to. I also get paid in cash right away, not have to work all week, then hope to get paid on collection day."

"Gran, you're worrying Mama sick, boy."

"Mom said it was okay, and we have a plan if there is a problem."

"Right, you were supposed to call before venturing into some stranger's house."

"Mom and I talked about it, I apologized. Promised that I wouldn't make that mistake again."

"That is just not good enough!"

"Levi, I'm not..." *your son!*

"You are going to stop this foolishness. Every time we look around, you are out there causing trouble. Mom had to lose hours at work to rescue you at school. How many times did she have to do that? Then, threatening the entire neighbourhood with her gun to save you from a race mob on the front door! You, out there trying to take on that mob all by yourself! Who do you think you are, young Nigger, Super-Nigger? King of 3148?

"Now, you're out there trapping around the West side, white hood, shining shoes in some businessman's cafe, on your own; house full of young women, shining shoes. Little brother, we all know better than to swallow that lie."

"It's the truth, Levi."

Thump. "Boy, don't lie to me!"

The blow to Granville's head hurt, his ears rang, eyes watered, even though it was open-handed. He recoiled instinctively, stepping back out of range. Levi moved to further close the gap. Granville side-stepped and brushed Levi's outreached hand, more than twice the size of his, aside.

In the same motion, driving a hard right jab to Levi's exposed chest, under his heart. The precision of the blow stunned Levi; not the power of it, but the fact that Granville was readily fighting back, paused Levi's tirade.

"YOU are NOT my father! Don't you ever touch me again! Mom tells me what to do. YOU DON'T have a FUCKING thing to do with it!" Granville screamed, through his tears.

Crack! Stars this time. Granville barely saw the blow before Levi rang his bells. "FUCK!" Granville went low, and went for his tall, big brother's hanging fruit in easy reach and rang both his bells. Levi grunted hard and buckled over, to be met with a volley of rapid blows to face and throat.

Granville's elder brother went down to one knee, trying to protect his face, throat, and balls at the same time. Levi's surprise had turned to shock.

...

Levi had thought of himself as his mom's resident male figure in the family. He was determined to keep his unruly little brother in line.

Granville had become a lightning rod for issues in his mother's life that was consuming precious resources within the family. He felt that his fatherless little brother of a different father seemed to go out into danger as quick as danger seemed to come and find him. To save his mom's sanity, he felt he had to step up and do what needed to be done, provide some guardrails for his little brother. Before he got himself killed or kidnapped. "Nothing's too good for Gran! Mom has doted on her love child so much, he's out of control!"

Levi loved his brother as the air he breathed, yet tough love seemed to be the order of the day.

Levi leaned hard against the small frame of his brother, briefly pinning him against the wall of his kitchen. Slipping into a low crouch, Granville squirted out of the vice and away toward and through the apartment's front door to the long hall that ran the length of the building. Half staggering, Levi followed in hot pursuit.

Granville careened off the wall opposite the apartment, heading for the stairwell up toward home. Levi managed to snag a trailing t-shirt tail as Granville rounded the staircase entrance facing the opposite direction.

Tripping while pulling away, Granville clambered up on all fours, gracefully scampering up the rest of the way to the next level and home.

Ines's closed front door stalled all forward progress while reigniting the struggle between the brothers.

Ines opened the door to the sight of Levi slamming Granville hard against the opposite wall and pinning him there as her second son fought hard to be free of the first.

Both froze under her instantaneously writhing glare. "Levi! GET your hands off that boy!

Granville broke free first, giving Levi a parting embarrassment by kneeing him in the balls, ringing his bells, one last time. "Ugh!" Levi instinctively clutched his crotch, now throbbing with pain, as Granville moved in the same motion to stand beside their fuming mother.

"Gran, that's enough!"

The fight was over as quickly as it had begun.

"Levi, I know you mean well, but I and I alone set the standard here as far as your brothers are concerned. You are not the father here. Gran does not need a surrogate father, he has me. Besides, do you think he will want to babysit for you and Beatrice now that you've beaten him?"

"Who's beating who here?" Levi still felt the deep ache and burn, while inwardly cursing the pint-sized source of this current indignation, the little shit, now defiantly standing next to Ines.

"The point is that there will be no more of this. Levi, you damn well know better. A grown man beating on a kid! Apologize! Both of you, now!"

"I'm sorry, Mom." Spoken in unison.

"And to each other!"

"Sorry, Levi!"

"Sorry, Gran!"

In Ines's kitchen, later that night, the three boys now sleeping, Levi found his voice to ask the burning question that had been chewing at his gut for far too long.

"Why, Mom? Why do you protect him? Treat him as if he is so special? Let him get away with all the crap he stirs up?"

Ines looked carefully at her eldest son. Could she trust him to perhaps understand a secret she had kept for so long? She decided that being the oldest and the only mature man in her immediate family, he deserved to be trusted.

"Levi, when Gran's father died, it almost killed me as well. I thought that I was going to have a heart attack, the pain was that great. My baby, Gran, was kicking, striking, twisting, and tossing, trying to turn in my womb, with the horror of it.

Suddenly, when I felt death would be preferable to this acrid misery, Gran went quiet, deathly quiet. I thought I was going to have another miscarriage or stillbirth. The thought of losing Granville's child, all I would have left of him, brought on another bout of raging panic. This time, Gran remained quiet. I felt all around till I felt his heartbeat, beating strong like a little drum. I felt I could almost hear it. Gran's quiet, his calm, his strength seemed to permeate my entire being. My child, in my womb, amid this tragedy, was soothing his mother! I laughed, and a deep, gut-wrenching joy enveloped me, and I understood.

"This child, this precious child is special and would need to be protected, for he would demand all I have to give and more, yet the world would benefit greatly from that love and understanding given this wondrous baby. I am preparing Gran for the burden he carries."

"What do you mean?"

"You've felt it yourself. There's something about Gran that rubs people the wrong way."

"Got that right."

"It's nothing he says or does. His presence demands your attention . . ."

"He's too damn pretty, and smart, and fast, and charming."

"Yes, he's all of that and more, much more. Gran just has to walk into a room, and everyone takes notice, men and women, adults and children.

"He carries the instinctive first-hand experience of death, the death of his father, my beloved Granville Howard, before he ever knew life. The taint of that deep knowledge, of death itself, branded him with a certainty that terrifies people.

"Especially those who carry an unrecognized death-wish in their subconscious. The fearful, the hateful, the perpetually angry or mean, are driven to seek him out and attack whenever the opportunity presents itself. They can't help themselves.

"His beauty attracts, then they look into his eyes and see that calm assurance, that cold, deathly Grim Reaper gaze that peers into their soul and finds them wanting, revealing their pitiful lack of self-awareness that they're trying so desperately to hide. Gran has that deep sight. He can't unsee whatever or whoever is before him. He is marked, for what I don't know. In truth, I don't want to know.

"I gave him my maiden name on his birth certificate. His father's name Granville, with my maiden name Johnson, so his father and I would forever be joined together in him. It's his birthright."

"Does he know about his true name, that it's different from ours, and why?"

"No, I've never told him. Neither will you. He needs to feel that he is as much a part of this family as each of you. He's an Andrea, that's all he knows, and that's enough for now. His true identity will be part of his self-discovery when he is ready for the weight of it. He's my love-child, the only child that bears it. He is my calling, to keep him alive and away from harm as long as I am able. He will seek his fate. He will survive, so others, in the future, will thrive."

"Is that the reason you divorced my dad?"

"No, your father was a bigamist; ours was the second marriage, therefore illegitimate. He already had another wife and children. I owed no allegiance to Luther Andrea whatsoever!"

"I know. I understand. Mom, I will support you, and look out for Gran's welfare the best I can as well . . ."

"Thank you, Levi."

CHAPTER FIVE:
Join . . . Move . . . or Die!

· · · · ·

GRANVILLE'S TRAVEL IN, through, and around the neighbourhood became more and more hampered by the rise of the Black gangs. His fight with Levi only heightened his awareness of the risk of walking the streets, which somehow now belonged to the groups of gang members. Small yet dangerous groups that casually patrolled their "territory" looking for strangers they deemed had no right to be there.

These were his streets. He fought in them. Shed blood for the right to walk them. His family paved the way for the presence of Black people.

The freedom they enjoyed was his to have given. How dare they try to take his away? He and his brothers were among the first to breathe this used-to-be-whites-only air. Defended against the bigots because it was the right thing to do. Now he must pay a blood toll to these self-appointed Black ass-backward-holes!

...

The Black gangs . . .
The night fights and flights of hunted prey.

"Mighty Vice Lords! Roman Saints.! . . . Up in here!"
The Black/white gangs'. . . cattle calls to battle.

.

Nigga . . . Join! Move! Die!

Supreme Gangster am I!
Too stubborn to do either. Day to night . . . . I . . . alone . . .
fight for my life.

-I Am an Honourable Man (Excerpt)... by Granville Johnson

...

[[Author's Aside]]

*The overarching potential violence of the gang mentality coloured
every aspect of ghetto life in the 'hood. No longer a neighbourhood, which
implies a populace of unrelated families, neighbours, living in a common area,
with commonalities between them that creates an ad hoc bond.*

*Granville's world had now devolved into the 'hood, where everyone was out
for themselves, inherent in the extreme need to survive, and life was cheap.*

...

Part 1: Love on Wheels

The place that became a safe zone, an uncontested service that benefitted all the intermediate-level elementary and high school boys and girls, was the YMCA. The community service that everyone enjoyed within the building was the roller-skating rink. There you could rent skates or bring your own. The gang members frequented the rink's skating sessions, particularly on Friday and Saturday nights. No one would create a problem in the rink proper during sessions for fear of losing access to the facility.

Though outside, after closing, there were the inevitable confrontations between rival gang members, especially if a boy had the gall to skate with a girl from a rival gang's turf during the occasional couples-only skate session songs.

Granville took to roller skating like a baby duck takes to water the first time, all enthusiasm, little control. Nevertheless, he knew this was his dance on wheels, though he found the rental skates to be awkward and clumsy.

Using his shoe-shine income, it wasn't long before he bought a pair of precision skates that had enclosed grease-packed ball bearings and were very smooth for effortless speed and precise control.

All the skate guards wore precision skates and danced in the centre of the floor while everyone skated around them in a tight oval. The flat wooden floor was worn as smooth as slightly textured glass.

The coolest boys would skate with a partner on couples-only songs.

They would glide through the room with long, languid strides and glides timed to the beat of a love ballad being sung: "Ooo Baby Baby" by Smokey Robinson and The Miracles, for instance, was a favourite.

It was a tribute to the ability level of a young boy skater's skill set to skate couples' sets. It was the boy's job to lead the dance, which could be as simple or as intricate as the couple's combined skill level could control. Boy-girl skate partners and boyfriend-girlfriend couples were the norm.

The R&B ballads pumping out of the speakers was always excellent for grooving around the room on wheels.

On occasion, it could be the opportunity to meet and connect with a girl or boy that you had been admiring from a safe distance.

Unlike in other social situations, where Granville kept to himself, a young Black girl sometimes happened to invade the tight circle of his awareness and thus snared his attention. This was the case when he found himself hopelessly attracted to Astra Pearls.

In between days at the rink with his new skates, he would glide forward and backward up and down the long hall outside his apartment for endless hours. Practicing "rubber-leg," spinning, and stop-go dance moves in the railing area at the top of the stairs where the hall widened to accommodate the two stairwells. Discovered painfully that the skillful application of the toe stops was even more effective and important than the wheels in spin control and direction reversal.

Granville went from rank beginner to a skate dancer, proficient in forward and backward movement, in either direction, in a matter of a few months.

Astra could skate, dressed in pleated knee-high skirts that sometimes flared open and flashed muscular calves, thighs capped by full, rounded hips and buttocks. Her upper torso boasted broad shoulders, a straight back, and firm, blouse-filling breasts. A tall girl, compared to Granville's diminutive height; this only increased her allure. Her skating style was powerful without exhibiting any overt effort. The girl could move around the floor as effortlessly, in any direction, as the other advanced skate-guards on the floor.

Astra's athleticism was self-evident. She was captain of the cheerleading squad at Frederick Douglass High School. She was also the only female skate guard at the rink. She moved with relaxed, unchallenged authority.

Soft, coffee-cream brown complexion; soft, loose, jet-black curls that caressed her round features; big, dark, night-black eyes that seemed to look through you, rather than at you, whenever your eyes would incidentally meet her gaze.

It was her full-lipped, brilliant-white toothy smile and full-throated laugh that grabbed his heart strings and began to play the sweetest melodies in his mind whenever she was in the rink. Try as he might—and he did try, hard—he could never stop watching her every move, especially as she glided across the floor.

Granville noted carefully that she seldom skated with anyone during the couples-only songs, only cruised the floor as a guard, shepherding the traffic.

Astra's presence became his motivation to attend the rink every week.

Her smile became his dreamed recollection each night during the days in between. He practiced his moves on the rink floor, working quietly, repeatedly, to become smooth in every gesture.

Eventually he could skate smoother and faster backward, watching over his shoulder with certainty, weaving in and out of the other slower, less skillful skaters during the open skates. Hoping each night that somehow, she would notice.

All the while thinking about, dreaming of, planning to somehow, some night, ask Astra to couple skate in that romantic, perfectly controlled glide around the oval, sweep her off her feet as he held her tight, just right, and together, skate into her heart.

...

[[Author's Aside]]

At an early stage, Granville had already developed a preference for strong women. It is said that a boy-child's heart is forever chasing the attributes of his first love, his mother, in the woman with whom he is attracted. This was never truer, and remains so, in Granville's life.

...

The couples-only skate was announced just as Granville was passing the double doors leading to the skate rental room, office, off-floor rest area, and restrooms. He had to go around the oval once more to leave the floor smoothly with the other traffic. He spied her standing in the corner opposite the entrances, leaning casually against the wall, waiting alone in the music-less soft whir of many wheels coming to an intermittent pause, as the floor crowd reorganized itself.

It was his chance, his time, to be accepted into her world or be crushed by her rejection. Heart beating like a trip-hammer doing double-time, gliding to a smooth stop in front of her, he asked, "May I have this skate?"

A pause, a refocusing, as if seeing him for the first time. She returned his smile with her own, a fullness, easy expression, open, welcoming.

"Thought you'd never ask."

Granville, completely flabbergasted, stammered, "I . . . I," and almost stumbled as she left the wall in one smooth motion, gliding into the couple position beside and slightly in front of him. They were away, effortlessly matching speed and direction.

Fortunately, the music started up at that precise moment, and all his endless hours of practice rescued him from embarrassment, as his muscle memory kicked in and matched her position at just the right pace, forming unison, two becoming one.

Holding her close, right hand resting on her powerful right hip, her left hand resting in his outstretched, upturned palm, their dance began.

Granville felt light-headed with the feel of her. He wanted to jump for joy, then backflip through the sky, life being quite wonderful, just being this close to his heart's wonder. Yet he focused on the task at hand, leading this incredible, beautiful young woman around the oval as flawlessly as possible.

Astra needed no leading. In truth, she was a much more powerful and elegant skate dancer than her oh-so-very-cute partner; still she let him lead, as was his role in the dance and smiled to herself at how well he was doing. At the very least, she felt, he would not embarrass her in front of all the other skate guards. After all, she did not skate the couples-only songs as a matter of professional policy.

To break her self-imposed code, and then skate poorly as a result of her partner's inept performance in front of everyone, was unthinkable in its potential for embarrassment; in a word, disastrous, that the other guards, now green with hostile envy as they watched the couple, would never let her live down.

The Commodores crooned, "Sail on down the line. Sail on, honey, good times never felt so good. Sail on sugar, good times never felt so good. Sail on," through the loudspeakers in perfect harmony with Granville's heartbeat, as he and Astra sailed around the room as if no one else existed in their universe. And to him, no one else did.

All was Astra, all was her, here and now. Her perfume filled his mind with a deep, heartfelt longing for more of everything. Astra Pearls! Precious pearls around her delicate, svelte neck encircled Granville's life like none other. Granville, once again, was in love.

To say this was puppy love was to say that first love is not meant for young adults; puberty fed a furnace of wanton desire and naive expression. Better to temper the desire until expression has had a chance to mature in life lessons learned through the harsh taskmaster of trial and error.

Granville had much to learn. Astra, unbeknownst to herself, was to become his first teacher.

"Thanks."

"Don't mention it. You're pretty good."

"I practice a lot, outside the rink."

"Where? You mean outside? I only see you here on Friday and Saturday nights."

"I skate in our hallway outside our second-floor apartment. It's a long, wooden hallway with stairs to the entrance at one end. I've been skating the hall since I bought my precisions, two, maybe three months ago. My mom thinks I'm crazy to risk falling down the stairs, if I miss the turn at the top of the stairwell."

"Sounds like she might be right. What's your name?"

"Granville, Granville Andrea. You're Astra Pearls, right?"

"How did you know?"

"Asked the guy renting skates, long time ago."

"Granville? Never heard that name before."

"Astra never heard that name before either. Could it be taken from the ancient herb Astragalus, used in traditional Chinese medicine for centuries? It's believed to prolong life, treat the common cold, fatigue, allergies, even used against heart disease and diabetes. Wouldn't it be cool to live a hundred years and never be sick? Astra as in Astragalus."

"Really? Never heard of that either. How do you know?"

"I read it. Mom bought me a complete volume set of the Encyclopedia Britannica for Christmas last year."

"For Christmas?"

"Yeah, I read it all the time. It was the best Christmas present ever!"

"What does your name mean?"

"It's French, big city, Grande Ville!"

"How about he's a Gran Ville, for his big brain! You know being smart is sexy."

"It is? Never thought of it that way. I'm in the honours class at Saint Philips Basilica HS. The class is full of smart kids, all boys, all white. I wouldn't call them sexy, just a bunch of mostly uptight Catholic nerds from the suburbs."

"Ha, ha, ha! Maybe because they aren't as cute as you."

"Thanks! You're captain of the cheerleaders at Frederick Douglass High School, aren't you?"

"And how did you find that out?"

"Same source, I think he likes you."

"Well, I like you. Let's skate."

Together they rejoined the oval traffic, still chatting, as he skated mostly backward, facing her as they went around and around holding each other's hands, and at times both. Weaving through the undulating throng of skaters was effortless for Granville, though Astra, skating forward facing him, occasionally steered him away from imminent collisions. Soon conversation became irrelevant and utterly unnecessary; just the flow of their shared presence was enough.

George, the skate-rental guy, watched them from the darkened skate storeroom's open half-door, adjacent to the office. Simmering rage well hidden behind his ever-present flat expression. A tightly held mask of disdain and disinterest worn to hide his crushing shyness. Women, girls, terrified him. His father, a devout Methodist fire-'n'-brimstone preacher, taught him that all women couldn't be trusted.

A real God-fearing man never let a conniving female worm her way into his life, into his heart, where she would control, use, and abuse him until she would cast him aside in search of another unsuspecting fool to take his place at her beck and call. Just as his mother had done until she was "caught" by his father in their bed with his best friend one Sunday, when he had returned home unexpectedly from service sick with a slow-burning peptic ulcer.

His mom and her lover had died together that day.

George, who at seventeen had never so much as held a girl's hand, dreamed of Astra, day, and night; she ruled his every fantasy. He had watched Astra grow into her role as roller-rink queen during his three years working there, initially as a skate attendant in the early days.

The rink was the only racially integrated establishment in the neighbourhood, owned and run by the YMCA.

The Y never discriminated against its patrons, which simply reflected the colour of the community's demographic. George had watched its patrons transition from white to mixed, when he had joined, to Black.

Once Astra skated into his consciousness, he had applied for the open skate rental supervisor part-time position. He had to be there every night on the off chance that she would be present to feed his internal life with new images.

The flickering snippets were hoarded in his mind, frozen in his cold heart. The place where, like his father, he hated himself for his hunger for her. The hunger that defined his weakness and lack of "true" manhood.

He barely knew Astra; in fact, not at all. Yet there she was, smiling, chatting, holding hands, embracing this little wimp, this chimp on skates, half his size and stature, clearly undeserving of his queen's attention.

What in the hell does she see in him?

George wasn't much of a skater, though he had open skate privileges at every session and event. He rarely strapped on his skates, being somewhat obese from habitual consumption of comfort food; he only graced the floor with his bulk after closing time, when prying eyes could not judge or, worse yet, mock him.

George had another part-time position that paid no real wage but gave him a sense of being somewhat special, even unique. On weekend game days, George was the water and towel assistant for the Frederick Douglass High School varsity football team.

He was privy to the relationships of the cheerleaders and the members of the team, of which there were several. One of the most famous relationships between the two groups was between the team's centre lineman, Frank "Tank" Fraser and Astra Pearls, cheerleader captain.

...

Tank was crazy about Astra, letting all who would listen, know how he would make that uppity girl his girlfriend, period.

Astra seemed to like Frank and did not entirely spurn his attention but did not care for his assumption that she was his just because he said so. She did not consider herself as property to be claimed by the loudest, perhaps crudest, bidder at an auction.

Tank's intimidation factor was legendary at school, on the team's front line, and in the neighbourhood. Built tall, thick, low, and wide, like a Tiger tank, the source of his moniker, he made a habit of mowing down the opposition in the centre of the front line, protecting the quarterback, or making way for the running backs following his lead to gain running room sans opposition.

George had some news for Tank, his hero, that he couldn't hardly wait to divulge, about what his "girlfriend" had been up to. *That'll teach the bitch; put her in her place. She'll know better than to fuck around when Tank slaps some sense into her!*

...

Granville and Astra were waiting, silently dreading their imminent separation. It was closing time, and most of the skaters were leaving, saying their goodbyes. Some of the guards had started a game of barrel-jumping, using a short bench and several chairs from the rest area as a "barrel" to clear for bragging rights.

For the couple, having to recognize on their first "date" the freshness of their connection, was both celebratory and exasperating.

To live in separate neighbourhoods, attending vastly different school systems—one public and nondenominational, the other private and Catholic—they were worlds apart.

At the same time, the physical distance between their homes meant crossing several dangerous turfs controlled and patrolled by warring street gangs intent upon attacking any stranger, in this case Granville, who dared to cross their warren.

Granville was aware that his life suddenly was faced with yet another *West Side Story* choice. Visiting Astra could very quickly become more dangerous than any foray into a whites-only neighbourhood. The thought did not worry him; it was just another source of unease, something he had long ago learned to live well with. Black-on-Black violence had become as common as pavement cracks that eventually devolved into craters.

"What are you doing tomorrow afternoon?"

"It's Palm Sunday. I'm serving in the Alms Offering Mass presided over by the archbishop. It's a big deal and only the advanced altar boys are allowed to serve."

"An altar boy? Smart and religious, a young leader. Aren't you full of surprises!"

"I'm working on the final draft of a book report, after that."

"Clearly, I'm a bit down the line with you."

"That is in no way true Astra. I have not been able to think of anything other than you, hoping to meet you."

"Well, now you have. You may have to alter that busy schedule a bit to make room for me. I'm not used to waiting for any boy. Usually, it's the boy doing the waiting. Yet I've had to wait, just to meet you. This will take some getting used to, Granville."

"Call me Gran, that's what my family calls me."

"Thanks. I will, Gran. Just don't call me Ass, I won't be impressed. It's strictly Astra."

"No problem, Astra, Can I call you beautiful or gorgeous? Maybe one day, my girlfriend?"

"A comedian as well, all in such a small, deadly, cute package."

"Big things can come in small packages."

"Gran, next week then?"

"Absolutely."

"Yo, George. Who's this young punk trying to date my girl?"

"Tank, his name is Granville. They meet at the YMCA every week. They skate together all the time. He's the only one she skates with on the couples-only songs. I heard he goes to that Catholic boys-only private high school, Saint Philips, bull-honky-shit. He's the token Nigger with the rest of those off-fay fags."

"Where does he live?"

"He lives on Harrison and Kedzie. 3148 Harrison."

"That's Vice Lord's turf. Is he a Lord?"

"Nope. He was one of the first Black families here, living over that storefront church. Nobody knows much about him, 'cept they say, all alone, he fought the white gangs and faced down an off-fay mob, before the crackers moved away."

"A little badass, is he? How does he live there and not get recruited?"

"Knows the 'hood, manages to be invisible, avoids traffic and our hangouts, knows how to move around without notice. The only place ever I see him is at the Y."

"Consider him noticed, right down into the fucking pavement!"

"What're you goin' to do?"

"It's Sunday, her folks are probably at afternoon church services. I think I'll pay my girl a visit."

"Come in, Gran."

"Thanks, your parents aren't home?"

"They're at afternoon church services."

"Do they attend the Christ's Shepherd Southern Baptist Church on Harrison Street?"

"Yeah."

"That's the church in my building. We live on the second floor above it. Do they know that you have company?"

"Interesting. Yes, they trust me. Don't you have company when your parents aren't home?"

"My friend, Craig, used to visit. His family moved back to California to be with his dad, who's in the navy. I don't have visitors now."

"No visitors, no friends?"

"No, I've always been a loner. Mom says it's because I was born knowing about death before life; that made me different at the beginning of my life."

"How so?"

"My dad died, unexpectedly, of TB when Mom was seven months pregnant, so I experienced his death with her, in her womb."

"Right. I get it. Were you born premature?"

"Yes, Mom says I hung on for one more month and helped her get through it, says that I'm the reason she made it at all. I reminded her of what was truly important in her life. My dad was the love of her life."

"I can believe that. So, have you always had this effect on people?"

"My blessing and my curse; her words, not mine. I'm a lightning rod for trouble. My presence antagonizes some people. Bullies, gangsters, no matter the colour. Mom says it's my "truth sight," the knowing, the wisdom; says I tend to see right through them, seeing fear within; the cowardice that they are trying so hard to hide. Makes them need to attack to prove what I'm seeing is not the truth."

"What do you see in me?"

"Beauty, light, courage, strength, a love of life that I want to be a part of."

"You do know the way to a woman's heart."

"My mother taught me well what truly matters to a woman, to anyone."

"And what is that?"

"Truth."

"Would you like to go for a walk?"

"Sure."

They walked along a side street off the busy commercial thorough-fare that was Roosevelt Avenue. It happened to be a tree-lined residential street and relatively quiet, graced by its closeness to Garfield Park. Enjoying the soft breeze scented with the hint of leafy green oak trees that peppered the park's landscape, they drifted onto the welcoming foliage lined path, holding hands. Once more, words faded to insignificance. The warmth of the shared silence held them close.

Tank approached from the rear, watching them from a safe distance to observe the connection and interaction between the pair. Rage burned deep in his eyes; he wanted so badly to destroy this young punk touching his girl. He knew she had been somewhat unresponsive to his advances. Yet he felt he could and would cajole, threaten, and, if need be, use force to get from her what he wanted. His blood turned cold, and a hard-edged plan blossomed in his dark mind.

"Hey Astra!"

Surprise jolted Astra out of her quietude; the feeling of Granville's new closeness vanished, replaced by a deep dread.

Then she felt the presence rumbling toward her, a rhino in human form, head down, horn up, approaching in long, low strides covering ground, sizing up Granville from a closing distance, menacing, frozen shark smile writ large on his wide-set jaw.

"Hey, Astra, want to introduce me to your friend?"

"Hello, Frank. Granville Andrea, this is Frank Fraser."

"Tank to you. Call me Tank."

"Hey, Tank."

Standing in the bright sunshine, suddenly facing this hulking horror, created for Granville the sense that this would not end well. A grim surety that this test would not end well for him. *Fuck, this is going to hurt.* Every fibre within screamed, *run to fight another day,* yet he could not. Some fights were worth losing. The idea was to survive; that would be winning.

Granville felt the adrenalin climb up his throat, the taste sharp, and bitter, as always. To be beaten down by Tank in front of Astra was what concerned Granville the most. In that instant, he decided that giving as good as he got was the only path to survival. *Show no fear. You got to bring ass to get ass, my ass will cost you dearly, Tank!*

"You live at 3148 Harrison, above that church?"

"Yeah."

"I heard about you. You're supposed to be the little badass that faced down a white mob back in the day. Boy, I thought you were an urban myth."

"It happened."

"Heard you were a good skater as well, skating with my girl," grumbled Tank.

"I'm not your girl, Frank!"

"Well, about that, I would say it's left to be seen. Just wanted to see if we're going to the dinner and dance celebrating the end-of-season district championship. After all, you're my date."

"You're ordering me?"

"I'm suggesting that you might want to reconsider; his immediate health may depend on it."

"Fuck you, Tank!" spat Granville.

"Pipsqueak punk, Nigger, I could stomp you into this shit pile you're standing on without breaking a sweat or dirtying my shoes!"

"Leave him alone, Tank!"

"That's more like it. That's my girl! Now, I'm sure that I can be under-standing; what a distraction this bit of business must be for both of you. So, to show you I'm not a total monster, I will let pretty-boy here go about his business on this bright sunny day. While you and I, Astra, will continue this stroll to discuss the coming festivities. And pretty-boy! I know where you live in Vice Lord's 'hood. Black Jesus, you know him? He's a friend of mine. If you so much as look back while you turn tail and hurry your ass away, I'll get BJ and his crew to pay you and your little brothers a pain-filled visit. Don't want to get my shoes dirty!"

"Kiss my little Black ass," cussed Granville.

"Gran, no!"

Suddenly, Granville was on his back, and not altogether certain how he got there, for he never saw the pile-driver jab into his sternum that had left him breathless, gasping for air.

He stared up wide-eyed at his grinning assailant. Tank had struck without any warning other than seeing Granville begin to bridle at the insults. In the blink of an eye, Tank's speed, power, and point was made. Granville never had a hope in hell of avoiding the blow or its result.

"Beatdown done, check. Now, boy, you crawl the way home while you still can."

"All right! All right! I'll go with you; do not fuck with him or his family. That includes your gang. If you do, I'll report this to the head coach, the principal, and the amateur athletic association. You'll kiss your college scholarships goodbye. Understand? Nigga!" cried Astra.

"Deal!" crowed Tank through clenched teeth with a sickening smirk of triumph. "I'll hold you to it and anything else I want."

Granville rose slowly from the damp grass with the heavy heart of resignation. Looking deep into the tear-filled eyes of his lady, the subject of his young love, he was painfully aware that Astra's capitulation to this monster's demand was to save him from what would have been a vicious beating.

He could not protect her from this sacrifice. Alas, he could not even protect himself. He was never more aware of his limitations: not big enough, not bad enough, not strong, not tough enough! A big brain meant little in this violent 'hood if you didn't have the muscle to back it up.

Granville knew of Black Jesus, leader of the Vice Lords. He was not surprised to discover that this bastard was affiliated with the gang. The Lords ruled the neighbourhood surrounding his home. He had managed to elude their notice so far. Once on their radar, the streets would become a very dangerous place to walk anywhere outside of his home.

He went to her, held both her hands briefly, a silent kiss paused, held close between them. Like became love, mutual and strong. Touched foreheads, in a soft nod of assurance, embraced his heart and soothed his troubled spirit as he wordlessly walked away, unable to bear seeing her with him. Granville never looked back, nor did he ever see her again.

Granville hung up his beloved skates for many months, as he buried himself deep within his dreams of Astra. It seemed pointless to care, to dare to ever try living a life that did not revolve around using someone or being used by someone. This was life in the ghetto, and he was disgusted by it.

Part 2: Supreme Gangster

Granville was walking in an unlit alley of a dark back street some blocks from home. He had been out for a walk to clear his troubled mind, contemplating whether to stay in this cesspool of Black-on-Black gang violence or to run away from home, which had itself also become a deepening source of emotional pain since his rape at the hands of Dyak Jihad, his mother's cousin.

He had become a night owl, nightwalker, travelling through alleys, vacant lots, and business, commercial, and industrial areas. All places that gang members seldom gathered or traversed. He was, for all purposes of survival, invisible to the world around him, nondescript, intentionally small and unremarkable to the casual passerby.

Now and again, the gangsters would cross his path, or he theirs. Still, he would will himself ever smaller and non-threatening, not worth bothering with, as he passed, shoulders hunched over, head down to avoid eye contact, shrunken to beneath notice, to move on his way, invisible.

Halfway down the length of the rough gravel and garbage-strewn length of the alley, a blue light began to bounce off the garages and garbage bins on either side of his elongated shadow. Granville, lost in inward focus, ignored this harbinger of imminent trouble for someone, somewhere. As he exited the alleyway turning toward the final three blocks before home and relative safety, he barely noticed the approach of the source of that flashing blue light, until the patrol car parked abruptly beside him.

"Hey, boy! Stop where you are!"

"We said stop! You deaf? What's your problem?"

Suddenly they were there, one cop in front of him, blocking his path, the other just behind him, poised, waiting, blocking possible retreat.

Blocked on all sides between the cops, their car, and the adjacent buildings, Granville was effectively cornered.

"What is it, officer?"

Their response was to push him against the rough stucco wall of the building, face-first. Then to search his pants and jacket pockets for weapons. Not finding anything in either pocket, he was turned to face them, before being hustled into the back of the patrol car. In silence, ignoring his brief questions as to the cause of his arrest, they drove to the district police station and parked in the rear of the building.

Granville was ushered into a well-lit room the size of a very large dormitory. There were Black teenagers scattered about, some sat in rows, others gathered in small groupings. Granville was led to one of the rows of seats and told to sit wherever.

Looking around, it took a few moments to recognize some of the faces and make the connections that each group had to the other. Once it was clear what he was observing, he wanted to be anywhere, anywhere at all, other than here. His fear of what was about to happen chased his eyes away from his perusal of the other Black teenage faces that stared back at him with veiled, somewhat amused curiosity.

He focused on the cops behind a large, sparsely covered desk with an open file drawer, several folders, and a camera off to one side. One cop was sitting at the desk; another was sitting beside the desk, straddling a chair back-to-front, cowboy style; two others were standing back from the desk on each side of an exit door, looking like back-up security. The cowboy-cop was handling the camera. The other was making notes in a ledger as the process continued.

It took a while for the familiarity of the cowboy-cop to sink in. When the memory of the policeman registered, Granville's heart did a belly flop and suddenly he needed to use the washroom in the worst way.

The cop behind the desk motioned for the Black teens to approach the desk, one by one. Once there, each was questioned, noted in the ledger, and his picture taken, before being allowed to return to his group.

"What's your name, address, school, street moniker, gang affiliation?"

Each boy grudgingly gave the information, except when it came to gang affiliation. That information was proudly, sometimes loudly, shouted, "Roman Saints! Up in here!" for all to identify where his allegiance lay.

"Next."

"Mighty Vice Lords! Up in here!"

"Next."

"Roman Saints! Represent!"

"Next."

It was obvious that the cops knew it was pointless to try to moderate the braying; in fact, they seemed to mildly tolerate the show of affinity. At least this way, the whole process was less boring and gave everyone a mild diversion.

The gangsters were as proud of their block moniker as they were of their gang affiliation, yet sometimes resisted revealing their birth names, as if those names had become foreign, belonging to someone else, who they no longer could or would recognize, for it held no power. The cameraman took their pictures in a candid array, hardly noticed by anyone at all.

"Next."

"John Jones, Black Jesus, Mighty Vice Lords! Leader in charge!"

"So, you're the Lord's boss man."

"Damn straight!"

"Good to know. Next!"

The room was slowly shifting as the rapid-fire interrogation ran its course. Eventually, there was only one little Black teen that had not been registered in the ledger. Granville, still sitting alone in his row of one, was the last to be called.

"Next."

"Granville Andrea."

"Address?"

"3148 West Harrison Street."

The cowboy-cop cameraman looked up. "School?"

"Saint Philips Basilica High School."

"Street moniker?"

"I don't have one."

"Gang affiliation?"

"None."

"What gang do you belong to?"

"None."

The sergeant's face twisted into a smirk that Granville noted as recognition of a memory better forgotten. Yet he knew that look. *The same expression that had crawled over his mother's torso by none other than Officer, now Sergeant, Hal Cronus.*

"Whoa! Hold everything! Boys, we are in the presence of an urban legend!" Un-mounting his chair like he was getting off his horse, he stood in front of the desk between Granville and the cop behind the desk, taking command of the proceedings, clearly relishing what he was about to say, the story he was about to tell.

"Back in the day, before any of you jungle-bunnies invaded and destroyed our neighbourhood, good, hard-working white families lived here. We tried to encourage the first Nigger families to move on, preferably to go back under the rock they crawled out of.

"We tried. Our children fought long and hard to make that happen. To no avail, eventually our people gave up and moved on one by one before their homes became worthless.

"Then you all arrived, and our community went to shit.

"The one who was there, who fought us tooth and claw, blood and guts. The one who, alone, fought our little white gang to a standstill, who faced down a mob of angry, law-be-damned white people to a standoff, all by himself! I was there to give witness! I present, ladies and gentlemen, this little, very badass Nigger! Granville Andrea!

"No gang affiliation, no street moniker, yet he has more street cred than all of you clowns put together. He fought for his home, for his family, and won against incredible odds!

"Not trying to rob liquor stores, which is why you all are here this fine night! Not to go out and create havoc because you have nothing better to do and are too lazy or stupid to try to better yourselves.

"Now he attends a private Catholic high school, the best around. Nigger must be damn smart to have even walked in the door. I wager he's probably the best in his class as well.

"This young man walks alone head and shoulders above all of you and follows no one! I give you Granville "Big City" Andrea, Supreme Gangster!"

The room, full of young Black gangsters, was deathly quiet. All eyes were on Granville, glaring, contemptuous expressions of hate and rage raking his form with a determination to destroy, to kill at the first opportunity this affront to their reputations, their power.

Black Jesus growled under his breath, "Yeah, we heard of him, thought it was a myth. Supreme Gangster, my ass. Gonna kill this little be-itch!"

Granville knew that the stupid fucking cop, in his self-indulgent tirade, had just handed out a wanted poster in his name. *"Granville 'Big City' Andrea. Wanted Dead or Alive. Preferably Dead!"*

Once again, the hunt was on, and he was the prey. His life and that of his brothers, from this moment on, was forfeit! They now knew his address, school, and the fact that he always travelled alone, without back-up. He quietly asked the sergeant if he could be the first to leave.

"Sure, Big City. I'll give you a running head-start. Just ask to use the restroom and the officer by the door there will show you the way out."

"Thank you."

"How's that fine mother of yours?"

"She's fine, sir."

"Yes, fine, she truly is one fine specimen of Niggra womanhood indeed! She still single?"

"Yes, sir."

"Tell her Sergeant Cronus says hello."

"Yes, sir. I surely will." *Fucking bastard!*

Granville, the first to be released, ran home as fast as he could, acutely aware that this was the last time he would be able to go anywhere, anytime, without looking over his shoulder, invisible no longer.

Part 3: "Brothers: The Good, Bad and Dangerous Ugly"

His younger brothers, at twelve and thirteen, were no more than a year apart in age, yet were very close to the same height and stature as Granville, three and four years their senior.

David particularly saw this as an advantage through which he would tend to challenge his "big" brother's authority during those infrequent occasions when Granville was left with the responsibility of taking care of them in their mother's absence.

It's the common lament of younger brothers, cursed with sibling rivalry, exacerbated by the dysfunctional influence of Sergeant Major Mark, and Rain—David and Joseph's absentee fathers.

The sibling hostility between Granville, David, and Joseph boiled over one sultry summer afternoon while their mother was at work, many months before the Showdown at 3148.

They were sparring with the tools that their Great-Uncle Prince had fashioned for each brother. "Oww! Shit! Dave, that was my hand!"

"Tuff shit, Gran! What's the matter? You're supposed to be the badass Supreme Gangster. Can't take a tap on your wrist? Try this on fo' size, pussy!"

Dave went low, aiming to clip his big brother at the knees or ankles. Quick as a cat, Granville hopped over the rod's path, while swinging at David's exposed shoulder "Fuck you, too, Dave!"

David barely avoided a badly bruised shoulder by rolling away from the rod's trajectory. Now both brothers were on their feet facing each other in a slow, stalking circle, looking for an opportunity to strike.

What the fuck! This is stupid! I'm outta here! thought Joseph, stepping up on the stairs leading to the third floor and out of the fray, realizing that his brothers had begun to fight in earnest.

Granville, noticing that David had inadvertently moved into a corner between the wall and the railing, side-slid into David with his lead leg, parting David's wide-legged stance, dropping to his knee, while jamming his rod into David's midsection, knocking the wind out of his surprised younger sibling.

Granville then straightened, lifting David off his feet to slam him to the floor while moving on top of David's chest, pinning him and using his free leg to tie up David's arm and fist that held the rod. Granville then pressed his rod across David's throat, underneath his chin, threatening his windpipe. "Yield! Asshole! Yield, David!"

"Fuck! Fuck you! Bitch!" was David's reply through clenched teeth. Granville applied careful pressure with the rod. "Give it up, punk! You started this, I'm gonna finish it! Last time, yield!"

David sucked what breath he could but said nothing.

"Yield, David! Don't be stupid! Yield!" cried Joseph.

David gritted his teeth, glancing at Joseph, realizing that his younger brother was not going to come to his aid. "Get off me, fucker! Get the fuck off!"

"Yield! Bitch!" Applying slightly more intense pressure, Granville waited for the inevitable.

"Fuckin' bitch! I . . . I . . . yield!"

Granville carefully released his brother, expecting retaliation at any time. When David seemed to be resigned to the cessation of hostilities, he moved to his feet and relaxed from the effort, though shaken by the realization of how close he and David had come to critically injuring each other.

Reaching out to shake David's hand, he said, "I'm sorry, Dave, didn't mean to hurt you; don't ever want to fight with my little brother."

David shook hands and started brushing himself off. Granville did the same and then said, "Whew, that was far too close to doing some real damage toward each other," as he turned away from David to enter their hallway.

"Not fucking close ENOUGH!" hissed David, striking the back of Granville's head at the base of his skull with the full force of the rod.

"Fuck! NO, Dave!" shouted Joseph, who was following his older siblings into the hall, as Granville fell in a heap like a discarded sack of overripe potatoes, unconscious.

...

"I told Uncle Prince that those damn rods would lead to trouble. These kids don't need to have those kind of weapons, Aunt Leena!"

"I know, Ines, but you know your uncle, believes that the boys need to be armed, have the tools, as he puts it, to defend themselves if attacked. The old fool thinks that he is some sort of sensei, mentoring them in martial arts."

"He's going mentor them into the hospital!"

"'Better the hospital than the grave,' would be his reply."

"If you hadn't found him, it might have been the grave. I'm so glad that your nurse training and years of experience were able to do what needed to be done."

"The forty years in that profession does come in handy now and again. He has a concussion, but I believe if we keep a close eye on him for a few days, after the headaches pass, watching for swelling in the area, temperature spikes, light sensitivity, double vision, disorientation as signs, we need to get him to Cook County General."

"Yes, I know the drill. I'm going to dispose of all of those bloody rods."

"Ines, I understand you're feeling that way, and I agree with you as a course of action. Remember, Ines, even in this hellish ghetto, they're still brothers. They'll be good, bad, and the dangerous ugly.

"Still, Ines, I think that the danger your boys are living in, especially Gran because the gangs are hunting him, requires that he has access to a tool for self-defence.

"How about hiding them in a place that only you would know? That way if he ever does need it, he would have to come to you to get it. Tell him that you've put them away until the need arises. Gran won't like it but I think he'll come around to your point of view; just explain how close his injury came to being permanent brain damage."

"Gran will listen, and he trusts me."

"Absolutely! He's your favourite."

...

Part 4 "Mom! Where's My Tool?"

[[Author's Aside]]

The following is a short story, the second autobiographical fiction to be included in Backstory, penned prior to my having the courage to begin this novel. The names and some associated references have been revised to fit the overall flow of Backstory. Nevertheless, "Mom! Where's My Tool?" represents the essence of the novel's developmental backstory and, as such, is relevant to the larger story, as a tree is relevant to the seed from which it evolves, since all is based on real events in the life of Granville Johnson.

...

"Mom! Where's My Tool?"
by Granville Johnson

Whatever *is that boy doing now?* thought Ines. It sounded like her son was trying to tear his closet apart without opening the door. From the sounds of cascading clothing, tumbling boxes, flying bags, and clanking hangers, he was ransacking his room—or a marching band had just moved in while she slept.

Ines was soul-tired. She had worked the evening shift that too often ran till early morning. Last night had been one of those nights. One of the men on her shift replacement had been caught DOA (drunk on arrival) and an hour late.

He had earned the night off. Of course, she was volunteered to do his work down in the hole cleaning sump traps. She wasn't, by far and a bit, low on the coach maintenance crew's pecking order; in fact, her seniority placed her very near the top of the heap. But she was the only woman in the crew, and they never tired of reminding her of her proper place with all the dangerous, filthy, and demeaning jobs that were beneath their precious male egos and therefore only suitable as "woman's work."

While there, her super had dropped in to check on her condition; or maybe it was to offer her an early pass home with a bit of overtime thrown in for good measure, equalling the approximate length of his pencil dick down her throat. It would have been a short suck, indeed.

While she squeezed his balls, held in the iron grip of her left fist, beneath his coverall clad perm-a-pregnant beer gut, she reminded him with the heft of her rock hammer poised above in her right hand. Her hammer was a handy multipurpose tool that she always kept in her kit: light and razor sharp, it had many uses. It was painfully clear that if he tried to touch her again, she would bury its head where his wife would have to suck on it next time she was on her knees.

His face lost all colour: beet purple red to pasty yellow, then ashen white. Trembling lips stammered, spat, then hissed, "Bitch! Y . . . y . . . ya, you are some CRAZY bitch." Through his brown chewing-tobacco-stained teeth, half under his putrid breath, so as not to be heard by the leering crew, waiting to witness her "comeuppance," as he scurried, as fast as he could, up the ladder and out of range, backwards.

She worked straight through another full shift, no overtime.

"Gran, what is the problem?" Ines called as she approached his room, having to stop to absorb a painful lower back spasm in the kitchen.

Holding on to the top of her high-back chair at the table, she continued, "You're supposed to be at work by now. Boy, we both know that you cannot afford to be late for work, any time, period."

"Mom, have you seen my tool?"

As she slowly entered the earthquake epicentre that, a short time ago, was his meticulously organized room, a disembodied voice echoed from under the bed.

Granville Andrea, a fine-featured, beautiful, cheerful man-child, strong and lithe, yet so small and somehow feminine, he was often teased about his sensitive nature and graceful movement.

He was her love-child, her middle child, her mediator. He looked all of twelve until you noticed his eyes, ancient in their wariness. Dark clouds loomed in their black depths. A spectral agony clung close to his heart.

She couldn't remember any longer when the shroud wasn't there. Nor could she imagine what was behind it.

These days, with her diabetes stealing all but her will to live, her swollen legs and feet throbbed a bone deep ache that resonated behind her eyes in endless migraines. She longed to whisk this evil away, soothe the awful pain and fear that grew within the shadows.

Those eyes, mirror images of her own, now peered up at her, seething with repressed rage and fear.

Her son, a cornered beast at bay, bloodlust vivid in a curling upper lip revealing the split gums above bloodied, snarling canine fangs. A slow trickle of bright red life oozed along a dark, jagged welt from his nose over and around his cruelly distorted mouth to cascade down the front and side of what was his brand-new, ultra-stylish, deep blue linen shirt jacket. That shirt jacket was Gran's pride and joy.

As in most things, Granville had an acute sense of style that set him apart from his peers. He, the proud individual, seldom followed the crowd, pop fashion, or, in most cases, the ghetto mentality. He chose to stand apart, to listen to his own counsel and that of his mother above all others—dangerous ground for a teenage man-child in the Westside Chicago inner-city Black ghetto. Thus, he reflected her sense of propriety, integrity, gritty determination, positive self-worth, and pride. Like her, he tended to walk his talk.

His sixteenth birthday present to himself, which he had purchased with the earnings of his first real job, was now torn badly at the left shoulder seam where the epaulette had been ripped away. His left side and shirtfront, she now noticed, was slowly being saturated with his life essence.

An ugly purple and black bruise rippled across his clenched lower jaw and neck. His eye on the same side, blood red and swelling rapidly, as if to hide from sight or seeing the horrified awareness and abject resignation on his mother's face.

Her son no longer resembled himself, but a poorly assembled 3-D jigsaw puzzle, a combination of two desperate images: one beautifully familiar, the other grotesque, and familiar only in the horrific sense of Dr. Jekyll sharing a body with Mr. Hyde.

Silence.

He did not have to ask again, nor explain what had occurred.

She knew the answers to all her questions. She would not delay nor try to dissuade him from what he had to do. Moving his chest of drawers, she reached behind it to retrieve his tool, a foot-long steel alloy shaft, fashioned by her Uncle Prince in his metal shop. It was smooth and shiny, about one half-inch thick with a slightly rough series of raised ridges scored into one end that served as the handle. Though both ends could easily be used for striking or thrusting. It was light and strong.

Each of her boys had been given one and taught how to use them effectively by their Great-Uncle Prince. He had schooled the boys well, practicing all the time, and cautioned them to never use their tools until they had tried every other way that they could to "fix the problem."

At first it had been a game for the fertile imaginations of young boys, until they'd had to use them during the block-busting race war that welcomed the family to this neighbourhood.

Then, it all had been white, poor white.

She and her children were the only Black faces that had dared call this place home.

The tools had helped to "fix the problem" during the final battle: her three Black children versus all twenty of the other white children on the square block. Their parents had also turned out to cheer and jeer.

Hopelessly outnumbered, outpowered, yet led by the courage of her oldest, her boys had faced them down and won their right to live in this rat- and roach-infested three-story walk-up. Fortunately, no child, white or Black, was truly hurt in the confrontation, though lives changed forever as a result of it.

Now war once more had claimed their home. The neighbourhood had transformed from poor white to poorer Black. A situation Ines had few problems with. The schools were good, the neighbours, white and Black, were reasonable or they simply left her family alone. The local merchants liked her boys, especially Granville, who sometimes earned extra money cleaning up in the butcher shop next door or serving customers in the corner convenience store.

A new enemy had gathered and targeted her son. The enemy, now, was the Black gangs living all around them. They went by many names: Vice Lords, Roman Saints, Black Stone Rangers, etc. A plethora of violent stupidity feeding upon themselves and others they felt threatened by.

The gangs had targeted Granville and hunted him with impunity because he was the first to live in the 'hood. And his role in the subsequent race war during the block-busting scam was a local urban legend. Granville had had the nerve to be here, moving among them, but refusing to have anything to do with them.

"Like some Supreme Gangster," the cops had labelled him, in bitter jest, that fateful day. "Granville don't need any gang. He's already proven that he's the baddest-ass young Nigga in the 'hood. He was here before any of you, an' you heard how he whipped a whole block fulla white crackers, almost by himself. You best be smart 'n' leave him alone. I'd hate to see any of y'all get hurt. Y'all have a good day now."

Their mocking laughter had echoed off the hardened, maleficent rage of Black Jesus, the Vice Lord gang boss, as he glared through the backs of the fat salt 'n' pepper "poke-rinds" in their retreating "pig-mobile."

Since that infamous day, Granville's presence in his home world was taken as a personal insult to every gang member itching to prove himself. "Join, move, or fuckin' die," were the choices. He chose to do none of those. The war had begun.

Ignoring the blood and bruises, as he was now doing, for they would heal. She honoured his courage and pride, now ready, once more, for battle. Kissing his beautiful side as she handed him his tool, she whispered, "I love you, fight well, and we'll be here when you're done."

He returned her kiss as best he could, brushing her cheek with his full lips,

"Love you, too, Momma. Thanks for everything." His lips were twisted; his words, his eyes and his heart were clear.

Hugging her with all his might, as she did in kind, he turned to open the front door leading into their building's hall. Before closing it, he turned once more to face her, hearing the chant.

"Mighty! Mighty Vice Lauds! Up in here!" Careening through the hallway, raising the hackles at the base of his neck. Their eyes met, he smiled crookedly. "Work to do. Gotta fix it. I'm late."

Closing his front door softly behind him and grasping his tool firmly, he went to work.

. . .

Part 5: Showdown at 3148

Granville stood with his back to his front door, watching the gang idly gathering to lounge on the corner, celebrating each other's success at running that little punk-ass Supreme Gangster to ground. So much for that little badass reputation; the "urban legend," in their eyes, was just a little snotty nose battered and bleeding Nigger running home to Mama, crying all the way. Each Lord had managed to get a piece of him during the running battle and steeple chase. The hounds had treed the rabbit and were braying at the base, hungry for more.

Black Jesus was there, so was Frank "Tank" Fraser; together they had been able to corner him several times in a dead-end alley to inflict some serious pain before the kid's small size and speed was able to squirt through an opening in the chain-link fence to sprint away.

There were ten Vice Lords, the failed fruit of a poisoned tree, happy, even giddy, from the hunt and steeple chase. "Mighty Vice Lauds forever!"

"Supreme Gangster! Here motha'fuckas! Come get me, fuckin' be-itches!" roared Granville.

The gang went silent, not sure they were hearing right. There stood the still bloodied "rabbit" on his front doorstep alone cursing the "hounds," calling them out.

They looked at each other momentarily. ". . . Little Nigger must have a death wish or maybe he's still upset cause I fucked his 'girl'! Had that pussy even though she didn't want to give it to me. In the end, that sweet cunt was mine!" loudly crowed Tank.

"Let's finish this, once 'n' for all!" Black Jesus smirked as the group began to leisurely approach their prey, fully expecting Granville to duck back inside his house or, better yet, run again.

Granville did neither; instead, he stood his ground. His running days were done. Eyes narrowed in concentration, he passed his tool from hand to hand, flexing in a tight fist, then relaxing each momentarily empty hand, as he watched the gang's approach. Deep within his throat, he growled, "Live or die, bastards, it ends here!"

"Gran, let me tell you about the advantage of one," counselled Great-Uncle Prince during a break in their practice session.

"You mean the majority of one?"

"No, that's a political catchphrase. I'm talking about a winning strategy in a fight."

Granville's ears perked up, grateful for any advice from the man who had become his mentor.

"Location is everything. Most people think that the best place to fight is in an area where you have lots of room to move around and to even escape if need be. That is all well and good. But if you are in a fight alone against numbers, the best location could be a confined space."

"How so, Great-Uncle?"

"Two reasons: the first being, if your back is to a wall, your back is protected. Now, if you're up against that same wall with multiple attackers trying to get at you all at once, they are all trying for the same target at the same time. They are bound to get in each other's way, perhaps even striking each other inadvertently in their haste to get at you.

"While, because there are many of them surrounding you on three sides in reach of whatever weapon you may be wielding, you will be able to make contact with anyone in that half circle. Defence is also in your favour because it is easier to redirect their missed strikes toward the other attackers with your blocks."

"I see. What's the second reason?"

"You've heard of the saying, 'An animal is the most dangerous when it is cornered'?"

"Right, a cornered animal is trapped and will fight to the death because it can't escape; with everything to gain, like freedom, and nothing to lose, other than its life. In that situation, its life is already lost if it's overwhelmed."

"Exactly, that is the second reason, extreme motivation to fight till the end; whereas your attackers may not be nearly so motivated."

"How do I set that up?"

"First, you must choose your location, one that is to your advantage, so you can fight on your terms. Second, goad your adversaries into a fever or fury, so incensed that their need to get at you, to hurt you individually, cancels their desire or tendency to operate as a group. Gangs are generally loosely structured groups of disorganized individuals. Thus, in the heat of battle, you wind up fighting each member individually, especially in the case of hand-to-hand warfare."

"Got it, the advantage of one."

"One last thing: to kill a snake, you crush its head. Same with a gang. Take out the leader, the rest will crumble.

"Amen ... sermon's over."

...

Granville watched the gang organize itself as it approached in power positions: leader and most dangerous in the front, lesser members and lackeys hanging back, hoping for some "tender morsels" when the bosses were done, like jackals waiting on the lions to finish a kill before gorging themselves.

As they reached the halfway point between the corner and his doorstep, Granville lit the fuse to blow the formation apart, bellowing at the top of his lungs while being careful not to let his voice bounce into his higher register with the effort.

"You blowhard bitches need ten-to-one to feel brave, bad, and bodacious! You're nothin' but a bucket o' bullshit cowards! Your daddy dropped you down a flight o' stairs when yo' mama couldn't flush you down the toilet the day you were born! And she tried! Lord knows she tried! You hear me, you dumbass bitches? I'm the Supreme Gangster! Up in here! I fight alone! I represent!"

Their walk became a full-on charge. Each trying to get to him first, determined to strike the first deadly blow.

Granville was set in a low crouch and easily dodged the initial onslaught. Swinging his tool in a semicircular arc, he established a fighting perimeter, striking several of the first to arrive before they could get their balance to avoid impact.

The rest were suddenly upon him; the blows came so fast that Granville could not recognize them individually. Still, the blur of pain blended into a blur of continuous motion. Slowly, as if in stop-motion, all reality contracted to a tight cone of grunts and shouts of startled pain, of which he felt little.

His left eye closed altogether, swinging the tool high and low, crossing in front to form a mobius loop of angry steel in the air directly in front of him. Instinctively closing his remaining eye, he fought on in a blind rage. He did not have to see where he could strike.

They were simply everywhere. Now striking each other as often, if not more so, than they hit him. He sensed the gang's mounting frustration. The "rabbit" was no longer easy prey. *Bastards! Gotta bring ass to get my sweet little ass!* He knew that they weren't prepared to go this distance toward his destruction.

Granville realized there were less and less of them and redoubled his efforts. His speed was the weapon of his ferocious inner demon, loose and hungry for Vice Lord blood.

"Niggas! Open up!" bellowed Black Jesus at the top of the circle near the curb.

Granville's eye flashed wide open and saw the daylight open in front of him, seeing Black Jesus break a whiskey bottle on the pavement at his feet, then throw it at Granville's face.

Throwing up his left arm to partially block the missile that shattered on his elbow, Granville lunged into the opening to strike at the base of Black Jesus's outstretched right arm, contacting and breaking the gang leader's right collar bone.

Hardly hearing the loud crunch and louder scream, he spun, losing little momentum to his right side, raking the tool across Tank's lower jaw above him with a backhand strike, aided by the full force of his spinning form, shattering the big man's mouth and lower jaw in flying teeth and spewing blood. "Ahhhh, ahhhh!"

"That's for my Astra! Shrivel-dick fuckin' bastard!"

[[Author's Aside]]

There would not be any words, at all, formed by that vile mouth for years to come. His football future died that day, as he himself would die in prison several years later, followed in quick succession by his buddy, Black Jesus, in a fight over a pack of cigarettes.

...

As the 'snake's heads' fell, so did the enthusiasm of the gang for mayhem. They gathered their wounded and limped away toward Kedzie, crossing against the light as a city bus screeched to a stop in avoidance of the battered, bleeding, defeated gang.

Granville watched them go, as he had watched others that had come before them. It was only then that he noted the river of blood seeping with each heartbeat down the front of his ruined shirt jacket, pumping from a two-inch gash that had cleaved his left cheek from the corner of his mouth to his temple. It had nearly penetrated completely through to his inner mouth lining. Only a thin film of interior tissue had prevented the through and through. Amid the blood and gore, he could taste the hot, bitter bite of the whiskey.

Ines had also watched the gang's ragged retreat, her 45-calibre pistol resting on the wide bay window ledge next to her chair. She had watched the entire battle, as she knew her son would have expected of her, to be there to back him up if needs be.

Her heart almost burst as she witnessed the broken bottle being thrown into his face. She let out a not-so-quiet cheer as Granville lowered the boom on that ass-wipe and in the same motion took a huge chunk out of the face of the Vice Lord leader's buddy, Tank Fraser, who was bragging about raping Granville's girlfriend, even though he was three times the size of her son.

She was not prepared, however, for the sight of Granville's gaping cheek wound when she opened the door to his soft knock. One look, and the blood drained from her face as she slumped against the wall next to the door. Granville's quick movement caught and held her before she slid down the wall to the floor. He hadn't seen that reaction in his mother since they stopped attending Christ's Shepherd Southern Baptist Church, where she often almost fainted after dancing with the Spirit.

"Oh my God! Gran! Gran, oh Gran! Your beautiful face is ruined!" All she could see before her, was that the flawless beauty of her love-child was gone forever. Her beautiful man-child was now a man, having left his childhood with his blood in the grit and grime of this ghetto's shattered dreams.

"Mom! It's all right. Mom, they won't be bothering us again. We can get it sewn up at the hospital. I'll get a different shirt and wash up."

Ten stitches in Cook County General's emergency ward repaired Granville's face, along with the assorted cuts and bruises which were also tended to. The on-duty doctor insisted on reporting the incident cause of such an ugly wound.

The news of the street fight involving the notorious Vice Lord leader and his gang brought in the police liaison to file a report. Ines had to complete a witness statement in support of her son's testimony.

Finally at home, Granville, exhausted, slept twelve hours straight. Ines, watching over him as she had when he was in diapers and sick with a fever, hardly slept at all.

...

Part 6: No Body Knows . . .

[[Author's Aside]]

"No Body Knows . . ." is the first autobiographical short story written in my vainglorious attempt to excise the demons of my first of many rapes and other sexual perversions over time; that ushered my youth into the universe of guilt and pain that dwells within the survivor of long-term sexual abuse.

The scars of that past still inhabit, and in some ways rule, my presence, to this day. Though I feel emotional intimacy, affection, love; I cannot feel the love, the lust, the need, the want, the heat, anything within the sexual act. I am devoid of that capability within emotional physical intimacy. Such is my curse, within my legacy, the imitation of life. The universe of the abused, the world of the damned.

"No Body Knows . . ." speaks to the world's awareness outside of the abused individual; the scars within being invisible to society. Yet the title is also an untruth, for the body of the rape victim always knows. Sixty-six years on, I can attest that the body still, always knows, never forgets. Nor, perhaps, forgives . . .

The names have been changed to fit within the larger context that is Backstory . . . as have all insertions throughout this novel.

...

No Body Knows . . .
by Granville Johnson

SQUEAK.

"Shit!" hissed Dyak Jihad. *Damn door, I've got t' get it fixed. It would be just my luck if David or little Joseph had to make an untimely trip to the can. Worst yet, if Granville awoke—that is, before I want him to. Though in due course, he'll awaken. But by then it will be too late, far too late.*

Dyak Jihad crossed the darkened room silently, sweating in eager anticipation, his mouth watering ever so deliciously for brown sugar.

Sweet meat, so close, his for the taking. A pasty thickness filled his throat. Swallowing became difficult.

"Ines, thank you," he whispered under his breath as his thoughts revisited his cousin's unfortunate flare-up and abrupt hospitalization. He was familiar, from experience, with the acute pain and possibly life-threatening reality of a bleeding peptic ulcer.

A steady diet of worry, about her boys, mostly, will do that to a body.

Dyak Jihad had been more than happy to rush his sadly overwrought first cousin to Cook County's emergency ward.

Chuckling quietly, he replayed her parting words. "DJ, please take care of my kids for me . . . ahhh!"

A white-hot bolt of pain had claimed her breath. Ines, now reduced to a fetal ball of searing pain and sweating profusely, had gripped the gurney's side rail with shaking hands and continued to voice her concern.

"Especially Gran, lately he's been acting up so. Lord, I wish I knew what was wrong with my baby. He does worry me so. Ahhh! Sweet Jesus, help me!"

"Don't worry, Ines, I'll take real good care of them." His fervent promise. "You can trust me, cous. You'll be home as soon as this passes in a day or two."

Now he said, "Real good care indeed," greed dripping from his tone. "Especially Gran," he growled, a low rumble within the darkness. "Come here, boy. Now we know your sweet ass is mine."

At puberty's threshold, gifted and talented far beyond his or his loving family's awareness or comprehension, Granville was a "too-beautiful" child. Small for his age, his lithe muscularity rippled beneath satiny, silken skin of rich cocoa brown. Soft, large black eyes radiated compassion, faith, and eager intelligence. Having his mother's eyes, he was thought, by critics, to be too vulnerable, attractive, alluring, even feminine, to be a boy child.

The same was often said about his mouth: his lips, a sienna fullness, made for kissing. An expressive pout reflecting deep-dreamer thoughts would, in a giggle's instant, caress a brilliant ivory-white toothsome smile.

Common family opinion was that Granville was too pretty, perhaps too smart, or just too different for his own good.

Easy now, easy, thought Dyak Jihad. The pale grey sheet rose and fell softly amid the deep night shadows.

It did not take long for Dyak Jihad to remove the cotton barrier. Neither did the boy's pajamas pants pose a problem.

My, my, what do we have here? I see from the trail of sticky dick drool that you have discovered how much fun your new toy can be. You could have waited for me to have some real fun. Oh well, never too late to have a good time. Dyak Jihad could not help but wonder if the boy's bedtime fantasies had been about him. He liked to imagine that they were, as he deftly kissed, licked, caressed, and possessed his prize.

"Ughhh, ahhhh, ooooh . . . Wha . . .what? DJ! What are doing? Noooo!" Granville cried in growing awareness. "Please stop! Let go! Get off! Please don't! Stop!"

Full-blooded lips between clenched teeth gave salted pungency to Granville's mounting hysteria.

"Does it feel good, Gran? Hmmmmmm. You know I can't stop now. And I know you like it. You like it a lot. If you don't, you have a funny way of showing it. A minute ago, you were moaning and groaning about how much you liked what I was doing. So why don't you just lay back, relax, and let me finish what we started. Remember, we don't want to wake your little brothers, now, do we?"

Granville tried his best to roll over and away from this nightmare.

Dyak Jihad was a brick-wall of a man, wide, square, and low to the ground. His movements often reminded Granville of a battle tank lumbering over rough ground. Yet he had the reflex quickness of a big jungle cat at feeding time, with temperament to match. And like a big cat, Dyak Jihad was always hungry for something.

The predator was well-prepared.

By simply shifting his prodigious weight and tightening his grip slightly, he inflicted a clear warning to the boy that escape was unlikely, resistance impossible, and disclosure dangerous.

Dyak Jihad's bobbing jowls and vacuous suction never paused a stroke in his slobbering rhythm.

Despite his cold fear and revulsion, Granville's body, still responsive to the residual heat of another of the erotic dreams that had begun recently to plague his sleep most nights, was resonating.

The horror continued unabated.

Granville was no longer sure of which he despised more: DJ, this monster that invaded, raped, used, and now controlled his life, or himself for seeming to enjoy, even relish this hell.

In the end, it didn't matter; only the heat mattered, the burning, exquisite, all-consuming fire flowing, careening, and climbing toward sweet release.

With release came the tears, enough tears to drown in, enough to die in. Though merciful death didn't come, only derisive laughter ringing in his ears. Dyak Jihad's laughter. "Young fool, what are you bawling about? You had a good time, didn't you? Or was that my imagination that just slid down the back of my throat, hot and salty? Beats the hell out of your stupid wet dreams. Can't you handle the real thing?

"Speaking of which, it's my turn. Come here and help me out. As you can see, I'm rock hard. If I don't get off soon, I'm gonna bust. Come on, Gran. I was very nice to you.

"That's it! Watch your teeth. Yeah!"

The horror began again.

Only this time the invasion was even more intimate. Dyak Jihad's overwhelming stench filled his senses, blotting out all thought, all feeling, except the shame and the pain. He was a sex toy attached to this thing. There was no heat, no place to hide from the bitter sense of rightful punishment for his pernicious lust.

Granville prayed, a child's prayer.

"Forgive me, Father, for I have sinned, and sinned, and sinned, sinned, sinned."

"Aaaahhhh! Yesssss, baby, yessssss!

"Good boy! God! You suck cock fine! I knew you had it in you. But you never give me a chance to really enjoy it. You're just too hot for me. How about a kiss to seal our little secret, baby? Tears again! Damn! Don't awaken your brothers, Gran. Look, you do what you have to do to feel better.

"Tomorrow, I'll take you all out for breakfast, that is, if you keep our secret and cooperate. Okay? Okay?"

"Please leave me alone."

"Sure, see you in the morning."

Granville cried for his mother, his brothers. He cried for the father he never had. Silent sobs wrung his body as he pleaded for death anew. The searing pain wrought spasms of living terror, hounded him, down, down into a bottomless black chasm of oblivion.

...

Part 7: Carmen, Clarita, and DJ

Carmen and Clarita Charles lived two doors down from Granville.

Their front door entrance was set midway down a walkway between two brick three-story walk-ups. The same walkway that Granville had used to approach the angry white mob trying to force his family to move.

That showdown preceded the arrival of the girls' family on the block.

Their family was somewhat unusual in its makeup.

Their father was a single parent, almost unheard of in Granville's neighbourhood, where single-mom households were almost the norm; two-parent families were the occasional exception. A single father raising two teenage girls alone was indeed rare.

At fifteen, with the voluptuous, well-developed physique of a woman, Carmen was the youngest of the two sisters. Clarita, slim and athletic, three years her senior, and in her last year in high school, worked part-time at White Castle. She was thoroughly addicted to their bacon and smoked cheddar cheese sliders, a Chicago delicacy.

"We're all getting fat, eating her take-homes," Carmen would complain, reaching for another slider in her ten-stack. The little square shaped hamburgers were very tasty indeed—tended to taste like "more."

Granville met Clarita as she served him and his cousin Dyak Jihad one night when DJ had taken him out for a drive and stopped in for a snack.

DJ had started flirting with Clarita behind the counter right away, taking advantage of the empty restaurant during her late-night shift. It made no difference to DJ that he was married to a beautiful woman twenty years his junior. His taste for young women appeared to be oblivious to the confines of the commitment he had made to his wife, Odessa. DJ was a "cock hound," completely ruled and driven by the demands of his gonads.

Granville had been spending occasional time with DJ whenever his cousin could manage to spirit him away from home on some pretext. He was now used to this passive aggressive, sexual-predator behaviour. He watched the charade but said nothing.

"My, you're such a sweet thing. Whereabouts do you live, darlin'?" drawled DJ.

"I live at Harrison and Kedzie, 3142 Harrison."

Granville's ears perked up, his interest sparked. "That's two doors down from my house. I live at 3148, above the church."

Clarita turned to face Granville, away from his handsome cousin, as if she were seeing him for the first time. "Really, we haven't lived there long. I still live with my dad and sister until I graduate next month. We moved in after he and my mom divorced."

DJ smirked—that was what generally passed for a smile when he was on the hunt, and the scent of prey was on the wind.

Granville ignored him, wanting to get to know this young woman, apart from the drooling behaviour of his second cousin, whom he had learned to sorely resent, in their "love-hate" familiar relationship.

"How old are you, if you don't mind my asking?" she asked.

"Sixteen. I know, I don't look it, never have."

"True enough. Carmen, my sister, is the same age, but she's pretty much a head taller than you, little guy."

"Yeah, I get that a lot."

"No offence intended."

"None taken. I'd like to meet her."

"Sure, come by tomorrow afternoon, it's my day off and Dad's at work. I'll introduce you."

"Great, Clarita. I'll see you then."

Granville awoke feeling bouncy and ambiguous following the night's carousal with his resident rapist, which is how he felt about his second cousin. Part of him enjoyed DJ's positive attention, while at the same time, he truly hated the man and did not trust him at all. DJ's touch made his skin crawl, leaving him feeling dirty, fearful, and somehow perverse. The heat of the sex came at the bitter price paid in self-loathing, a soul-deep, core pain, impossible to ignore. Yet he tried to not let those feelings surface in his dealings with the man. He was always keenly aware of his debts owed to Dyak Jihad.

...

DJ's appearance had been very timely when he happened to be driving by on his way to visit Ines and discovered that his little second cousin was cornered in a vacant lot by a marauding group of Roman Saints gangsters about three blocks from home.

The Supreme Gangster, once again, had been run to ground. Granville was holding his own, though he was alone as usual. Fighting, dodging, running in a hit-'n'-run helter-skelter pattern throughout the large lot as best as he could, given the fact that the gang was closing around him, cutting off any possibility of escape. It was a ring of disruption toward impending disaster; he was outnumbered ten to one, and the deadly trap was closing fast.

Just as Granville felt sure he was done this time and prepared himself for the imminent rain of blood, gore, and horror, DJ suddenly was there, attacking, fighting his way through the death trap. Together they were able to disperse the bastards, in a hand-to-hand melee. The pervert had saved his life that day.

Dyak Jihad was to be instrumental in getting Granville hired on as stock boy at the neighbourhood Sears and Roebuck department store, one of the largest commercial institutions in the area. It would be Granville's first real job.

Granville used the income from that job to buy Christmas presents for everyone in the family as well as an LP turntable for himself. It was a deep source of quiet personal pride to be able to share in his good fortune, in his love, with his siblings and his mom, his superwoman.

Though he was fired three months later when the white stock boy, who worked alongside him on the same shift, through his connections in the office, found out that Granville had been hired at a higher initial wage and complained to his father, the departmental supervisor.

Throughout this period, DJ inserted himself into every facet of Granville's home life, all part of the perpetual clandestine grooming process. All and anything to exert influence, to keep the boy indebted to him, and thereby be able to manipulate and exploit his young cousin.

DJ truly believed that he loved the boy, aside from the lust; thus, in his mind, control by any means necessary was appropriate.

"Hello, I'm Granville." He immediately noted that Clarita's little sister seemed to possess the stature and curvaceous figure of a woman more than a head taller than himself, with visually striking maturity, very much belying the reality of her youth.

"Hi, I'm Carmen. Clarita told me about you and your second cousin. She said that she met you at her job last night. I think she likes your cousin."

"No surprise there, DJ has that effect on women. He's mister charm himself. When he turns on his 'charm offence,' telling them exactly what he thinks they want to hear, in the way they want to hear it, the ladies begin to take notice. Big bad boy in a grown man. They almost melt out of their clothes and into his arms."

"You live above the church?"

"Yeah, we're neighbours, we were one of the first Black families to move here after the church opened."

"So, this block was all white people?"

"The whole neighbourhood was, pretty much . . ."

"No other Black families?"

"There was one, my friend 'Daredevil' Craig. Him and his mom lived a couple of blocks over from here. Craig was a sea cadet; his father was a captain of a destroyer in the navy. They moved back to California to be with his dad and near his sister, who was going to university there in San Diego."

"Heard that it was pretty rough."

"We had to convince them that we had as much a right to be in this brick-and-mortar, rat-and-roach-infested, hell-in-a-handbasket ghetto as they did."

"Did they need much convincing?"

"It took a bit of serious persuasion."

"Who did the persuading?"

"Our moms, Craig, my Great-Uncle Prince, my brothers, and me."

"So basically, two families against all those white people."

"Yeah, we all did our part."

"The church folk didn't help?"

"They didn't live here. Pastor talked about loving thy neighbour in his sermons. But that was about it."

"I bet. You're the Supreme Gangster! We heard about you. You're at war with the Vice Lords and the Roman Saints."

"Yeah, something like that."

"Why did you give yourself that street moniker?"

"I didn't. The cops did when they found that I still lived here but refused to be a part of any gang. Picked us all up one night when someone tried to rob a liquor store.

"We all were being interviewed in one room at the cop shop. One of the cops recognized me from the blockbusting fights. Feeling his malice, he crowed loud and long that I was a Supreme Gangster, trying to shame all the other gangsters in the lock-up. They've been hunting me ever since.

"Join, move, or die; that's the gang creed. I won't do either, so it's war. I attend Saint Philips Basilica High School."

"That's the Catholic private school?"

"I have an academic scholarship. I'm going into the Jesuit priesthood after graduation."

"You want to be a priest?"

"Yeah, if I can get out of here alive."

"You're pretty small to be so tough."

"Goes with the territory. Enough about me. Tell me about yourself."

"What do you want to know?"

"Why do you and Clarita live with your dad? Is your mom alive?"

"They're divorced."

"Mom says the divorce courts always award the mother the kids and the father pays support payments, like my little brothers' fathers."

"Yeah, I heard that as well from the lawyer. Our situation is different. Mom caught dad having sex with another woman."

"Who? Do you know her?"

"Yeah, it was Clarita."

"Fuck!"

"Yeah, when she discovered them at it, she screamed, raged, threatened to kill them both, then cried for a week. Eventually she said, 'You want the bastard that much; you can have him!' Then she left and sued for divorce. They sold our home to pay the lawyers and we moved here."

"You chose to stay with your dad."

"Not really. Mom didn't want me. Didn't trust me. Said I had probably fucked him too. She was so fucking angry."

"Did you?"

"Yeah, the asshole didn't give me much of a choice. I still do. We both do. He takes what he wants, whenever he wants it! Treats us like we're his private in-house pussy!"

"I know how you feel. DJ, my handsome second cousin that Clarita likes so much, he's married to beautiful woman half his age, yet he rapes me every chance he gets. He's a closet-fag pervert!"

"Fuck!"

"Exactly."

Part 8: Bigger They Come . . . Harder They Fall

Doris Kilogram lived at the opposite end of Granville's block. She was the middle child of her father's three daughters. Doris was athletic and drop-dead gorgeous. She excelled in two track and field events in her school, John Marshall High School: the hundred-metre dash and two-hundred-metre hurdles. Her prowess brought more than her share of attention from all the men, young and not so young, who had watched her exuberant performance from the stands at the local, regional, and statewide competitions.

Doris exuded strength combined with a lithe, feline movement in her walk, the bodily expression of a big cat, whose ferocious temperament was barely concealed or held in check. Doris's appetite for whatever passed her fancy knew little bounds. She did not beat her competitors on the field. She destroyed them as they ate her dust at every meet.

Doris's home was easy to spot. There were at least a half dozen vehicles parked in front and around the corner that did not belong to the family. In fact, Doris's father could never park his big Plymouth in front of his home. He had to resort to parking in the alley behind the house. The family lived on the second story of a two-story walk-up. A double door front entrance separated the two apartments. Doris's interior door rested at the top of the staircase on a small landing.

The cars out front mostly belonged to Doris's admirers. Gang members, mostly Vice Lords, and other gang-affiliated young men would lounge in the cars and on the concrete steps of the building's front portico. The building's front door at the top of those steps, leading to her family's apartment, was usually left open to facilitate egress for a line of Black teens stationed in single file on the stairs between the exterior and interior doors to her home.

Doris was holding court, and all the young men were waiting their turn to pay their respects to the reigning queen of track. Each in turn would give his all to curry favour from the young woman who expected and revelled in all that was given.

Granville liked to play tag with his younger brothers. He felt himself to be a bit old for the game, but cheerfully participated in the frolic, as it was one of the few things that he, David, and Joseph did that was fun together.

The game's geographic limits included the length of the 3100 block on which they lived, the walkway between buildings, as well as the back alleyway behind the buildings. Up, down, and around, the brothers would chase and be chased, until all had had his turn as pursuer and pursued.

Occasionally, the game would stray down the block to chase in amongst the cars parked in front of Doris's home.

It was on one such occasion that Doris noticed Granville as she sat in her home's bay window seat above the street, watching the chase in progress. Perhaps she was bored with the accolades being presented at her beck and call, or perhaps just peeved at the racket that the trio was making below.

"Hey, you!" shouted Doris.

Everyone below stopped what they were doing, talking, or chasing and looked up at the source of that shout.

"You, chasing those kids; what's your name?"

Granville thought to ignore her, then looked at the curious yet mildly suspicious expressions of the boys on the steps of the portico, as if they knew that there was something familiar about him but couldn't quite place the association.

Then he decided to respond, "My name is Granville," curious as to what this was all about.

"You live on this block, don't you?" she said, noting the heightened interest of the other boys lounging on her stoop.

"Yeah, above the church. Why?"

"I've wondered about that. Come up for a minute, I want to talk to you," she said in her most come-hither tone.

"Guys, go on home. I'll catch up," said Granville, after momentarily considering the invitation.

"You sure, Gran?" asked David, acutely aware of the interruption of their game, as well as the hostile stares of the gathered gangbangers.

They were like young lambs who suddenly discovered that they had wandered into a den of hungry wolves.

"Yeah, it'll be okay. Tell Mom where I am, so she won't worry."

"Okay." David and Joseph watched carefully as their big brother slowly mounted the stairs between the assembled gangsters and entered the open outer double doors, like David of biblical fame entering the lion's den. As soon as Granville was out of sight, they took off sprinting for all they were worth to tell their mom what had transpired.

Granville was mildly surprised to find the stairs were lined with more gangsters, mostly Vice Lords, some he recognized. Step by step, he passed each one on the narrow staircase. By the time he reached the top landing, he was sure that they finally had recognized him. The hairs on the back of his neck began to rise in a warning alarm.

Doris didn't help matters in her greeting when she opened her door. "Granville, right? Aren't you the one the cops call Supreme Gangster?"

Granville didn't reply; he didn't have to. The maleficent murmur rippled up and down the staircase occupants like the rumble of a landslide rolling down the mountain, grinding everything in its path to dust and debris. The sound settled in the pit of his stomach, igniting a lump of hot fear and determination.

Granville began to sweat in that instant, and he quietly cursed her in his mind and wondered if he'd be able to get out of this death trap alive, but still said nothing.

"Come on in. Sorry about interrupting your game of tag. Aren't you a bit old to be playing that kid's game?" said Doris, sarcasm dripping from her frigid tone, like melting icicles dangling from a dead tree branch.

"They are my little brothers; it's a game they enjoy. We like to play together, and it's fun," said Granville.

"You're pretty little yourself to be the big, badass Supreme Gangster that I heard about. Are you really that tough?"

"I survive," said Granville, biting his tongue to prevent further comment. *Again, with the sarcasm, as if it's any business of yours,* thought Granville, beginning to seriously regret his decision to accept her invitation.

"My name is Doris, I run track for the John Marshall senior squad.

"Yeah, I've heard of you." *It's obvious that many others have as well, reflecting on the crowded staircase and front stoop.* "Are all these guys friends of yours? You like hanging out with gangbangers?"

"Boys will be boys. Some are, some are just friends of friends," replied Doris, smug self-importance evident in every gesture, a prima donna holding court in a fools' paradise filled with criminals.

"With all your options, you'd think you would choose your friends more carefully," said Granville, acerbic temper rising like molten lava, bubbling just beneath the fracturing crust of a quaking volcano.

"You're one to talk. Word is that you spend most of your time running away from them," retorted Doris, tetchy attitude, probing for weakness on this unfamiliar ground: a truthful person, not interested in pleasing her by telling her what he thought she might want to hear.

"They hunt me in packs. I fight alone, only when I must." *They're cowards, I'm not,* thought Granville.

"Why don't you just join?" interrupted Doris, still not able to fathom the strangeness of this too-cute young boy's individual courage.

"I'm not a joiner, never was, never will be. Don't believe in it. Besides, I've got better things to do with my time, with my life."

"And what is that?" barked Doris, now truly interested in what that might be.

"I go to Saint Philips Basilica High School on academic scholarship. I'm studying to become a priest," responded Granville, growing bored of sparring with this uppity girl, so full of vacuous ignorance.

"A priest? What's the matter, don't like girls?" spat Doris, each word meant to wound.

"I love people and want to help them, to be better than this place will let them become," said Granville, exasperated, the simple truth that revealed the ache in his soul.

"Thought you weren't a joiner," whined Doris, in a tenacious need to discredit what she couldn't understand nor accept.

"Walking in God's plan is a solitary path that I walk alone; it's what's required to be as one with Him," said Granville, speaking of his faith, a soothing balm to the growing frustration within the wariness of self-defence.

"So, you're not at all interested in having a girlfriend?" asked Doris, probing further.

"I like girls just like you seem to like boys; like I said, I have better things to do than chase."

"You prefer boys?" Doris's certainty of discovery blossomed as a gotcha moment hidden in the question, the eye within a roaring tornado spiral clearing ground, reducing all in its path to rubble.

"I have friends that are girls. I have friends that are women and are students in university. I am not interested in boys, period." *Enough already*, thought Granville.

"All right, didn't mean to hurt your feelings." *Just needed to find out what makes you tick, so different, so infuriating*, thought Doris.

You didn't, though you tried your best to get under my skin, to unnerve me, thought Granville.

"Have you ever been in love?" asked Doris, reaching for familiar ground to smooth the ruffled feathers of this angered hawk perched on her forearm.

"Yes, that's my business," said Granville, still defensive.

"Do you think you could fall in love again? After all, you're still pretty young, smart, and awfully cute to be devoting yourself to the priesthood."

Can't you see that I like you? You're not like the others. So many boys would betray their mother to be this way, this close to me. Why won't you show me that you're interested in me? thought Doris.

"I don't know; again, my business." *You have a staircase-full, and more, of gangbanger admirers ready to do your bidding, why must you call me out to be in your menagerie?* thought Granville, somewhat befuddled by her question.

"There, see, there may be hope for you yet." *And perhaps with me if you wise up, pretty boy*, thought Doris.

"Why does it matter to you?" asked Granville, perplexed. *This conversation is like herding rats in a minefield*, he thought.

"Oh, I've just never met a Black wannabe priest before, especially one with your reputation." *Don't you get it? Must I spell it out for you?* thought Doris.

"I never sought my reputation. I'm just Granville; nothing more."

"Well, Granville, you are very different, difficult to read, and I'd bet you're much more, indeed. Thanks for the chat. Nice to have met you."

"Thanks. Nice to have met you as well, Doris." *Now to leave with my skin intact, if at all possible,* thought Granville, wary of who all were waiting for him on the staircase. They were probably counting the minutes he'd spent with her and getting more intimidating, in a darkening rage, with each passing minute. The passage would be dangerous, even deadly. Thanks to Queen Doris and all her priceless special attention. Damn!

Granville made his way down that same gauntlet towards the outside door. The gangsters, one by one, followed in his wake in silence until they had flowed out the door behind and formed a rough circle around him in the street at the base of the portico. Their silence made the procession more menacing than if they had shouted and cursed him every step of the way.

Granville steeled himself, not daring to make a sound that would set them off. The air was thick with violent intent. The biggest, ugliest hulk that would have made Frank "Tank" Fraser look small was leaning against the trunk of a Pontiac, "Nigger, bless your lucky stars that this is the queen's place," he said. "Otherwise, we would have messed your puny ass up somethin' terrible. Yo' momma would never recognize the pieces. You get me, boy?"

Granville thought, *In it for a penny, in it for a pound*, and deep within, his bubbling, gurgling pool of molten lava finally broke through the crust of fear, patience, and restraint. After saying a brief, quiet prayer—*Jesus, please help me fight this vile evil*—he answered the challenge.

"Boy, you are big, and you are ugly, Lord knows you are. But you, all of you assholes, are just another bunch of bullies! So, you cowards can kiss my sweet Black ass! Bitch!"

"Big Ugly," otherwise known as Goliath, sprung off the car to tower over Granville, like an enraged gorilla bent on crushing the little boy that dared defy him. The killing zone instantly grew to accommodate his girth.

Granville took one half step back into a low crouch, ignoring the growling grimace above his head. Instead, he focused on the behemoth's crotch within striking distance, a vulnerability that the big man was evidently oblivious to.

Granville waited a heartbeat for the behemoth's next move, which was to reach down. Feeling hot breath on the back of his neck, Granville struck as hard as he could, a pile-driving right javelin-jab directly into the giant's balls.

As David brought down Goliath, the big man fell to his knees.

Dodging the falling human tree with a quick sidestep, Granville peppered his throat and Adam's apple with right and left crosses, intent on cutting off his breath. It was like beating on the trunk of a big oak.

Big Ugly just knelt there, taking the blows with low grunts. Granville, in desperation, because he knew he was dead if this beast rose from the pavement, balled both fists together and battle-axe swung to strike him square on his temple.

"Ugh!" The grunts ceased as the "lights" went out, and Goliath hit the pavement unconscious, face first, nose bursting on the concrete like an overripe tomato, spraying blood.

It took a moment for the surrounding gangsters to recover from their shock. "Mighty Vize Lords! Kill this motha'fuckin' . . ."

"ENOUGH!"

Everyone froze at the bellow coming from the wide-open bay window above their heads.

Mr. Darth Kilogram, Doris's father, was leaning halfway out of the window, his barrel chest filling the width of the sill. He was pitch black, with a full snow-white beard and moustache, completely bald and in full rage.

"I warned you Niggers, when you started hanging out on my doorstep . . . pestering my daughter, that if any of you young bastards started fighting, ALL of you punks would be history. Now get the fuck off my property. I never want to see any of you FUCK-UPS again EVER!"

He then pulled out a 38-calibre pistol and aimed it at the group to make his point understood.

Slamming car doors and screeching tires signalled the gang's departure. Only Goliath's gurgle-snoring form was left, awash in his blood and gore, as Granville watched their retreat.

"Granville, is that your name?"

"Yes, sir."

"You best get along home now. By the way, good fight!"

"Thank you, sir!" Thank you, Lord!

...

Carmen could not stop laughing as Granville recounted the fight and conversation with Doris that had preceded it.

"That silly bitch has some serious nerve, holding court with those fuck-head gangsters."

"I didn't intend for that to happen, but I think I ruined her fun," said Granville quietly.

"A queen deprived of her adoring court full of suitors is a vindictive bitch indeed, worse than any woman scorned. She will burn your house down with you in it."

"I didn't start that fight," said Granville, through barely restrained giggles. "Mom was not pleased when I told her what happened. She's worried that the Lords will retaliate after I embarrassed them, ruined their chill time."

"Ahh, but you finished it. Doris set you up; probably knew who you were. Everybody and their mothers have heard of that showdown, bust 'n' dust-up. I bet she was bored and just wanted to see what those lazy Niggas would do if she showered you with any of her spectacular more-magnificent-than-thou attention in their presence."

"Well, she found out."

"What!" Both teenagers lost their composure in gales of laughter. "Ah, so, ho, ho!"

...

Part 9: "Be Damned With the Donkey You Rode in On!"

Several weeks elapsed before Granville dared pass the Kilogram house's front portico again. For days, when he wanted to get to the pedestrian bridge across the expressway, which intersected with the corner two doors down from her building, he used the alleyway behind her house. He figured it was prudent to heed Carmen's advice and avoid the possibility of being seen, let alone encounter her, by chance. Still, you can only walk on eggshells over quicksand for so long.

"Granville, will you walk me to my cousin's house? They just moved and live about eight or ten blocks away in the Roman Saints' 'hood," said Carmen, in her best come-hither tone. "I'm a bit nervous crossing their territory. Haven't been in that area of the neighbourhood before."

"Sure, the Supreme Gangster will be glad to provide escort," said Granville, in a mocking, sarcastic, self-deprecating tone.

"So, you are the badass to be feared now?" She was surprised at his response yet questioning his certainty.

"No, but the sarcasm helps take some of the bite out of the ludicrous nature of that ridiculous moniker. Would you like me to stay with you for the return trip?"

"Thanks, but I'll be there for the day helping them set up."

"Okay, call me if you want company for the walk home."

Their walk to Carmen's cousin's house was uneventful. Lost in conversation, they hardly noticed the dark shadow that noted and watched them intently behind the partially closed curtains as they passed Doris's house. No longer an edifice to be avoided, the building, and the associated memory of recent events, were rapidly fading to insignificance.

"There's Granville, that little private school punk that turned me down and ruined my groove. Black priest, my ass! Who's the bitch he's with? I'll fix that little dipshit!" murmured Doris, careful not to let her parents hear, as they were watching television.

...

[[Author's Aside]]

Caution is a fleeting bird in the near-constant barrage of threats, real and imagined, in the ghetto. Eventually the past violent encounters become old news, once survived, and soon nearly forgotten in the vibrant, dark presence of the current menace.

Reflecting upon his conversation with Carmen and the depth of their refreshingly deepening relationship, Granville was just passing Doris's front steps when the door to her building flew open and a vengeful harpy in the form of a butcher-knife-wielding Doris charged, screaming, "Little Nigga, I'm going to kill you! You ruined my life!"

Granville was shaken out of his reverie and totally unprepared for this powerful young woman as she leapt upon him. The weight of her attack, a butcher knife cleaving the air before her, drove him toward the street until he found himself bent backwards over the hood of Mr. Kilogram's Plymouth, which had finally been re-established in its true home sans the crush of gangster-mobiles.

Doris, with maniacal strength, held Granville penned against the big car's hood with her left hand in an iron grip clutched around his throat, while trying to stab and slash his face with the butcher knife held high in her right fist. Only Granville's quick reflexes in gripping the wrist holding the knife allowed him some space to breathe under the onslaught.

Doris's weight and leverage advantage behind that huge blade began to press the needle point and razor-sharp edge ever closer to his face.

Rolling out from under her proved fruitless as her steely grip began to close his windpipe. He couldn't fathom which was the most pressing danger. To pass out was to die, to lose his grip on her twisting wrist holding the glistening knife was a sure death as well. One would, simply, with finality, lead to the other.

Just as breath became scarce and his hand began to loosen its grip, an unseen force lifted her, and by attachment, him, off the car hood and back onto the pavement. The reprieve allowed Granville the opening to wrench himself free of her hold, while receiving several hard, flailing kicks to his abdomen and groin from a barely restrained Doris in the process.

Mr. Kilogram, bending Doris back away from the car and her intended victim, growled in a taut, guttural tone, "Boy, get yourself home! Doris, you ain't gonna' kill nobody on my watch! Girl! Do you hear me?"

"Let me go, Papa! He ruined everything!"

Granville limped away toward home and his worried mother as quickly as the ache in his balls would allow him. He hadn't been that close to death in a while. The reality that Doris was the source of this reckoning was a strange irony. He started to chuckle, which flipped into a choking gasp deep in his bruised throat. Instead, he croaked through his thoroughly bruised larynx, "Doris! Be damned with the donkey you rode in on!"

...

Part 10: Beatrice, Levi, Joshua, and Marcia

Granville's sister-in-law, Beatrice, was horny. Levi Andrea, her husband, Granville's eldest brother, was out doing whatever with his running buddy since childhood, his cousin Joshua Grahame. The two were virtually inseparable these days. The usual explanation was that they were shooting pool at the local pool hall, the Eight Ball Lounge on Roosevelt Boulevard. Truth be told, their evening usually would start out that way, while between them, over a game of eight-ball, they would casually plan the night's carousing, progressing from shooting pool to shooting for strange pussy.

Cock hounds both, being married didn't seem to be of the slightest concern to either man.

Beatrice and Levi had been wed via shotgun ceremony. Not the best portent of a successful joining or lasting bond. Each was itching to be free of the false bondage of pseudo-commitment. Two young children under four tied them together as much as their infants' presence kept them apart.

They were virtual strangers, uneasily cohabitating instead of living truly together, under the same roof.

Beatrice was grounded by the ever-escalating demands and responsibilities placed on a mother of young children, while Levi, working and financially supporting his family, rationalized his wanderlust as his rightful reward for support given.

Ironically, Beatrice also had a kindred spirit in Joshua's wife, Marcia Grahame. The two ladies would gather either in person or via phone to complain about their married state between gossiping tidbits about friends or other family members.

Beatrice, a thick-bodied woman, was broad of hips, butt, and shoulders. Birthing two children had not diminished the size or girth of her opulent breasts.

Low-slung and melon-sized, her orbs were a particular source of pride. She tended to dress in low cut blouses, dresses, and sweaters. At home, she often went braless all together.

Push-up bras that Marcia, who sported a leaner, more svelte figure, used to enhance her cleavage, were of no use to Beatrice, who had enough cleavage for two women.

Beatrice and Marcia were beautiful coffee-cream-coloured Black ladies, vibrant and eager to live well in the lives they had chosen.

Neither felt that they had made a poor choice of husband. Yet their men seemed to be constantly preoccupied with chasing other strange women, rather than being affectionate, much less intimately loving with them.

It was crushingly apparent that both cousins had lost interest in being with their wives once the challenge of the premarital chase was no longer an issue.

"This home-alone-with-the-kids business was old a long time ago. Damn it all, Marcy!"

"How long has it been, Bea?"

"Too long, it's more than I care to think about," whimpered Bea.

"We're so fucking stuck!" shouted Marcy, voice dripping with malice. "The question is, what are we going to do about it?" A low, guttural, angry groan, an open question that hung in the air between them like an unrequited fart.

"They do as they please, while we sit at home waiting on their pleasure that only comes home when they can't find some strange pussy to play with." Bea's lament danced with Marcy's rant, only to reemphasize their shared hopelessness.

"We need a substitute, someone that is available and reliable with as few complications as possible." Bea's furtive reach for a life preserver amidst their quicksand sea, tone bright with wishful, fear-laced hope, lit a smouldering flame of cautious determination in her beautiful cousin.

"I have an idea. It's risky!" Marcy's eyes, alight with careless resolve, belied the hazardous minefield she was about to cross.

"How risky?" whispered Bea, feeling her sphincter tighten in sudden awareness of the dangerous no-woman's land she had found with no recourse but to see where it all may lead. *Perhaps to hell and back in a handbasket*, she thought.

"Living dangerously, in the family, as close to home as it gets."

"Shit! What do you mean? Please explain what's on your mind," said Bea, momentarily thinking, *This woman has truly lost her mind*!

"I heard quiet-as-kept DJ, that slime-ball cock hound loving to crow loud and long about his supposed conquests, has something going on with young Gran," said Marcy, in a secretive, conspiratorial soft hush— yearning hunger, satirical sweetness, while yielding to the acrid taste of true villainy.

"Gran? Ines's Gran? You can't be serious!"

"Oh, yeah, Bea, you remember when you were watching the boys, cause Ines had to work a night shift? We were having coffee at her place, in the kitchen before breakfast."

"Gran came out of his bedroom, rubbing sleep out of his eyes on the way to the bathroom. He was barely awake, hardly noticed we were there until he finished and came out. I doubt that he was even aware that he was carrying what looked like about a nine-inch piss hard-on in his boxers."

"How could I forget! I almost wet my panties on the spot."

"Yeah, how such a small boy could be sporting that whopper is beyond me."

"How would you like to be riding that joystick? DJ says he's had him, and every inch is rock hard, and the boy can keep a secret!"

"What! Damn! DJ's such a slimy fucking fag! Chases women like nobody's business, but what really turns his crank is young boys!"

"Yeah, Gran is about as cute and luscious as they come, and a virgin to boot!"

"Amen to that!"

"Okay, Marcy, I'm all ears, what's your plan?"

"Tomorrow is Friday, payday, pool night, as in pooh-tang. The boys won't be back till the crack of dawn or till the pussy's been had."

"And?"

"You've been complaining about your limited wardrobe forever."

"Yeah, I left all my good clothes at my mother's in Elgin."

"So, suggest that this weekend, he go pick up your things for you. Tell him that you have already planned with your mother to have them ready. And suggest that he take Josh along for the ride. Road trip!"

"Strongly suggest that they take the kids so they can visit with their grandma. They'll probably resist that part, but make it a condition of the trip, with grandma being happy to spend quality time with the kids and being an instant overnight babysitter. They'll jump at the chance to be out of town on the weekend with our blessing."

"Got that right. Might they get suspicious of our rather sudden generosity with their time out?"

"Perhaps, but they're far too conceited, self-centred, and stupid to suspect that their housebound *frau* could be up to something nefarious. Besides, they'll never hesitate, in their dash to the car, long enough to look this 'gift horse' in the mouth."

"So, they're out of the picture. Then what?"

"You go downstairs and ask Ines if Gran could sleep at your place Friday night. Tell her that Levi's gone to Elgin for the weekend and you're feeling a bit nervous, being alone in the apartment. Truth being told, you'll be nervous, all right, but it won't have anything to do with fear. Do I have to spell the rest out for you?"

"No, sweet bitch, I think I can figure that out my damn self!"

"Now, come morning, you call to invite me over for coffee, and we'll share that long dong, with a side order of sweet dark chocolate creme-filled pole-sickle for breakfast!"

"Sweet indeed, you evil woman!"

"Takes one to blow one!"

Beatrice was standing at the door to Ines' apartment, nervous as a cat on a hot tin roof wanting to knock, yet giddy and somewhat fearful in the anticipation of what may transpire once the door opened and Ines would be there, curious as to the purpose of her daughter-in-law's late-night visit.

Breathe, Bea, just stay calm. Am I really going to go through with this?

What if she says no? What if Gran doesn't want to? Then what? Oh, shit, woman, too late to turn back now. Marcy's crazy idea's going to blow up in your face, and she'll never let you live it down!

It was at that precise moment that fate answered her call. The door opened on its own, sans knock, as if it had read her mind.

"Oh, hello, Bea, come in. I was just about to come up to check on you to see if you were okay with Levi being out of town. He called earlier and asked me to check up on you in case you needed anything."

He's probably hoping you would catch me out with Marcia chasing strange cock, like he and Joshua chase pussy. Takes one to know one. If they only knew. We're making a custom order for an in-house delivery! Bea thought.

"Hello, Ines, I was wondering if it would be okay for Gran to stay with me tonight. I am feeling a bit uneasy being alone."

"Of course, it's fine, Bea. Gran's been working on a class project for next month's science fair, but he's just watching TV with us now."

"Gran really takes his education seriously."

"Yes, he loves science, and his ideas are always so complicated and creative; likes to get an early start to avoid burning any midnight oil at the last minute and keeping me awake in the process."

"What's he working on now?"

"A three-dimensional erupting volcano, complete with lava flow rising through visible underground channels within the volcano. Gran, pull your eyes away from the television and come here."

"Yeah, Mama?"

"Your mom tells me that you are working on a rather ingenious science project for the regional fair. Tell me about it," said Beatrice.

"Sure. Every year, there are at least a half dozen volcanoes. Some erupt, most don't. It's kind of a 'so what' kind of display that the judges look at, nod, sometimes compliment, and ignore when it is time for the prizes. I decided that I wanted to do something different with a tired, overdone topic; kind of inject new life into it, add a bit of wow factor."

"How so?"

"I'm building a cut-away model using an old ant farm display case that I found in a second-hand store. I will glue a large plastic cone to one side to form a cut-away version of the volcano."

"The ant farm has chambers throughout that lead from the base, a chamber where the queen used to be living, eventually reaching the surface where there are small exits for the ants. In between the chambers, the space will be filled with multi-coloured strata sand to exhibit the layers of Earth's crust.

"I am drilling holes into the cone sides, through which I will insert clear plastic tubing that will connect to the chambers in the ant farm at different levels.

"I will fill the empty queen's chamber with dish soap, white vinegar, warm water, and food colouring. When I am ready for the eruption, I'll add baking soda wrapped in tissue. Voilà.

"The lava will erupt throughout the ant farm chambers, including the clear tubing leading to the sides of the volcano, not to mention the main opening in the cone's bowl at the top. Of course, all the areas will be properly identified and labelled.

"What's neat is that you'll be able to see the eruption from start, in the magma chamber, to finish, in the peak's cone, as well as the sides, the way lava actually erupts; rather than just what comes out of a decorated papier-mâché´ mountain."

"Gran, you are some kind of smart brother-in-law!" Beatrice's brilliant, bright-eyed smile gave further credence to the warmth of her approval.

"Thanks, Beatrice . . ." replied Granville, basking and beaming in the glow of love shining upon him, a clear mirror of his sister-in-law's sentiments.

"Gran, I want you to sleep at Bea's apartment tonight. Levi's out of town and Bea would like some company. Is that okay with you, son?"

"Sure thing, Mom." An automatic acknowledgement of his mother's directive. Granville was flush with the enjoyment of Beatrice's closeness. Neither touching, yet close enough to share breath and scent. Her perfume scent tickled his nose and intrigued his mood.

"Go get ready. Wear your new pajamas. Don't forget to brush your teeth," called Ines. The spell broken, he hurried to change.

Granville had scrutinized his sister-in-law closely in the light of their conversation. Her eyes had reminded him of molten lava. Volcanoes being one of his favourite topics, a close second to dinosaurs—being that one was very much the dynamic environment that existed during earth's primordial period, when the other walked amidst the often molten, new, untrod earth that was born in its depths.

He had very much enjoyed sharing his avid interest, yet there was something in this request that struck him as odd. Something behind her eyes when they met his, suddenly, a twitchy nervousness that wasn't there while they were chatting.

Why would my overnight sleep in Bea's apartment help her be more comfortable in her own home? thought Granville.

The errant thought dissipated in the disarming radiance of Bea's welcoming smile, as she continued to beguile him while climbing the stairs to her home, holding hands.

Once inside the apartment, Bea led him straight to her bedroom.

"Gran, I really appreciate this favour. Sometimes I miss just having someone next to me. With Levi away, that bed feels lonely. I'll sleep much better with you being there. Do you mind sleeping on this side of the bed? That's where Levi sleeps. It's a king-size bed, so there's plenty of room to stretch out."

...

The bed was firm yet soft under his new PJs, the covers cool to his skin. The unease flowed from him, and he became drowsy. Sleep claimed him easily. He never consciously felt the silk-covered, firm yet soft in all the right places form that curled up to his back, then wrapped itself around him, spooning, till he unconsciously snuggled into to the lightly perfumed warmth.

Granville was having a wet dream. With the advent of puberty, his testicles had become testy, a subconscious tingling itch that could only be scratched with long smooth strokes, till the lava rose, erupted, and flowed.

The rising fury now seemed to consume his consciousness, since DJ's vile touch had set him afire. DJ's ever-present desire and attention fed Granville's need to incessantly self-satisfy the urge at every opportunity.

"Is this the dream? What's happening? Feels so good, oh! Oh! What! Bea! BEA!"

Having awakened to his soft moaning, and the slow rocking of his hips against her belly in his sleep, she had impulsively grasped and caressed the boy's wet dream expanding boner hidden under the cotton sheet.

Beatrice now knelt straddling Granville's legs, knee to knee, large thighs and bum resting on his lower legs. The top of her head was slowly rising and falling, from his point of view, nestled between her large melons on either side that stroked his thighs with each piston cycle. Granville, held in place by the weight of her, couldn't halt his rocking hips in concert with her sliding, sucking mouth and twining tongue. He didn't want to.

Granville reached down to stroke her loose curls, until her head rose from her ravenous succour to meet his eyes, breathlessly asking, "Is this okay, Gran?"

Nothing to be said, his throbbing, blistering heat choking any hope of speech to a sighing silence. Granville nodded in assent, open mouth, eyes half-closed, wishing he was any other place except here, yet praying she'd never stop.

With that submissive approval, Bea rewarded him by sliding her mouth down the length of his sweet cock as far as she could reach, ceasing as the bulbous head massaged the very back of her throat to the point of gagging. She held him there, caressing the throbbing beast with throat and tongue.

Granville felt that all this was wrong! So wrong, yet there was nothing to be done for it. Abject acquiescence, to his hunger without end or form, was the best he could manage.

Once again, he felt used, by his cousin and sister-in-law, betrayed by his longing, by the woman's touch, unrequested, undesired, undenied, never ever to be forgotten, a lifetime to forgive.

Fellatio ceased, replaced by a new heat, a white-hot moistness enveloping the fullness of his man-sized length and girth. A hardness that he would spend his youth through adulthood growing in symbiosis with its effect on men and women.

Bea, once mounted, rode him: high and low, long and slow, quick and hard, pause, suspension, to begin again, and again!

Sweat ran in a rivulet, cascading down between her breasts over her ample belly to pool in his navel before rolling over his hips, around his pumping cock to squish-squash slap beneath and behind her bouncing, vibrating ass cheeks.

Building momentum, speed, and intensity: the climb higher and higher still, abs taut, ass rock-hard, thighs straining to reach the sky, lifting her high off the bed despite her size, in pumping eruption before collapse; breath slowing, heart hammer quieting.

Granville looked at Beatrice's glowing face, deep into her questioning eyes, and began to cry.

Neither heard the soft knock on Beatrice's front door until it became more insistent. Bea knew that knock, and she couldn't have come at a worst time.

Bea bent down over Granville and kissed him hard yet tenderly to quiet his tears. "Baby, I didn't mean to hurt you. I just wanted your first time to be special, not thrown away fumbling with some young girl who wouldn't know any better. It's okay, no harm, no foul." A second kiss swallowed his lips and fed him tongue to claim his breath. Breathless release calmed his fears, though not his confusion; that would come later, as would he, many times over.

...

"My, my! Whatever do we have here?" snarled Marcia in mocking indignation, though she had been delighted to the depths of her moistening pussy with the sight of Bea and her young cousin's lips locked, entwined together, both oblivious to anything outside of that heated embrace.

Satisfied with the obvious success of her plan, she felt that things were definitely heading in the right direction.

Shocked at the voice and the intrusive presence, Beatrice and Granville bolted to sitting positions, remaining only partially covered by the thin cotton sheet.

Marcia, who had entered the apartment unbidden, stood in the door at the foot of the tousled bed, leaning against the doorframe, a wide, smirking grin spread across her mouth in a vain attempt at contrived indignation.

"So, you started the party without me," said Marcia, her mouth beginning to salivate at the sight of Granville's penile bulge evident beneath the clinging sheet.

"I was going to call you," replied Beatrice, her reddening face burning with self-conscious concern as to what Granville's reaction might be to Marcia's interruption. The fear that the boy might realize his familiar seduction was a premeditated plan, proposed and carried through by the two women rather than a spontaneous occurrence, was unnerving.

"Well, that ship sailed two hours ago," snapped Marcia, becoming more careless of exposing the details of their plan.

"What time?" questioned Bea, wishing to delay, perhaps divert, the situation's seemingly inevitable outcome.

"Ten thirty. I hope you saved some for me," said Marcia, impatience with Beatrice's delaying tactics resonating in her tone.

"Maybe we should take a break, have coffee, maybe breakfast," whined Beatrice, a last-ditch effort to defuse the sexual aggression emanating from Marcia.

"I've had my coffee, don't want breakfast. I'm ready for dessert!" Marcia's low, guttural tone declared: Enough small talk, no more words necessary, resistance is futile, deal with it!

All during this conversation, Marcia had been slowly unbuttoning her ankle-high, form-fitting deep purple frock. Her hourglass athletic figure was highlighted by her small Barbie doll waist. No bra was needed to cover her perky, high-breasted chest; she had svelte hips with long slender legs that seemed to go on forever. A purple G-string panty could not hide the dark curly hairs protruding out from all three sides.

Naked, she approached the bed.

"Someone likes what he sees, Gran!" purred Marcia, in her best come-hither tone, eager to possess Granville's hardening cock, now forming an undeniable indication of imminent, sensual sexual gratification.

True enough, looking down, Granville was surprised, even shocked, to find that he was fully erect once more. Marcia's heady scent preceded her physical touch as she reached out to softly trail her fingertips from his temple to his chin, deftly guiding his gaze from her breasts to her eyes. "Well, little big-man, I like what I see as well. The question is what we are going to do with it."

Bea, sitting quietly on the bed next to him, was clearly comfortable with letting Marcy take control of the situation, content to follow her cousin's lead.

Granville, once more, was afraid to breathe. Every iota of his weakening willpower rang in alarm, yet Bea's equally deft touch stroked inside his upper thigh just at the base of his surging penis.

Granville stiffened visibly at the unexpected invasion, causing Bea to hesitate, yet she continued to softly squeeze the growing cock-sleeve, her touch synchronized with its rhythmic pulse.

It was one thing to take advantage of the boy's wet-dream-induced boner in his sleep. Another thing entirely to aggressively manipulate the boy, to overwhelm his uneasiness and unwillingness to repeat a sexual act that he knew was wrong in the first place.

"It's now or never, baby. I say now." Bea's hand lightly encircled and caressed Granville's shaft, slowly sliding toward the head and down, as Marcy slowly pulled the sheet down, uncovering Bea's stroking manipulation with one hand while stroking her own clitoris, in small circles, with the other. Bea's hand glistened with her spent juices, still flowing.

Marcy carefully leaned forward and down to the cap and replaced Bea's stroking hand with her mouth in the same motion and pace as was her cousin's hand.

Granville, brother-in-law to Bea and cousin to Marcy, in frozen silence drew a deep, ragged sigh of resignation and fell backwards on the bed, his head half buried in the soft pillow.

Bea's mouth followed him down to swallow the fullness of his ripe lips, filling his mouth with her thrusting, sucking tongue.

Pinching and twisting his hard nipples, without breaking the oral assault, she carefully moved to where she knelt beside him.

Coming up for air only to whisper in his ear, "Close your eyes, open your mouth, baby; I have something special for you. Dessert, and it's delicious!" Then, her knees on each side of his head, she lowered her pussy to his soft lips and guided his chin to her folds, then hissed, "Lick, baby, lick me. Yes, right there!"

Marcy soon shifted as well to guide his fullness into her folds. Facing each other, they rocked together, eyes half shut. Lost in their mutual lust and blissful ride to satiation, they reached out to lovingly caress the other's breasts. Then, leaned into a long, deep, open-mouthed kiss of celebration.

Granville rode the exquisite rush of orgasm several times more, as did both women through several position changes. There were no more tears. The time for that had passed, for now.

The three shared a hearty brunch while unabashedly discussing DJ's foibles in depreciating Black humour, the lecherous part he had played, and how that had brought them to this point.

Granville realized that, for better or worse, in hell or high-water, he had been initiated into a family sex ring. Family with benefits and risks. Where the sexual predators were actively sharing information about potential opportunistic targets and collaborating in the use and abuse of the family bond to their own perverse ends.

The question that reverberated through his conscience was, "What was he going to do about it?"

Part 11: Molliah . . . I Hope You'll Dance

Molliah Stevenson was light enough, with fine features, to pass for white. A true high-yellow beautiful girl, sporting flowing auburn ringlets that cascaded down her long neck and back, who had her hazel eyes on Granville long before they met.

She noted that there was something different about him. Though he actually was a bit shorter than her, and rather slight, he carried himself with quiet assurance, as if he could handle himself and was not deferent to the gangbangers that populated the skate rink on Friday and Saturday nights.

He tended to always be alone without seeming concerned about it.

In a neighbourhood where there was strength and safety in numbers, due to the gangster creed, "Join, move, or die," lone wolves, as they were sometimes called, were rare. Lone wolf, he definitely was.

Molliah was curious as to why.

She had watched him take up with Astra, the cheerleader captain, and wondered how long that would last. Astra tended to shed suitors like a dog shed fleas. Seldom without ongoing male attention, she never suffered fools lightly. Still, she was with him long enough for every teen in the rink crowd to notice. "How did he sustain her interest? Capture her heart? What was his secret?"

Rumours abounded that he was known as some kind of Supreme Gangster. She thought, *That pipsqueak? No possible way!*

Yet, the rumours were persistent enough to pique her curiosity.

What is his game? What's his play?

He showed up again alone, as usual, about two months after Astra quit coming. Molliah was not aware of the cause behind Astra's absence, until she heard the rumours about how "Tank" Fraser had raped her.

The boy was "drop-dead" cute, with bright doll-baby eyes that seemed to exude intelligence. It was said that he attended a Catholic private high school, on an academic scholarship, no less. She wasn't aware that there was such a school in the neighbourhood.

Molliah decided that it was time to introduce herself. The question being, how? She had an idea, just needed someone to help set the scene.

She knew someone that was always eager to please. And would be happy to have her indebted to him.

She skated over to the rental office that was also the DJ nook. "George, what's your problem? You have something against ladies?" said Molliah, feigning indignation.

"No way, Molly! You know I do love my ladies." He mimicked her tone in a theatrical exaggeration of wounded pride.

"So, when are we going to have a ladies' choice skate?" Each word exalted by her brilliant playful tone and smile.

"Ahh, at your pleasure, madam. When do you want to have it?" replied George, happy to comply, sensing a chance to curry favour with the 'rink prima donna.'

"Ooh, how about for the next couples-only skate?" suggested Molliah, presenting the languid epitome of nonchalance in body language and expression, all belying her true interest and end goal.

"Deal! Save one for me later?" Eager hope for dreams coming true danced across his mind's eye: Molliah in his arms, lithe, lovely, naked for the taking, forcing, fucking, forever!

"Sure thing, George!" That time would never come. It was common knowledge among those in the know that George talked big and loved to bellow like his surname, Bellows, but was terrified of women. It was the reason he always hid in his booth peering out at what he coveted with all his cold, perverse little heart but could never have.

"Attention ladies and gentle peoples, this skate is for couples only. Ladies' choice! Ladies, this one's for you."

Granville left the floor right away; sans Astra, he had lost interest in skating the couples-only songs. He took up a space against the corner wall to listen to the song while he watched the couples on the floor. That's where Molliah found him.

She noted that, standing there alone, he seemed sad, self-absorbed, disinterested in his surroundings, as if that solitary corner of the busy rink, where he often had relaxed with Astra while she was on duty watching the traffic, had become the place where his dreams came to die and be buried deep within.

"Hi, my name's Molliah, would you like to skate this one?"

Granville was startled out of his reverie, his bittersweet remembrance of Astra. This was their space. How he missed her warmth, her strength of purpose. He so loved her, longed for her, needed her in his life to feel whole. Felt so special in her love for him and he for her.

"Happy to," was the quiet, halting response that was more an unconscious anodyne for his dark, soulful mood than a welcome diversion.

The Temptations hit, "My Girl," started as they glided into the flow of sparse traffic, typical of the ladies' choice skate. It just so happened to be one of the easiest ballad songs to skate, with lots of room on the floor and an easy rhythm to follow. Granville led Molliah with ease.

He skated with her as an equal partner, not trying to overpower her with his control. She was able to relax into his rhythm and understood why Astra had chosen him as a skate partner over others.

His confidence allowed them to glide in and out of the other couples while maintaining a smooth flow that was effortless. Molliah followed him as he danced with her skating backwards, facing her in a confident, gentle embrace.

His spatial sense avoided collisions with the others like he had eyes in the back of his head. She found herself feeling breathless in the embrace of this calm man-child.

"You are quite the skate partner," said Molliah, instinctively sensing his quiet depth of character; the subtlety of his perceptiveness intrigued her.

"So are you, thanks for inviting me," replied Granville, expressing his gratitude, honestly impressed by her brief, transfixing presence, and casual, confident intimacy, yet acutely aware of being closely scrutinized by envious eyes throughout the rink.

"Dibs on the next couple skate?" Molliah spoke without thought, followed by a sudden awareness that she never had, or wanted, to make that same request, which was so often requested of her, and just as often gently refused. She chided herself, acknowledging that his reticence was something she had never encountered. Was that what made him so fascinating?

"Sure, no one has ever called dibs with me before," said Granville, quietly, seeming to be speaking to himself, again feeling Astra's memory, its indelible brand upon his heart.

"No one has? Not even Astra?" Her inquiring tone was probing, yet gently challenging, forcing him to define his feeling about her absent friend.

"Well, it became a given. No invitation necessary." *It's my business, period.*

"Perhaps, it will be that way between us as well." *There, I've said it,* admitted Molliah to herself.

Granville hesitated, uncertain of what she was saying. "Are you inviting yourself into my world?"

A slight tilt of her head accented a soft smile, and calm, clear hazel-eyed silence that spoke wonders, as if to say, *"Must I spell it out for you?"*

Once again, surprised and caught off guard, unsure and somewhat uneasy, unprepared for what she was implying. He had seen her often at the rink. She was so beautiful, unmistakable in her commanding presence, desired by every boy; true enough, yet he didn't know her.

All his attention and affection had lived with Astra. The thought of her only brought the pain of that day in the park and his humiliation at the brutal hands of Frank "Tank" Fraser. His eyes began to burn, tears welled; he willed them not to fall. Molliah noticed the tension, the abrupt sadness.

"You really liked her?" said Molliah, hoping that he would admit to his true feelings. So wise and sensitive, was this beautiful boy as mature as he seemed? If so, for whom did his heartbeat now?

"Yeah, loved her, she was my girl," replied Granville, owning his feelings, stating a simple fact, a quiet, shy pride, sans regret of any kind.

"Astra told me that 'Tank' Fraser raped her. He beat her pretty bad to do it." Instantly realizing, by his reaction, that he had not known his deepest fear for Astra had become a horrific reality, Molliah felt deep remorse for her dear friend and the boy who loved her.

It was too much. The sadness evaporated in the heat of instantaneous boiling rage, a killing rage. Without a word, Granville turned away and skated into the washroom, lest he say something he would only regret.

Molliah did not deserve to face what murderous intention was consuming him. Cursing long and loudly through his tears, he swore at that moment that Tank would pay by his hand even if he had to trade his own life to do it. When he came out, Molliah was still waiting.

"I'm sorry." Surprised once more by her unexpected attentiveness, he managed a soft, twisted half-smile that did not extend to his large, deep, near-black eyes, where pools of salty tears still rested, ready to fall until he flicked them away.

"No problem, I understand. I wish someone cared that much about me." *Could you be that someone in my life?* thought Molliah.

"You don't have a boyfriend?" said Granville, not sure how that could be true; why wouldn't she be with someone?

"Until now, I haven't wanted one. The boys around here seem only interested in gang banging and other forms of dangerous, destructive stupidity." *Enough said*, thought Molliah.

"Amen." Echoes of his many battles flashed through his mind.

"Supreme Gangster! You have a strange rep not to be a gangbanger." A slight hint of disbelief floated through her tone.

"Yeah, I know, the cops gave it to me. It has nothing to do with me, who I really am." Granville could not suppress his disgust with the irony of the moniker and role he had been forced to play by being, living, fighting, just to stay alive.

"I would like to find out who you really are, Granville."

"I'm hunted by both gangs in this neighbourhood, the Vice Lords and the Roman Saints. To be with me could be dangerous. That's why Astra was targeted." An exhausting sense of hopelessness chewed at his words. A tight knot of frustration formed in his gut.

"Not so. Tank had it in for Astra long before she met you. She knew she was playing with fire when Tank approached her, and she didn't reject him early on."

"He had no fucking right!" Granville's mood darkened anew, anger flared just beneath the surface, behind narrowing eyes.

"I'm not saying he did have any right to do what he did! I'm just saying it was not because of you, even though it happened after she met you."

She spoke rapidly in Astra's defence, consoling Granville and imparting clarity in the evolution of the catastrophe.

"I'm a lightning rod for trouble." He was resigned to his fate, destined since birth.

"I'll take my chances. Being with you likely will not be boring." She spoke to Granville's gathering storm cloud, hoping to instill a silver lining.

"No, it won't. I'd give just about anything for a little boring in my life." He was speaking now almost by rote, not really listening or attending to Molliah's implied meanings.

"Please, not when you're with me. I could use a little excitement." Exasperation coloured her tone.

"With you?"

Suddenly, Molliah was there, within his cloud, a shimmering, silver lining, its brilliance shown everywhere. "Yes, that is what this is all about, isn't it, Granville?" *Last chance, accept me or lose me,* thought Molliah.

Granville stared with a wide-eyed, openly dumbfounded expression, finally realizing where this conversation had been going, and for a long moment he was speechless. In the silence, the cloud dissipated, his smile blossomed in the light and grew to a big, pearly white, toothy grin. "Call me Gran. My family calls me Gran."

"Gran it is. Call me Molly, only my mom calls me Molliah."

"Deal, Molly."

Their partnership was formed, and they became inseparable at the rink.

Granville and Molliah were accustomed to being watched as they went about their daily endeavours as part of their individual presence. Each tended to command attention simply by entering a room. This was particularly true of the glamorous Molliah. Many in the rink's break room had intently watched their conversation. Thus, the obvious personal interchange between them was being carefully observed and noted by boys and girls alike.

Granville, who had been recognized as Astra's skate partner, held a unique primacy among the skaters, within the ranks of the boys, an object of envy, while amongst the girls, a subject of wonder. Now watching him in an intimate conversation with regal Molliah, the reigning roller rink queen, was unnerving for some, mesmerizing for others.

The stares of those around the entranced couple were completely ignored and of little consequence to either Granville or Molliah. They had found succour in their grief, shared pain, mutual respect, and recognition. Nothing and no one else in the room mattered.

Glaring through veiled fury, leaning on the open service window ledge of the adjacent office to appear as nonchalant as possible, George trembled inwardly with the urge to break the punk in half, then throttle the bitch into submission and rape the whore till she bled in front of him. His seething, hate-filled rage mattered.

Once again, George Bellows felt that he had been made a fool, this time by the beautiful Molliah. When he realized that her ladies' choice request had been a ploy so she could choose the short-fry Nigger to be her partner, George's admiration of her as being something special, unattached, and thereby open to possibilities and fantasies in his mind, digressed into his age-old general fear, disgust, and resentment of all things female.

His manipulation of "Tank" Fraser had been all too successful. He felt empowered to strike once more for revenge's sake. "Bitches just can't be trusted. She will pay and pay dearly, like Astra. My dad was right all along."

Mrs. Obedia Stevenson had welcomed Granville into her home when Molliah brought him home after a Saturday night rink skate session. She liked the clean-cut look of the boy.

"Hello, Granville, please do come in, good to meet you. I have heard so much about you. Well, Molliah, to what do we owe this surprise visit? Though I've wondered how long it would be before I'd meet the boy that had captured her interest so completely, when so many others had failed."

"Hello, Mrs. Stevenson, it's great to meet you. Molly . . . ugh . . . Molliah and I were chatting after the skating session when we saw that there might—well, likely—be a gang confrontation between the Roman Saints and the Vice Lords over a slight that occurred during the session.

"A Vice Lord was skating with the younger sister of a Roman Saint during a couples-only skate, very much a violation of the unwritten and thereby informal skate rink rules that forbid any romantic interaction between the rival gangsters, entourage, and their family members. Think *West Side Story*.

"There was a heated verbal confrontation within the rink that I was concerned would develop into a violent confrontation between the gangsters afterwards as a result of the perceived transgression.

"Since you live in Roman Saints' territory, I asked Molliah if I could walk her home, just to be sure that she would be okay."

"And then what happened?" asked Obedia, wondering where the story was going.

"As it turned out, a running street battle did develop that we were able to avoid by using an alternate route through the industrial warehouse area. It's a route that I use often to avoid the gangs when going to and from work. Neither gang ever traverses that district. It's much too boring, security is very evident, so theft is not feasible, thus of no interest to the gangsters."

"Would you like to sit awhile?"

"Thank you, ma'am, but I'd best get home, I'm one of the acolytes serving the daybreak mass tomorrow, starts at eight a.m. See you next week, Molliah, Mrs. Stevenson. Goodnight."

His obvious intellect impressed the single mom, who worked as a legal assistant in a small firm located downtown on Lake Street.

Obedia worked a forty-hour week immersed in a sea of legalese and the high-powered lawyers who interpreted the professional language of state, law, and commerce.

Obedia had cautioned Molliah to be careful in her selection of friends and associates in the community. Gangbangers and other malcontents, bent on a life of crime, prison, or early suicide by cop, would never be welcome in their home, period.

The social reality of the ghetto did not allow many choices or options for Molliah.

Molliah had spoken of Granville with her mother after she heard of Astra's assault and rape. At the time, the exceptional qualities of Astra's new skate partner were somewhat envied by Obedia's daughter. "Why can't I meet someone like that, Mom? Astra says he's really smart and nice, easy to talk with, and interested in furthering his education to university and beyond, which he takes very seriously. He's religious and very respectful of women. Not interested in chasing girls, gang banging or the criminal lifestyle."

"Don't worry, baby, boys come a dime a dozen; many are not worth bothering with. Yet there's always a good one to be found amongst the rest. Just be patient, persistent, and determined not to settle for less than the one who exhibits the qualities you want, the high standards you deserve."

Granville's language dexterity was a skill set; Obedia knew that it had to be a combination of nature as well as nurture. His having achieved an academic scholarship at Saint Philips BHS, a private boys-only Catholic high school, the last of its kind in the area, meant that he took his education seriously and would probably be one of the few Black teens who had a valid chance to do something important with his life.

"Gran, I have an idea," said Molliah, her eyes bright with anticipation.

"Cool! Molly, what's on your mind?" He was eager to entertain any ideas this deep woman, who reminded him so much of his mother, had to share; she was just another superwoman and Granville did luxuriate in the easy comfort they'd come to enjoy with each other. It was like a cool, deep drink from a fresh spring, an oasis, after a long trek through searing desert dunes.

"Does your mother attend the church in your building?" She knew her mom wanted to meet his mom and the church was the perfect place to spend time together; it'd be safe. Besides, it was her mom's idea.

"Yeah, she does pretty regularly, even though she became a Catholic so we could attend Our Lady of Sorrows when we first moved here."

"Great! Mom and I want to attend next Sunday." No need to say whose idea it was; besides, she was happy to have her mom's support.

"Sweet! Mom and I will be there. For sure, you can join us for brunch after services, visit our place. Mom to mom, sorta speak."

"Great idea! Thanks for inviting us." She was pleased that Granville supported the idea and was willing to go one step further, without trepidation or question.

"Yeah, a good way for our moms to get to know each other on hallowed ground, sorta speak."

"Ya thinks?" agreed Molliah, her teasing tone implying the obvious.

"Both of them being the only women working in an all-male environment and holding their own, they will have some war stories to share about their jobs and the men they work with and for. For starters, some men on my mother's work crew call her Mighty Mouse because she is so small and so strong. She also does not suffer fools for very long. Mom is tough," said Granville, filial pride looming large in his deep brown eyes.

"Mom says that some of those lawyers are either kissing ass, hunting for it, or both, always on the prowl."

Male psyche on the prowl, fearful in their threat, fearless in their stupidity, fragile in their egos, desperate to prove otherwise.

The image of a large jungle enclosure filled with prowling, preening cats flashed through Granville's imagination. Lions, tigers, leopards, and back-alley tomcats, all hungry and horny, extreme appetites seldom satiated in either case.

"Common, uncommon ground," interjected Granville, rueful irony framing his crooked half smile, recognizing once again the deeper, perhaps more far-reaching, depth of their love and its effect upon the most important women in both of their lives.

"Should be interesting," concluded Molliah, welcoming the wisdom embodied in this young man, as any doubts of his sincerity and integrity evaporated. Molliah felt her heart smile in relief as the effect spread across her face, a big, bright, toothy grin, from cheek to cheek.

Their kiss sealed the deal, as hearts beat in tandem, rhythm calling to the joy of discovery and wonder. Loving is a way unknown, lives unfurled in white flags of surrender to glorious golden sunsets and clear, star-bright, full-moon nights.

...

Sunday morning, bright and sunny, Granville was feeling his oats, giddy energy, butterflies in his stomach that felt like bats flitting around refusing to land.

Molly and her mother were paying a visit. This first contact, parent-to-parent, of boy and girlfriend could be quite an experience. This was brand-new to him. It felt a mix of intense anticipation and total panic. *Never done this before: hold breath, breathe, release, relax, you're safe in your skin.*

Molly thought of Granville's smile as she lay in her bed, staring at his face etched on the ceiling of her mind. The boy was so nice and fun to be around. *Open to whatever I have to say, values my opinion, no matter the subject, so easy to talk to and funny, wicked humour. Mom will be easy today, loves to talk, great storyteller.*

If Gran's mom is as good a storyteller as she is, the stories will last all day. They'll still be swapping stories at dinnertime. Okay, day's begun, girl, get up to meet this new boy of yours and all that life entails. Feels good, strange though, now that I have him, or is it that he has me?

At some point, I'll have to tell Astra about us. She has to hear it from me first, before the rumours reach her ears with the stupid lies about Gran and me. I love Astra. She's my best friend. We have always been attracted to similar boys. She has always been active, dating a revolving door of boys coming and going since she was fifteen. I've always kept them at healthy distance, waiting for the right one.

It couldn't be helped that she connected with Gran first. She was always more confident, more assertive, going after whomever piqued her interest right away. Those traits brought "Tank" Fraser into her life, briefly enjoying the status of being with the leader of the pack, the bad-boy charm, till she realized what a bastard he really is and bailed, too late to avoid the repercussions of his unwanted attention. The assault and rape broke Gran's heart and hers.

I've always been more reserved. So, of course she met Gran first, even though we both had been watching him. I know she still misses him. I didn't begrudge her romantic connection with him, though I was dying of envy. Still, I wished her well and meant it.

I'm sure that it'll be hard for her to appreciate that Gran and I are together, to accept that her intimate time with him has passed, sad as it is, and let go. I really hope we can still be friends; we'll see.

Now I'm with him and I love him; love everything about him. I need to be with him. And I know he feels the same about me. It just feels right.

...

"Mom, their car just pulled in. Let's meet them before they go in." Granville hurried out of the apartment, down the stairs to meet Molliah and her mother just after they exited their vehicle.

"Hello, Mrs. Stevenson, Molly, it's good to meet you again. Glad you could make it."

"We're pleased that you invited us, Granville," said Obedia, *noting once again how this beautiful, rare—by ghetto standards—young man was easily a head shorter than her daughter yet carried himself with an easy, affable charm that was quite disarming. His presence welcomed engagement without affront of any kind.*

"You can call me Gran, that's what my family calls me. Wow, so young, you could pass for Molly's sister, and evermore gorgeous, rather than her mom. *She's so beautiful, the lady has serious style.*"

"Yes, I stand corrected. Thank you Gran, it warms a mother's old heart that you should think so. It's nice to be considered as part of your family. I see Molliah wasn't exaggerating. Young man, you're a tall drink of cool water beneath the desert sun."

"Thank you," replied Granville, looking up at Mrs. Stevenson and Molliah towering over him in the bright sunlight, not used to being described as tall in any context, though the analogy pleased him.

Ines arrived to join her son and the mother of the new young woman in his life. She was encouraged by the look of Molliah, a tall, svelte, beautiful girl who carried herself with a calm self-assurance that clearly was an echo of her mother's prominent spectacular presence exuding intelligence, strength, and wisdom. "Hello, Mrs. Stevenson, Molliah; I'm Ines."

"Please call me Obedia; your son has made quite the overwhelming impression on my girl, Molliah. She hardly speaks of anything else since they met and became skate partners at the rink."

"I believe our meeting was planned as a signal to both of us that they want to be more than partners on wheels. I'm hoping that this means they wish to proceed toward a fulfilling, mature relationship that may enliven their lives as well as it seems to have begun," said Ines.

"I suspect that that's definitely the direction they're heading," concurred Obedia, immensely comfortable with Granville's mother, who clearly exuded confidence, strength, clarity of focus, and purpose in her slight yet curvaceous frame, which she held ramrod straight.

"It's good that we have met and can work together to encourage them to be responsible and honourable in their relationship with one another as well as with us," continued Ines, pleasantly pleased with the simpatico response of this striking mother and her gorgeous daughter.

"Ines, I like you already."

"Same here, Obedia; shall we go in? Service should be starting shortly."

Granville and Molliah shared an affirmative glance, accented by brilliant smiles, having witnessed their mothers deftly confirming their contextual relationship, which included mutual support of each other and their children's love affair.

Part 12: Pastor Jeremiah Robison's Sermon

Ines and Obedia entered through the heavy double doors of the church, held open by Granville who, holding hands with Molliah, followed their mothers to a vacant pew near the rear of the room.

Christ's Shepherd Southern Baptist Church's Sunday service was called to order by Rev. Pastor Jeremiah Robertson.

Rev. Pastor Robertson was not new to the pulpit. He had been a very active assistant pastor at the original and main Christ's Shepherd Southern Baptist Church prior to his current assignment.

He was very active and responsible for the church board's decision to purchase this building and to establish this satellite ministry. He had been witness to the social and cultural upheaval that resulted from the church's arrival and the evil practice of blockbusting that occurred in its wake.

The transformation from an all-white neighbourhood, then mixed racially and culturally, to a now-predominately Black enclave, had been both tumultuous and violent. The community was now a ghetto with family cohesion and integrity under a devastating downward spiral in living conditions and quality of life of its inhabitants.

The pastor also had recently received a life-changing medical diagnosis, after six years of escalating health issues that seemed to be primarily cognitive yet defied clear explanation.

He had been diagnosed with early onset dementia. Dementia, in the ragged rancour of the disease, weakens the social/cultural restraints that define what is appropriate speech and behaviour. The process, a mixed bag of good, bad, and ugly, can reveal the innermost dreams and aspirations of the person living with dementia.

If the person living with the disease is supported by positive reinforcement within his/her environment, it can become an evolutionary experience by facing and working through the natural fear of the unknown within the terminal eventuality. A life direction may emerge that challenges as well as enhances life quality by building resilience toward a defining sense of courage that the journey engenders. The past is forgotten. The future is uncertain and irrelevant. The present is omnipotent; now is all or never.

Thus, after much prayer and professional consultation, the terminal disease was no longer seen as a death sentence by the reverend; instead, it had become a wake-up call to himself and the community over which he had presided, as a shepherd to his flock, for more than twenty years.

He was on call to address the malignancy of spirit and cultural practice that had devolved the neighbourhood residents' quality of life, especially the loss of hope and dreams among the children, personified by the growth of the gang-land subculture and its socially cannibalistic criminal lifestyle.

Walking in the biblical footsteps of his namesake, Jeremiah, the Old Testament prophet bewailing the evils of the day or prophesying disasters to come, Rev. Pastor Jeremiah Robertson had self-resolved to use his terminal illness as an introduction and vehicle to address, head on, the malignancy within his flock. A process that would begin with today's sermon.

Rev. Pastor Jeremiah Robertson's Sermon

"Hello, everyone: God bless and keep you well. I'm sure the Lord welcomes you to his house on this beautiful sunny Sunday service. I am pleased to see such a large turnout today. It warms my heart to see almost every pew occupied with parishioners who take their love of God and each other seriously, enough to gather regularly to share in the celebration of Jesus's love and devotion. May we all reflect that love within each other, believer and nonbeliever in kind.

"On a personal note, I wish to share something with all of you that came to my attention recently. I am sure that many of you are familiar with the cognitive disease dementia, a terminal disease with no cure which can afflict anyone from their fifties through their nineties. The earlier age range, pre-sixty-five, is called early onset dementia, with its own patient-specific symptoms, issues, and challenges.

"Several months ago, I received a positive diagnosis of early onset dementia. Some would look at this diagnosis as a preordained death sentence and spend their remaining life setting their affairs in order, in preparation for their imminent demise. All that may be true and the business of it is valid and should be looked after.

"One of the more public results of living with dementia is the loss of your social-cultural filter. What I am about to share with you may offend some, outrage others; if so, so be it. Chalk it up to my dementia, to the loss of my social filter. All the same, please indulge me by listening with an open mind and heart. Our children's welfare will be blessed by it.

"There is also another, somewhat lesser known, approach; I feel it is a different call that must be answered within the situation. Take it, as you will, to be an opportunity to rise to the inherent challenge of living more fully than ever before by celebrating the life you have been given. Face the challenge of the truth that has been all too easy to ignore when you thought: 'What I can do? It's just not my problem. Is it?'

"The questions I wish to pose to you today are similar to the same questions our Lord Jesus asked of the Father on the mount, when he entreated, 'Father, please let not this chalice be mine.'

"I see the questioning expressions on many faces. Yet we all have been touched by the problematic malignancy we have nurtured to epidemic proportions within our world. The cancerous malignancy is gang-land culture and its criminal lifestyle, a growing blight within our culture and society.

"Perhaps some would say, 'Reverend, with all due respect, this is not news and it's nothing that I respect or contribute to, so what do I have to do with it?'

"Mostly, we complain loud and long when it touches our lives. Yet grow silent and insular once the incident passes, hoping the problem will magically go away, or that the police will 'do their job' and deal with it.

"Gang banging is not a problem onto itself. It's a symptom of a cause that is hidden deep within: our culture, our society, our community, our families. The cause, which eventually metastasizes into the very public cancerous tumour of gang violence, which must be excised, is child abuse.

"Child abuse begins at home, within the environment that we assume will nurture and protect us throughout the early beginnings of each and every one of us.

"Child abuse may occur in physical abuse: 'Spare the rod, spoil the child.' Neglect is another common form of abuse: 'Children bearing children with no inclination, time, experience, wherewithal, or knowledge of how to raise a child.' Then there's, perhaps, the most heinous form of all, sexual abuse: 'Just trying to show him/her how it's done, just an education so they'll know what to do when their time comes.' That perverse education, by a man or woman, is called rape.

"Rape in the family is called incest. There's no rationale for incest.

"These dysfunctional parenting practices are assaults upon the child. These forms of violence beget violent children, nurtured in rage, fear, and confusion. The child is permanently damaged in body, spirit, and soul.

"Love is perverted, trust is nonexistent, rage and fear remain the only emotions the child is capable of feeling, if the adolescent can feel at all. To hide their fear, the children strike out at anyone, and everyone in general.

"The result, the anatomy of a gangbanger: biting the hand that should have fed it. Hating the life that hated it. Resenting the family that wounded and betrayed it.

"Our many sins have come home to roost, people. No one here is above and beyond this. The proof is out there walking the streets that you wouldn't be caught dead on after nightfall for fear of winding up, just like that, dead.

"You must understand it's not too late. The change begins and ends with you.

"The question is, what are we going to do about it?

"We are starting a workshop in positive parenting techniques and practices. 'How you can prevent and fix child abuse!' We will be meeting weekly on Sunday afternoons, after service, and Wednesday evenings. The meetings are open for those who can attend at least once a week, on either day. The registration book is located at the back of the church. Please leave name, phone number, and the day of the week you can attend. Don't be shy; we all know each other. There aren't any strangers here, just our church family."

Rev. Pastor Robinson paused.

The silence among the congregation was deafening, only punctuated briefly by the soft sobs and murmured curses of denial and regret. Pastor Robinson was encouraged, yet not surprised, knowing there was hope in all responses. The awareness and need for change among his gathered followers were self-evident. He had struck a nerve that might begin to save the children through the courage of their parents. The rest was up to God's mercy, and that, his faith dictated, was beyond measure.

"Let us pray. Our Father, who art in Heaven . . ."

The congregation prayed with their pastor, some loudly with deep affliction. Others whispered quietly through bitter tears of recognition. Still others cried through the joy of knowing that they were not alone in their confusion of what could be done to help their children. All prayed to help themselves and each other save their families.

The remaining service was somewhat anticlimactic after the pastor's insightful, powerful sermon.

The workshop registration list was quickly filled and took up several pages of the big book.

The departure ritual, as the pastor bid them farewell at the front doors, was protracted by the membership's expressions of heartfelt gratitude for his sharing.

...

Granville had listened to the Pastor's sermon with sinking dread deep in his soul. So afraid that his culpability, his role in the abuse, would be revealed and he, too, would become a pariah in the community, in his family.

Could he have fought harder to prevent DJ's initial attack and repeated rapes? Could he have rejected Bea and Marcy's seduction? Confessed all to his mother? He had never lied to her before.

With his mother, Molliah, and Obedia on either side, Granville quietly, deep within, shed burning, bitter tears over the innocence he had lost and would never regain. The wisdom of this knowledge was indeed hateful without hope of recourse.

Now, he was living a lie that was corrupting him from within. The corrosive effect upon his sense of self was a poison seed from which a deep-seated self-hatred was taking root. This poisonous weed would eventually bloom from a barb-laden vine that would wind itself around his heart and destroy his life as he knew it.

"Some sermon!" said Molliah, turning to Granville, feeling somewhat taken aback, even a bit shell-shocked and unsure of what to make of the pastor's forthrightness and eloquence. "Talk about too much information, why don't you! He makes it sound like the whole congregation is rife with child abusers, perverts that are beating and raping their children. How could that be? Where did he get that information? What business is it of his, anyway?"

Her tirade, a monsoonal downpour of condemnation, heaped upon the brittle, fragile, guilt-edged delusions of her newfound love. Granville shuddered, his world became a slow dance in a minefield, as intimate as it was deadly. There would be explosions.

Granville cried, within his racing thoughts. *It's true, all of it! They use and abuse us at every turn. It doesn't matter that you are family. It's all meaningless, that they're the ones whose purpose is to protect us from the very people who are determined to destroy us. We are their children. They claim to love us, while their true intention is to twist our love, our self-awareness, our lives, to suit their obsessive perversions! How is that love? How's that family?*

He fought his heart's earnest truth, in thunderclap drumbeats, for his life and her love. The desire to confess his compliance within his familiar, prurient, pornographic world, his secret abhorrent life of sex toy and plaything for his cousins and sister-in-law to rape at will. He choked and coughed on the rising bile crawling up his throat, yet remained silent, eyes downcast. Thankfully, Mrs. Stevenson spoke and rescued him from her daughter's silent, intense, confounding gaze.

"Whew, is he always so assertive?" queried her mother, breaking the glacial moment.

Ines looked at her counterpart. "Actually, until today he was quiet and reserved. I suspect that even then he was trying to work with some of the member families on a more individual basis. I guess the magnitude of the problem finally reached its boiling point, facilitated by his dementia diagnosis, and the pot boiled over. Decided to address the congregation in a more effective process. After all, we were here with him early in the blockbusting ghettoization of this community.

"Gran has fought many of those battles with the gangs, white and Black, on the church's very doorstep. Blood was shed; hate, rage, and violence were on full display.

"Pastor Robertson witnessed all of it, yet it has taken till now to face the contributing factor of it and get the members of the congregation on board to address the source. I welcome Jeremiah to the war on child abuse. The real change that may get at the core cause of the violent culture we have had to learn to live with; it couldn't have come sooner."

"Amen!" agreed a much-relieved Granville, pride in his mother shining in his tear-filled eyes.

Later that balmy evening, with the bright daystar just beginning to set, the teens relaxed on the smooth concrete steps of Molliah's front portico.

Inside, Ines and Obedia were still swapping stories over their dinner preparation. They behaved more like sisters, comfortable with one another and appreciative of the camaraderie. The bond between the women had been immediate.

The bustling kitchen's sweet, savoury aroma filled the apartment and promised a culinary delight to relish with their new friendship's celebration.

"What do you think about our mothers' time together?"

"All things considered, I think it went really well. Sure smells like it," quipped Granville, breathing deeply.

"Thinking with your stomach again?" teased Molliah. "Actually . . ." She took a long, slow, deep inhalation, filling her senses, relishing the resplendent kitchen scents wafting from the open window. ". . . Yeah, me too."

"T'was a Sunday well spent," declared Molliah, deciding that though the sermon was unsettling, the reality that was being addressed by it was horrific and needed to be called out.

"Well, if that sermon gets the congregation mobilized, maybe some of the street warriors will give peace a chance. A little kumbaya would give me a breather from having to be looking over my shoulder whenever I'm out and about," said Granville, relieved to discuss that aspect of the sermon, a role that he could relate to and express in a positive way, bereft of his demeaning, emasculating guilt.

"Said the hare to the fox," chuckled Molliah.

"This is one quick hare; my fleet feet saved my bacon on many an occasion, sprinting to my lair," retorted Granville, quick to defend.

"Ahh, so there's a poet among us. Can you write as well as you run?"

"Speaking of running, you've seen pet mice in a cage running on a circular treadmill, haven't you?" asked Granville, though he had never shared his poetry with anyone other than his mother. His poetry was intensely personal, a journal of his innermost thoughts and feelings. He decided to risk their friendship and love by sharing something he had recently written about the endless cycles of hopelessness that seemed to be everywhere in his ghetto world: the abuse, the violence, within and without, overwhelming, all consuming.

"Yes, why?" queried Molliah, wondering where this was going. Perhaps a story?

"It's just a poem, called 'Treadmill.'" Granville began to recite his poem of desperation, in a breathless, rapid rhythm, the racing tempo and pace of a hundred-yard dash, sprinting to the finish line.

"Rats on a treadmill, the circle goes round.
Time passes ignorant of the sound of my racing feet
As I claw my way toward the illusion of freedom
Over the hill, 'round the bend, up the wall.
The track runs on and on toward an ever-distant horizon
The end of this world made square then round by edges worn smooth
A glass house filled with hungry piranhas swimming fast,
Toward dinner left warm in the fridge turning green with mold
Growing rotten, too long left unplugged without meaning.
To be foolish or wasteful, yet I must run this course. And worst to be near and dear for former enemies,
Now friends sans friends that never should have been trusted with family members so loving . . . the children.
Too far away . . . out of control, my life lives in ashes of the past
A past forever to be my present that haunts my future Running on, around and 'round . . . my claws are sore
My heart cries no more, yet the track rolls uncaring
Souls, without ears to heed, or heart to beat the pounding of my tired bruised bleeding feet.
Treadmill . . . Treadmill . . . Treadmill."

-TREADMILL . . . By Granville Johnson

"You wrote that?"

"Of course, and that's not all," and with that, Granville began a slow, sultry gospel rendition of, "A Change is Goin' to Come," morphing into, "Easy," the Commodores' mega hit. "That's why I'm easy." Both of which happened to exemplify Granville's call to living life.

"Can sing as well! You are a deep well, full of surprises."

"Learned to sing in choir, first soprano in grade school at Our Lady of Sorrows, now first tenor at Saint Philips BHS since my voice dropped. My family is musical."

"Ever thought of making it a lifetime thing?"

"Course, would love to, it's so much fun, making music with your voice."

"Try this: 'That's What Friends Are For.'" The melodic tones of Gladys Knight's sweet aspirational ballad of hope, faith, and inspiration floated lightly from the beautiful girl's svelte throat. Her voice enraptured Granville, and he wanted to cry through his wide-eyed grin; such is the way of happy tears.

With a little generous, gentle coaching, he joined her for a duet rendition of the song, each realizing how special was the linking of their lives together.

Their melodious vocal lilt brought their mothers to the open window to listen secretly to the clear celebratory joy of their children. Both felt warmed by a mother's joy in the unique expression of the young couple's affection for one another.

...

Each mother was painfully aware that time is a fleeting thing, and that it's most precious indeed. "Yes, they are moving that way; methinks they're a little further along than 'skate partners,'" surmised Obedia.

"Amen, and I approve," concurred Ines.

"Ditto," said Obedia, nodding in mutual approval.

...

Part 13: When One Door Closes . . . Another Opens

Saint Philips Basilica HS was a breeding ground for potential acolytes, boys who lived to serve in the church at mass and other 'godly' minor roles. Since Granville had been already serving in that capacity since elementary school at Our Lady of Sorrows Elementary, the next rung on the gilded climb to heaven's Godly purity was the priesthood.

Jesuits were the sect that taught at Saint Philips.

They introduced themselves as warrior priests, the sect given the responsibility of defending the faith against all threats. The true believers and emulators in Jesus Christ and all things Catholic including martyrdom, which could and did lead to the path of sainthood.

Granville felt that he had spent all his young years in some type of warfare, both without his family and now, within that very same family.

Most of his battles to date had involved some type of violent, pointless gang warfare, white, Black, and otherwise. Now his fight, the fight of his life, seemed to be literally for his body and soul, against the predators within his home. His second cousin, who'd raped him repeatedly in his own bed. His cousin, who'd seduced him in hers with his sister-in-law.

The newly minted, embraced Catholic sense of guilt and sin was choking his sense of self. He felt that the freedom to be himself was facing an attack that made that awareness of self to be unclear and unclean.

How could he allow himself to be DJ's sex toy while having sex with women in the family, and somehow think it was okay? Was it because, in the seduction, there was no force or intimidation involved? Was it because he felt more of an affinity with the women, because of the "female" sex role he was subjected to in DJ's rapes?

Was he submitting to DJ to protect his brothers? Was he submitting because his sexual craving was so strong that any sexual activity was welcome to scratch the ever-present itch? Was he a bitch or a whore in sheep's clothing?

The priesthood seemed like a way out, a way of focussing outside of his self on a path that left his body alone while giving his soul to something bigger than himself, a spiritual sense of purpose, the worship of a forgiving God.

To explore the truth, Granville took advantage of an opportunity to spend part of his summer in the seminary: an open opportunity to briefly experience the inner sanctum of the cloistered priesthood firsthand for two weeks. The result surprised and troubled him.

He loved the quiet, the ascetic clarity. Yet he felt uneasy at times when several of the fathers exuded a vibe with which he was all too familiar, that of predacious sexual interest. It unnerved him; fear, fight, and flight became the overriding emotional remembrance, derailing his expectations of the cloistered calling.

He returned after that trip feeling confused and depressed.

What clarity did come was that his fantasy of being a priest had little to do with reality. He did like and prefer women and he wasn't gay.

Sometimes when one door closes, another opens. This was the case when Granville felt his desire to remain in Saint Philips BHS and to become a priest had died.

The priesthood had lost its call for the boy. It was one of the truths that had bothered him since he had spent the two weeks of his summer vacation at the Jesuit seminary.

Though he had continued to excel in all his subjects, his school days immersed within the Catholic mythology only reminded him of the drabness of the seminary, its lack of vitality, its false humility that passed for piety, and, by association, the lack of female energy in that life.

The time surrounded by supposedly devout men, devoid of any female contact, had left him wondering how a life such as that could be fulfilling.

He had been raised by his single mom. He was truly ever more comfortable with and around women than men. Maleness devoid of female energy: to soften, strengthen, make relevant, significant, meaningful, alive, was an imitation of life and, thus, lifeless.

Granville had no idea how to tell his mother what was really bothering him.

Granville had developed a kind of subconscious awareness of that hunger in men and women; a sense of the danger and desperation roiling just beneath the surface of their smiles, words, and actions toward him.

What he could not share with his mother was how he had felt in the cloistered atmosphere of the seminary. Feeling some of the similar sexually predatory and perverse focus that DJ had emanated whenever they were together, at any time, in any place. He hadn't yet told his mom the truth about DJ.

Was the evil you knew less fearful than the one you didn't?

Perhaps to be in an environment that did pose obvious potential for physical, even violent, threats from gangbangers, was preferable to the lurking, hidden reality of the sexual perversion he sensed within some of the cloistered adults around him.

Granville felt the enveloping, urgent need to escape. His growing affection for Molliah was a new life within his heart and spirit. Her love was the brightening light warming his tired bones at the end of the long, cold dark.

...

"When you get the choice to sit it out or dance, I hope you dance."
-Gladys Knight

...

"Mom, can we talk?"

"What's on your mind, son?"

"I don't know how to say this."

"That's okay, just say it.

"I want to transfer to John Marshall." *There, I've said it out loud. No backing down now. I must see this through. Mom will understand.*

"Why, son, that's where all the gangsters that have been hunting you attend. Gran, you can't be serious?"

"I don't want to attend Saint Philips anymore. I really do like the classes at Saint Philips, and some of the teachers are great, all except the catechism class." *Mom, please don't be angry with me. I must tell you the truth, at least this truth. I'm in for a penny; in for a pound.*

"That's because a kid in that class, whom I liked and thought wanted to be my friend, asked if I would let him suck my cock when he saw it as we were using the restroom urinals side by side after school. He said he'd never seen one as big as mine. I refused. He tried to pay me to let him suck it. When I refused again, he said that he would tell his parents that the little 'welfare' Nigger in his class propositioned him. His family is rich, with powerful positions in the diocese, and would get me expelled."

"Did anything happen then or later?" said Ines, holding her instant fury in check, despite her darkening mood, in order to hear her son out.

"No, Mom, I avoid him. I moved to another desk in the class, even cut the class sometimes, because I don't want to be there."

The dam had been breached; nothing could abate the flow of long-held recriminations and revelations that poured forth from Granville. Ines relaxed into listening mode, intent on letting him say what needed to be shared in his own way and time, no interruptions nor questions need be asked. She would hear it all, the good, the bad, and especially the ugly.

"I don't want to be a priest anymore. I didn't like the seminary. It just didn't feel right . . . so dank, dark, and depressing." Granville continued in his confessions, in much the same tone he spoke in confessional every second Saturday, after choir practice.

"A life in a world of constant prayer and supplication to God seemed tiresome and boring. It just didn't feel like it was a part of the real world.

"Sure, there were activities and even athletic games to participate in. The focus, however, was on loving Christ and through him God the Father, with the help of the Holy Spirit.

"I'm having real trouble believing in any of it anymore. I spoke with the counsellor at school a couple of times, and his advice was, 'God is everywhere and in everything. Follow your heart and obey your conscience and do the right thing in all things.'

"'Jesus will be there. He will understand and he will love you for it. If for some reason you have a problem or make a mistake, the Holy Spirit will be there, through prayer, to help you find your way.'

"'If you really feel that the priesthood is no longer for you, it's best that you find your way through other pursuits.'"

"All of that is well and good, but you realize that Saint Philips is a much better academic school, normally would be very expensive to attend. You have an academic scholarship in order to attend. That has been very fortunate for us," said Ines.

"I know that Mom, and I appreciate it. Still, John Marshall also has an honours class that I'm sure I would qualify for. The school also has a wrestling team that I would like to join . . ."

"A wrestling team! Before I speak to that, I have a question. Other than the boy who propositioned, then threatened you with lies and expulsion, does any of this have to do with Molliah? Is it because of your new girlfriend that you want to leave the all-boys school?"

"Yes, and no. Molliah does not attend John Marshall. She goes to George Westinghouse College Prep on 3223 West Franklin Boulevard. So, no, it isn't to be there with her. Though, yes, if I could transfer to her school I would; unfortunately, it's in a different district.

"I am not comfortable with being in an all-boys school any longer. Sure, I kinda know a couple of the boys, but I don't have any friends at Saint Philips.

"All my real friends have been girls, except for 'Daredevil' Craig. I am most comfortable with girls, as friends. Like the university students I met. Like you, or my sister Laura, or Carmen, Astra, or even Molly."

"Those girls were girlfriends, Gran," retorted Ines.

"Carmen's a friend. It's also true that both Astra and Molly were my friends first, before they became my girlfriends. I want to go to a school with girls. I want to have that energy in my life all the time, like I do at home. You are my mom, the centre of my universe, you are also my best friend."

Son, you absolutely do know your way around women, thought Ines. *I've taught you too well. And, perhaps, created a beautiful monster, if you ever decided to turn your considerable charm offensive against some unfortunate female. If you ever chose to be a user of women, you would be fearsome and frightful, yet beautiful to behold.*

"Mom, I just don't want to feel like I am being prepped for a life without women."

As if that were entirely possible, son. You couldn't live a life without women. They wouldn't let you. Women will be your blessing and, probably, sooner or later, your downfall. There'll be hard lessons to learn; fortunately, you've always been a quick study. She was seeing her lovechild in a light never realized; the unbridled power of his blossoming manhood stood before her, persuading, pleading for her blessing, for this new direction from which there would be no return, yet a path he was destined to walk to an uncertain future.

"So, you are absolutely sure about this? It's something that can't be undone."

"I'm sure, Mom. I wouldn't have brought it to you if I weren't. I know the risks, the danger of attending the same school as the assholes I've been fighting for years. Yes, I'm jumping from the frying pan into the fire. Still, it's the only way I can be in an honours program and on the wrestling team."

"Right, the wrestling team. Think you'll be good at it?"

"Well, I'm quick, and I've had a lot of experience fighting. It would be great to learn how to wrestle. It will make me stronger, which will make me a better fighter, like it did after training with Craig, to deal with the assholes."

"Okay, we'll make the change in the fall."

"Thanks, Mom, you're the bestest mom ever. I love you!"

"Just don't make me regret this decision. I expect your grades to remain in the A/B range, understood? No grades, no wrestling team," said Ines, in her strictest no-nonsense, no-exceptions tone.

"Deal!"

CHAPTER SIX:
Meat on the Hoof

· · · · ·

JOHN MARSHALL HIGH School, a public institution, dwarfed Saint Philips BHS, its private Catholic counterpart. The building covered an entire square city block. Four stories, red brick alternating with huge concrete bulwarks towering up from pavement to sky-scratching industrial roof line, framing two sets of side-by-side double doors between each pair. On each level, the floor-to-ceiling concrete window frames held small-frame inset frosted glass plates that were covered with a heavy chain link mesh, creating, for some, an industrial facade that spoke of some mass production manufacturing plant, rather than a school built to shape young minds, hearts, and spirits.

Education was an incidental by-product that, when successful, was accomplished despite its environment, not as a result of it. JM, as it was fondly, sarcastically thought of by the students unfortunate enough to be incarcerated within its walls, was also referred to as "the cellblock," an acknowledgement of the prison-like appearance of the place.

The sidewalk frontage of the building was as wide as the street thoroughfare that adjoined it. The space provided a gathering area for students, those in-class and not, non-students, drop-outs, gangbangers, and other ascenders that hung out for purposes of their own that had nothing to do with the education of themselves or others.

It was a gauntlet of distraction and intimidation that confronted Granville on his first day and every day thereafter while he attended John Marshall. He was soon recognized by the resident gangsters that smiled with an ironic gleam bright in their eyes, knowing that now their nemesis was in attendance in their house.

No need for the wolves to hunt far and wide for their preferred prey, who continued to reside at the top of their most-wanted list; he had made the foolhardy mistake of moving into their lair. "Heads up, Niggas, meat on the hoof has just arrived . . ."

Inside John Marshall, the dark-walled halls were wide though well-lit by large florescent light-rows on the ceiling high above, as were the stairwells leading to each floor. The halls were lined with row upon row of student lockers sandwiched between numbered classroom access doors, each with partially frosted glass panes with view-plates for limited viewing without being seen by those within.

Teachers and administrators used the view-plates to check on the students within, in passing, for the maintenance of order.

The classrooms were generally well-lit as well by a combination of fluorescent lighting and sunlight filtering through the thick floor-to-ceiling windows, though the dirty glass tended to soften the sunrays' effect within the room.

Each classroom held approximately thirty desks and students. The exception being the art classrooms that held approximately twenty-five individual desks and several long worktables that doubled as project work areas and some storage.

The student presence that stood out to Granville was the girls. There were girls of all sizes, shapes, and colours of Blackness, as well as Latinas and Asians. They seemed to vastly outnumber the boys in each class.

He was to learn quickly that it was due mostly to the fact that boys tended to drop out more often, more readily, and much earlier than the girls. Thus, they sometimes would be moving to attend the "street school," along with the boys that regularly cut classes, which was held on the pavement in front of JM's main entrance.

The "street school" was not supported by JM's administration, other than a lone teacher's aide that drew main entrance monitor duty each day during morning, lunch period, and dismissal, and a police patrol car that slowly drove by the scene once a day, usually at lunch, but the students' daily gathering was not formerly discouraged either.

The hands-off unwritten policy had evolved out of a recognition of the power of the assembled gang members and their ability to exacerbate the sometimes-tenuous relationship between the administration and its students. A tacit policy of confrontational avoidance was firmly in place.

The police patrol, or "pig-mobile," as it was called by the gangbangers, was an annoyance that was easily ignored, as was the ME monitor.

So, between the chronic absenteeism and the drop-out rate among boys, the preponderance of girls populating the various classrooms, filling the desks, was very evident.

The initial impact upon Granville, of the preponderance of young women and girls swarming in his academic universe, was virtually euphoric, like entering a vibrant, verdant oasis after crossing a desolate wasteland bereft of feminine sexuality.

His honours class homeroom was particularly interesting, smaller than all the others, just twenty-two registered students. He was one of seven boys.

The homeroom teacher, Ms. Haghuana Houston, was a visually striking Somalian woman, with a six-foot, five-inch majestic stature; coal black skin of burnished silk; large, bright, almond-shaped, sky-blue cat eyes that seemed to pierce the surface to peer deep within your most inner sense of self briefly.

Granville found her presence to be intriguing, having long since become comfortable with his deep sight, his ability to look deep within others to see the true self hidden within, even cloaked, perhaps from the person's awareness of him or herself.

Yet, he found the teacher's gaze to be somewhat unnerving, to be on the receiving end of her apparent casual examination of his inner self. She gazed deeply without judgement or malice, more to simply observe, to get to know others. It was her visual shorthand approach toward establishing clarity in relationships.

It was school protocol to report to the homeroom for dismissal at the end of the school day to be acknowledged as still present, and accounted for, having attended all classes throughout the day. A protocol meant to counter the high rate of absenteeism.

The teacher would check everyone against the daily attendance report that had been faxed to her. All absentees were noted in her daily report to the vice principal after dismissal.

As the dismissal bell rang, reverberating through the halls and stairwells, the human flood that emerged from every door merged and flowed helter-skelter to the lockers and down the stairs. A thousand voices filling every nook and cranny, accented by the bang-clang of as many lockers opening and closing in a near thunderous rolling-rumble unison.

The "street school" kids tended to mix and mingle with the teenage tidal rush, flowing from the exits and dispersing in all directions. All were quick to intertwine with their friends and cohorts as they tumbled out of every door to the sweet air of freedom sans school restraint.

Clouds of cigarette smoke would rise from the throng, filling young, long-denied-habit-ridden lungs. Time to be cool for all to see. The occasional fight would break out, sparked by insidious rumours rife throughout the confined environs entanglement of the "factory" school day.

Granville had developed a purposeful pattern of nonchalantly dallying at his desk. He would go through his notebook for each subject, carefully assessing his homework assignments; reviewing any test results or instructor comments, criticism, or evaluations that he should be aware of to address at the next opportunity; checking to see if there was anything he might need in the library for any project or reading material; and, finally, observing the writhing throng of teenage student bodies below the homeroom's big windows overlooking the school's main entrance, paying close attention to the location of small knots of gathered gangsters before exiting the homeroom on his way to his locker.

Granville, seldom deferring from his dismissal bell stratagem, which included ignoring his other classmates as they quickly left the room and subsequently emptied the hall, preferred to wait out the rush-crush commotion and then to leave at his leisure in the deafening quiet. The added perk of his regimen was avoiding the gangbangers, usually gathered at the main entrance, who were always hoping for a bit of sport, boredom avoidance, at his expense.

Ms. "Double H," as her students had anointed her in her absence, had noticed her new student's avoidance pattern and was somewhat curious as to the cause. She also had noted how quiet he generally was in class.

All the others had been in her homeroom since freshman year and shared a boisterous casual familiarity. Being insightful, as was her habit, she knew her girls and boys well.

Now, being the start of their junior year, this transfer student from Saint Philips was the first she had ever heard of, particularly a Black student, who had held an academic scholarship. He was a different breed, to be sure; just how different was left to be seen. Her curiosity about the lad was very much piqued; she was determined to find out.

"Granville, how are you feeling about your new school?" An opening inquiry, with her deep sight in crystalline, though somewhat veiled, consanguinity to her young charge.

"Ms. Houston, I pretty-much like it." Feeling relaxed in the beautiful teacher's presence, grateful for conversational interplay to pass the time as he waited for the coast to clear, Granville welcomed her interest in him to perhaps get to know her better.

"What do you like better than Saint Philips?" Sensing his openness and obvious intelligence, which reminded her of her students in her home country, which highly valued education, formal as well as informal, and were always eager for more opportunities to increase their educational wealth in knowledge gained, Haghuana decided now was as good a time as any to press for a deeper awareness of what mattered to him in the greater scheme of things.

"That's easy: girls, and a chance to join the wrestling team."

"Ha, ha, ha, there's plenty of those in John Marshall. I know you did transfer from an all-boys school. So, I imagine that it's quite a change, being immersed in such a predominantly female population. You seem to handle being surrounded by all this eye candy quite well."

"I don't have many friends, never have. All but one of my friends are girls. I like having female energy around. I'm more comfortable around girls as classmates and friends than boys. My mother is my best friend.

"She says, 'Every girl is a growing woman, whom you'll respect just like you respect me.'"

"There aren't many boys your age that feel that way around girls. You have a relaxed maturity that helps the girls relax around you. They can be themselves. The girls certainly appreciate your presence in the class.

"You're quiet, not trying to impress them or flirt every chance you get. That calm attitude also makes you unique and equally attractive."

"I know, it's nice. I feel their energy. I like the attention, but I have a beautiful girlfriend; she attends George Westinghouse College Prep."

"An outstanding public high school, a true college preparatory institution. Saint Philips BHS is, by all accounts, an excellent school as well, with a high academic standard and excellent instructional reputation. Plus, you had an academic scholarship, which means you were one of their best and brightest. Do you find the quality of education at John Marshall equally challenging?"

"Honestly, yes and no. My mother taught me that the quality of education relies not so much on how the information is being taught, rather more on how you apply yourself with what you are being taught."

"The onus is on you to make the most of that information and how it enriches your life."

"There are some great teachers here. My history teacher is very good, makes the past important as to how it affects the present and future. 'If we don't learn from our mistakes, we are destined and doomed to repeat them.'

"Others are not so much. Still, the quality of work that I put into my assignments is strictly up to me to make the most of them, so, in that regard, I've made a determination to be self-taught to the absolute best of my ability."

"Mom derides me sometimes when I'm disturbing her sleep by burning the midnight oil working late on a class assignment or project, saying that every assignment or project doesn't have to be a masterpiece. I tell her that she created a masterpiece. How can I do less in the work I do, or things I create? She set the standard. All I can do is try to meet it."

"Whew, I like your mother very much already. You are a very lucky young man to have her kind of support at home."

"I know, she can be a hard taskmaster, but I love her for it."

"Well, she is turning out a wise young man, far beyond your years, and giving you an excellent start in life. I would love to meet her someday."

"Do you go to church?"

"Sometimes. Not as often as I should."

"She attends church almost every Sunday, Christ's Shepherd Southern Baptist Church, a storefront missionary church on the street level of our building at 3148 West Harrison St. Services are usually at ten a.m. We have brunch afterward at our place, and you'd be welcome to join us."

"Thank you, I'll keep that in mind."

"Sure, you're welcome. See you tomorrow."

Ms. Houston sat at her big desk in front of the window overlooking the school's main door and the 'street school' in full, seething bloom below. After a time, she could just make out a small, solitary figure exiting the school, pausing at the top of the wide staircase, walking down the steps to pause briefly once more, then walk straight ahead through the centre of the amassed student body. She marveled as the crowd of teens seemed to briefly clear a way, like Joshua parting the waters of the Red Sea in his path, as the boy slowly passed through the gathered throng. In his wake, all eyes watched him intently as activity unconsciously was stilled, only to resume in his trail, seemingly freed of his presence to go about their business once more.

The lone figure walked unhurriedly across the street, down the adjacent sidewalk, around the corner, out of sight, without a rearward glance.

Recognizing instinctively who that powerful, little-big man-child was, she reflected on her conversation with the young Mr. Andrea. Feeling that she probably had just witnessed the comet trail of a shooting star blazing a path across the sky toward a special kind of star birth, one based on service and benefit for all humankind, rather than on vacuous global popularity. She hoped to still be around to bear witness, if only to say, "I knew him when."

Part 1: The Gladiators

The Gladiators, John Marshall's wrestling team, met three times a week: Monday, Wednesday, and Friday. The basketball team of the same name met on Tuesday, Thursday, and Saturday. The alternating schedule was a result of having to share the same gym.

Several of the taller seniors were on both teams, thus benefitting by being at high level of fitness. As such, they set the training pace, level of difficulty, and challenge for the rest of the wrestling Gladiators.

Granville loved it. Wrestling was like partner-dancing on a gym mat. He was one of the smallest members on the team despite his age. Many of the freshmen were taller, more stout. Yet Granville was quick as greased lightning in a bottle. When slippery with sweat, he was almost impossible to hold on to, let alone pin down.

All this pleased the coaches enormously, as they were lacking some speed and developed muscle tone in his weight class. The tonal muscle in his lower body, developed through years of running from gangs, reinforced by natural age-related muscular development, gave the young Gladiator a competitive advantage, a force to be reckoned with.

Cardio development and enhancement were accomplished by running laps, lateral circuits to emphasize quick directional changes that were augmented by laps around the gym periphery.

Granville, in training, realized that his weakness was upper torso, lats, and arm and grip strength. To counter this important deficiency, he could be seen doing push-ups, pull-ups, chin-ups, plat suspensions, and resistance circuits whenever he was not active on the mat, paired in a practice match. The coaches were impressed with his work ethic.

Granville's heightened dedication to the training process was not to impress the coaches nor to improve his performance on the mat matches.

He was all about improving his physical arsenal and skill set in the expectation that at some point he would have to face the gangsters languishing on the doorstep of his school, waiting for the opportunity to attack.

This was an inevitability of the world he lived in; the wolves were always waiting just outside the door, hungry for the notoriety of taking him down. The Supreme Gangster remained a prime target for bragging rights.

The wrestling mat was a circular area in the centre of a room-sized, two-inch-thick padded gym mat. It was in some ways hallowed ground. It was the place where wrestlers proved themselves, to each other and to themselves.

John Marshall's team trained to develop the skill set for freestyle wrestling where, unlike the Greco-Roman style, a wrestler can use his/ her hands, legs, and feet to overcome and control an opponent. Tripping and tackling are allowed.

At the high school level, there are thirteen weight classes, starting at 103 pounds and going up to the heavy weight class of 275 pounds.

Granville, at sixteen years, weighed 120 pounds soaking wet. He was definitely a lightweight and far from the strongest member on the team.

Coach Sheer watched the work-out regimen of his newest varsity team member. He was doing his umpteenth set of push-ups augmented with chin-ups, while the others were enjoying the brief break in training to sit and chat while stretching.

The kid was small for his age, being a junior, yet showed promise in his quickness, work ethic and positive attitude.

Coach Sheer was true to his namesake, abrupt to the point of rudeness in his coaching style. Definitely not the warm and cuddly kumbaya type of leader. Still, there were no hidden agendas in Coach Sheer's make-up: what you saw was what you got.

The man was honest to a fault. His world was black or white, period. There were no grey areas, no misconceptions or misunderstandings. His commitment to his team was sacrosanct. He expected nothing less from his wrestlers. His word was law, which brooked no vacillation or noncooperation.

His Gladiators, the team named for the warrior slaves who fought and died in the Roman Colosseum of ancient times, performed with total dedication to the task at hand in the combat circle. The heartbeat mantra of every wrestler was, "Give all or go home."

"Granville."

"Yes, Coach?"

"I want you to work with Lionel on reversals. You can start with the side roll and switch. He knows how they work and is pretty good at them."

"Got it, Coach."

Lionel was nearly a head taller, though a year younger and in his sophomore year. He was solid, lithe, chiselled muscle and sinew, not an ounce of fat anywhere to be found on his body. Granville was impressed with the strength of his handshake; it hurt his hand without any seeming effort on Lionel's part. The lanky kid very much reminded Granville of his friend "Daredevil" Craig.

Craig had been a hard taskmaster, patient, yet tough when sparring.

He liked to spar almost full-out, progressively more intense and thus faster, as the bout continued to its maximum speed and tempo, then coast at that pace before full-tilt fight mode kicked into gear.

"Daredevil" used to say, "You may not remember or even see the move that bruised you, but you'll remember the bruise that move caused; eventually you'll discover and learn how to block or avoid it." Granville thought, *I see there'll be more bruises in my immediate future. I'm sure of it. Bring it on!*

Cool!

"Granville, I'll take the bottom position, you take the top," said Lionel, kneeling to all fours.

"You'll be kneeling behind me on one side with your left arm around my waist, holding my right arm with your right hand, just above the elbow, like this."

Granville could feel Lionel's well-developed biceps and triceps, both long-muscled, not bulky as you tended to feel on the bigger, more burly wrestlers. He had learned enough about wrestling and muscular dynamics to know that lean, long muscle indicated high reflex trigger speed, as was his secret weapon. He would have to be always on guard to defend against Lionel's serious speed.

"Yeah, that's right, perfect," said Lionel, aware that Granville was a quick study, and must be respected if he ever would have to face him in a match.

"Now let's go through just the roll. We'll go slow, step by step, and I'll talk you through it. Once we have it down, we'll move on to the switch as well. Ready?"

"Yeah."

"First, I lock your right knee in place by shifting my right knee to place my foreleg over your calf on that side; once there, I'll give it a little weight so you can feel the shift. Got it?"

The nearly imperceptible change in the wrestler's weight was very apparent to Granville, yet Lionel had barely visibly moved from his original position. *Very tricky indeed*, thought Granville.

"Yeah," said Granville, refocusing on the task and the opponent at hand.

"Now at the same time, I would grab your right wrist that's holding my elbow and lean into your right side, forcing you into a roll to that side with me."

"Right," said Granville, managing the weight shift and start of a slow roll.

"Your right knee is anchored to the mat by the weight of my body pressing on it," explained Lionel.

"Right." *Shit, I feel like my leg's sprouted roots in the mat*, thought Granville.

"In the roll, there are several options:

"One, I break your hold on my waist by turning counter clockwise into your body, so when your body hits the mat and you're on your back, we are face to face.

"Two, I switch to a perpendicular prone to your position, slipping my free arm, my left arm, under the back of your neck.

"Three, I spread both legs, wide as possible. My right leg wraps around your left leg to prevent bracing while my left leg is as wide as possible to support my base in a spread eagle. My body remains in that suspended position, transferring as much of my body weight onto your chest, thus countering your defensive arch, while my head lock prevents your rolling away.

"Four, from this position I can push, pull, or rock you to break the arch and hold your shoulder blades on the mat. That's the roll and switch."

"Right, I think I get it. Let me try a couple of times in slow-mo. Once I'm good with the sequence and timing, then up to speed without defence, then at speed with defence."

"That's not much practice in slow mo before doing it for real."

"I'm a quick study. If I fluff it, we can do it until I get it right."

"All right, you're on."

Granville and Lionel began with Granville on the bottom, and Lionel continued to direct and correct him from the top position. When Granville could go through the sequence without direction, they switched.

Then they exchanged starting positions after each had had a turn on the bottom. With each rotation, speed and defensive commitment was increased approaching full speed and full-out offence/defence until the entire strategic, and counter move, were being done for real.

It took ten rotations doing it for real before Granville successfully pinned Lionel on the mat for what would have been a three-point reversal.

The boys took a five-minute time-out to rest overheated muscles before moving on to the next stage in their practice regimen.

"Pretty good, boys. I want you to move on to takedowns. Lionel, will you show him the high-crotch takedown? Okay?"

"Sure thing, Coach." *This'll be interesting, and even a bit o' fun for the rookie,* thought Lionel, suppressing a chuckle low in his throat.

High crotch?" What the hell is that? thought Granville, his questioning expression clearly writ large, as he peered at the coach's retreating form, who was already focussed on another sparring match-up within the wrestling circle.

"Yeah. We call it the ball-buster; it's one of the reasons that crotch guards are standard protective equipment. Make sure your cup is in the right position. If it's not, it will be the last time you make that mistake."

"Sounds dangerous." Granville was not especially enthusiastic about what this movement might entail.

"Only for your ability to piss or get a hard-on without pain for the foreseeable future." *Don't sweat it, rookie. You'll live, albeit somewhat uncomfortably for a time*, thought Lionel.

"Fuck! Really?" *You've got to be kidding*, thought Granville, wincing in his blossoming unease.

"Real as your last wet dream." Lionel's off-coloured tease was a response to the obvious discomfort in Granville's body language. It was clear to Lionel that a nerve had been pricked. For an instant, he wondered, what was his teammate hiding? What was he afraid of?

"Okay, we go from standing. You grab the back of my neck with either hand. Using my hand on the same side, I grab the elbow of that arm and push it toward your chest to cock it, then, using it as a lever, I pull it out and away from my neck as I drop to my knee, putting my free arm between your legs.

"Being careful, in my haste, not to punch you in the balls or crunch your nuts with my shoulder in the process. It does happen sometimes. Thus, the inherent need for the cup and effective jewel protection.

"Before you can straighten your legs in a spread-eagle counter, I lock my hands together behind your knee or thigh. My head is to the outside of your body at this point.

"If you make the mistake of having your head on the inside, you wind up with my body stuck on the back of your neck, a very weak position with your head trapped in my crotch and all my weight suspended on your neck. No fun.

"Remember, head on the outside. I drive up to standing crouch position, crunching your balls on my shoulder and lifting you up with one leg trapped in my grip. With you off balance and in more than a little crotch pain (it's inevitable), I trip your standing leg for the takedown.

"If I do it right, I have enough control to place you on your back. If not, your side will do in a pinch, for the switch, and pin."

As before, the teammates, after briefly checking their cup-pieces, moved on to the takedown maneuver, again in rotation, each finding the sweet spot and balance point of the other.

From offence through defence, they worked their way to doing it for real.

This time, Lionel and Granville were even more evenly matched in speed and strength despite Lionel's slight advantage in size and a two-year age separation. Still, Granville was able to hold his own, literally.

Coach Sheer had watched the teammates competing and mentoring each other as they both honed their skills and was himself impressed with both young men. Strong, quick—lighting-quick—and very smart. No wasted motion or hesitation, no indecision or lack of confidence in their knowledge. Their mutual respect was evident. He realized that both were potential championship material and was pleased with their prospects.

Part 2: Doing It for Real . . .

Granville was nervous, more like scared shitless, "cat-on-a-hot-tin-roof-in-a-forest-fire" kind of petrified. The bleachers were full of John Marshall students come to see the first intra-squad meet. Granville spotted many of the Vice Lords in attendance; among them was Black Jesus, the Vice Lords' chief, and his deadly crew.

He had seen them in the "street school" most days, hanging out while cutting class. He knew how he performed in his match would be reported to the rest of the gang along with the reassessment of his reputation.

Though he hated his moniker and the rep that went with it, he was very aware that his rep as being a little badass was the only thing that gave the gangsters second thoughts about challenging him on the street.

He was matched with Lionel, his friend, teammate, and today his nemesis. They were well-matched, though Lionel had a year's worth of experience on the team in training and competitive meet experience. In the 132-pound weight class, he was also taller and stouter than Granville.

Coach Sheer tended to pair all the wrestlers with different categories, usually one or two weight classifications apart, as was the case between Granville and Lionel.

The difference between them presented a bit of a toss-up. Granville's only had a slight speed advantage due mostly to his smaller size and quick reflexes.

Granville faced Lionel as they circled the ring in a slow side slide, each bracing for the inevitable first move. The height disparity between the two made the difference; Granville had always felt his short stature was an advantage in that his centre of gravity was lower and closer to the ground.

He altered his trajectory slightly in the circle, which brought Lionel's legs in proximity for a double-leg takedown. Changing direction in the middle of his sidestep, Granville, who had been moving steadily to his right, slid his right foot in-between Lionel's feet as he was following Granville around the circle.

Once planting his foot firmly between his teammate's legs, Granville dropped to his knee on that lead leg, while locking both arms around Lionel's thigh. With his head on the outside, Granville then lifted the taller, heavier boy off his feet, suspending him briefly over his shoulders, onto his back, before dropping him back down to the mat for the takedown.

The move had been totally unexpected. Firstly, it was something seldom attempted by a wrestler of a smaller stature against a larger opponent, basically because of the size difference.

Secondly, Lionel had never taught Granville that move, and they had never used it in their drills or practice matchups.

Thirdly, Lionel knew that the boy was dangerously quick, but had no idea that Granville could be that strong. The move had caught Lionel flat-footed, and suddenly he was on his back, arching in a last-ditch defence against Granville's switch and press.

Granville had his head in a steel-vise headlock around the back of his neck that prevented him from rolling out of the near pen. Granville's spread-eagle stance had anchored the leg that he had used as his fulcrum for the takedown.

Every time Lionel arched or attempted to roll out, Granville broke his arch, pushing, pulling, shifting to prevent him from getting purchase or momentum.

Lionel, now approaching panic, could only marvel in wonder of where this kid's power had come from. How had he managed to keep this a secret? Had he not been going full-out in all those sessions that they were supposedly doing for real?

In near rage from frustration, he saw Coach Sheer call the match.

Granville had managed to pin his more experienced teammate. The rookie had beaten his mentor.

After Lionel and Granville shook hands and returned to the sideline with the rest of the team, who also shook both their hands in congratulations for a match well fought, Lionel raged, "Damn! What was that all about, Granville?"

Granville looked his friend in the eye and said simply, "I had to win. I didn't mean to embarrass you."

"Man, that's not my issue. I want to know how you learned that takedown. I never taught that to you. We never practiced it, and you timed it perfectly. Have you ever wrestled freestyle before?"

"A friend of mine, 'Daredevil' Craig Montrose, was a sea cadet advanced corps. In his training, he learned a lot of hand-to-hand fighting techniques. He taught me many of them so we could spar all the time.

"It was his practice. I was his sparring partner until his family moved back to California to be with his dad, who was a captain of a destroyer stationed in the South China Sea. I learned that takedown from him along with lots of other stuff.

"Why didn't you tell me?"

"You never asked."

"Right, you're a bundle of painful surprises. From now on, no more Mr. Nice Guy. You won't catch me off-guard again."

"We're still friends?"

"Hell yeah, but from now on, I'm going to whoop your ass every chance I get."

"Good luck with that, friend."

Granville's warrior's edge was no real surprise for Coach Sheer. He had done his homework—a little quiet investigation into the background of his newest recruit. He didn't have to scratch the surface too deeply to unearth the rumours about the boy.

He had been an honours student at Saint. Philips BHS, yet he was known as a gang fighter, a gangster without a gang, a Supreme Gangster, a target for every gangbanger for square blocks around. He had fought white and Black gangs to a standoff, and was now wanted dead or alive, preferably dead.

With all that going against him yet showing none of the easily recognized postering that usually went with that kind of rep, there had to be much more to him than what he was revealing in practice, even in the heated sessions of the full-out matchups.

He seemed to be holding something back, staying deep within himself, as if he was afraid of being found out and recognized for what he was, a no-holds-barred street warrior.

The boy could be deadly in a real fight. That level of contained violence was fearsome to behold. Lionel had just gotten a taste of it.

"Were you wrestling or fighting in there?"

"Wrestling, Coach, I was wrestling, I just didn't want to lose."

"Why? You've never worked that hard in practice."

"I couldn't afford to lose. I was being watched."

"I know; I know about your street rep. I want you to work that hard in every practice and even harder in your matches. I want you to push yourself and your teammates for all you're worth."

"Your teammates need to know what and who they're up against so they can trust you. Save the surprises for the other school's team. You understand? And Granville, great match! Keep it up!"

"Thanks, Coach, will do."

Part 3: Black Jesus's Revenge

Black Jesus had watched the match while sulking silently apart from the cheering, jeering students, in his seat high above the gym floor on the highest bleacher row with his tight crew. Underneath his heavy, hooded eyes, a sardonic smirk that passed for a smile; he also was not surprised at the outcome.

241

The sissified punk had always proven hard to kill. Black Jesus bore the proof in a metal pin inserted in his shattered right collar bone, an ache that always foretold rain or chill, to forever remind him how badly he wanted the little bitch dead, by his own hand.

Black Jesus had found that his hunger for revenge against the Supreme "Punk" Gangster, and the removal of the disgrace on his rep as the Vice Lords' undisputed leader, had been elusive.

Watching the remaining intra-squad meet gave him an idea that might serve a similar purpose of dealing with the little bastard by proxy.

He recognized the combatants in the heavyweight class. One of them was a slow-witted, fat, flunky ass-kisser that "Tank" Fraser would use now and again to spy on the rival Roman Saints at the skate rink and run errands as a "go-for."

There's more than one way to skin a cat or deal with this little bitch, thought Black Jesus, unconsciously licking his lips, like an over-fat cat eyeing an unsuspecting mouse just prior to pouncing.

After the meet, Black Jesus was waiting in the "street school" area outside John Marshall's main doors, surrounded by a gaggle of students, hanging out with his crew.

George Bellows was in a vile mood. Wrestling at 285 pounds and as the heavyweight on the team, he had lost his match to John Joseph, who tipped the scale at 190 pounds. JJ was an even match for George in height, though much more muscular in stature, quicker, and more skilled.

George was not particularly strong or fit, given his girth, relying on his size and weight to do most of his fighting, and the overpowering of his opponents. George was also lazy and mostly unmotivated. If he couldn't out-wrestle an opponent, he would eventually fall on him for the pin.

He liked to impress the girls with the fact that, being the only wrestler in his weight class on the team, he was guaranteed a match-up at every meet, with opponents often smaller and more vulnerable than he.

His courting and bragging to his latest potential girlfriend, sadly, had fallen far short of his guaranteed victory. "JJ's no way a match for me, sugar, I'll squash that little Nigga!" George had been pinned by JJ in two minutes flat of the first period. He was a very sore loser.

Black Jesus spotted "Big" George as he was quietly passing, head hanging down, looking rather small, which was quite a feat for someone of his size. "Big George! I missed your match. How did you do? Heard you really wasted JJ."

"It was a good match, I did okay."

"Look, George. I need you to do a favour for me . . ."

"Sure, BJ, what'd you have in mind?"

"You know that lil' punk that calls himself Supreme Gangster?"

"Yeah, why?"

"He's the lil' fucker that stole Astra from you, then there was the ladies' choice skate with Molliah at the rink; the one that she lied to you about, right?"

"Tank told you about all that?" George wasn't sure whether to be pleased or irritated that his private failures with both of those prima donnas had become common knowledge within the gang leadership.

He'd been bested for their affection by that lil' punk who now was working his way into an exalted position on the Gladiators. The fuckin' punk was no more a Gladiator than he was a Supreme Gangster. Yet there he was, Coach Sheer's latest pet prodigy. Coach watching over him, grooming him like he was going to be the next State Champion. If he ever got the chance, he'd snap the lil' bastard in half.

"Yeah, bro, we go way back, Tank and I; of course, he told me."

"Anyway, we all have a score to settle with that lil' high- 'n'-mighty Nigga. I think you're in a unique position to help, even take care of that problem for all of us."

"How so?" Hell yeah, BJ! Happy to oblige!"

"You're on the same team as him, work out with him three times a week including Fridays. Am I right?"

"Yeah. Well, what is it you want me to do?" *I can't kill the fucker!*

"Talk to the coach, suggest that you want to work on speed in your technique, given your loss to JJ, you need to improve in that area."

George bristled at the reminder of his most recent embarrassment in the Gladiators' circle, witnessed by John Marshall's entire student population, but kept quiet as to not antagonize the Vice Lords leader. This gang boss was not to be trifled with.

Black Jesus noticed the reaction and smirked inwardly, a bit of salt in the open wound tended to guarantee attention and submission without any real bother when dealing with over-blown chumps like "Blow-Hard" Bellows. "You have all the power that you need; that's not the issue. You would like to work with, what's his name?"

"Granville." To have to say the name galled George. Still, he held his silence, knowing better than to interrupt BJ. The boss brooked no rudeness from low-lifes.

"Granville, right, what a fucking sissy name," said Black Jesus, spitting, as if to clear his throat with the curse."

"They call him Supreme Gangster," said George, interrupting.

"I know what they fuckin' call him. I'm the only goddamn Supreme Gangster in this fuckin' 'hood. You best not fuckin' forget it!" snarled BJ.

"Right, boss!" George's instant reply, an inherent capitulation, was quick to acknowledge that he had blundered onto dangerous ground.

Black Jesus picked up where he had left off, as if George's interruption had never happened. "Cause he's so quick off the mark, like lightning in a bottle, I'm told. The two of you maybe could work on takedowns and reversals."

"Tell the coach that if you can get used to working with that kind of speed, your reflexes would improve. Plus, the kid would learn how to work with some real power and weight. Coach Sheer just might go for it."

"Then what?" The idea of cozying-up to the lil' bitch he wanted more than anything to kill sickened him.

"Work with the punk until the time is right and Coach Sheer is busy elsewhere, distracted, then 'accidentally' break him in two; take out his knees, at least, though a broken back would be nice.

"Probably won't have the opportunity right away. Take your time, be friendly. Let the wimp think he can trust you. Wait for the coach to see some improvement in your technique, your speed. Don't fake it. Has to look real, be convincing, then, and only then, fuck him up! Bad!"

"BJ, I'm at your service. I'm your man. When the time is right, I'll break the lil' bitch into even smaller pieces and throw him in the trash, where he belongs. Consider it done!"

Granville had been exposed, in the meet, as a true force to be reckoned with. He was under the gun to excel in every match and workout. He redoubled his efforts to build more muscle in the areas that were weak. Seldom did he rest during the short breaks in practice sessions.

He often thought of Craig's skill set, his friend's determination: to be bigger, faster, smarter, cleaner, more focused in every aspect of the task at hand, out-maneuvering, controlling, dominating his opponent whomever that may be. Craig had set a high bar in Granville's life that he was determined to surpass.

...

When Coach Sheer had suggested working with George Bellows, Granville didn't recognize him right away. Though, the following week, during a break in training, during a conversational discussion of the YMCA's recently closed roller rink, he did recognize George the DJ, the guy who worked in the office renting skates.

The memory only partially resolved the sense of uneasy familiarity that had plagued Granville since they had started working together.

"Now I remember you. I really liked your choice of music. Great songs, you never skated during the sessions. Though Astra, my skate partner, said you only skated after closing time. Said you had a choice pair of precisions; the most expensive skates she'd ever seen. Said you were as smooth as water over glass on them. She liked you."

The remark hit George like a lightning bolt, shaking his preconceived notions of Granville to the core. His memory of Astra's betrayal seemed trivial, suddenly false, somehow conceived by someone else, in another time and place.

"She liked me?" George's incredulity was an unstoppable force colliding with an immovable object, his fear and animosity toward all females, splintering in every direction.

Oblivious of the impact his revelation was having on his current sparring partner, Granville continued, "Yes, she did. She felt that you were hiding all the time, in your office; wished you would come out of your shell and be with the rest of us, just enjoying the skating. If you had, she probably would have skated with you too."

"You two skated together all the time," said George, fishing for the truth in murky waters.

"Yeah, we were good friends."

"Just friends?" George heard the boy's lie. Some thought him to be slow, perhaps stupid—not even, not ever!

"Yeah, I liked her a lot; we loved to skate together," replied Granville, briefly reflecting on how much deeper his feelings for Astra were and why.

"You miss her?" asked George, suspicious jealousy ballooning in his thoughts.

"Sometimes, yeah."

The death-like, bitter cold rage was suddenly there once more, like a well-worn and battered suit of armour, clinging to his heart, destroying in the bud all kindness, forgiveness, and empathy for his teammate.

Astra had chosen Granville, bonded with him, given her time and affection to him. Shown everyone that he was her preferred choice.

Astra had betrayed his affection. He couldn't punish her for her folly, her deception, her lies. He wanted more than anything to hurt her. Yet she was out of reach.

How dare Granville lay claim to her memory, inserting himself between him and her? Astra was his to love, to miss, to hunger for.

Granville had tainted her presence in his mind; for that, he had to pay.

George would exact his revenge for his loss upon Granville, even if it meant being kicked off the team. Grimly, he plotted for his chance to avenge his pain, to inflict his suffering upon this interloper.

George had been somewhat frustrated by Granville's quick trigger reflexes and general speed of response to George's reversals. For George, whose reflex speed had increased as a result of these practice matchups, it was still very much like trying to corral a greased eel that seemed almost boneless in his ability to contort his body to elude George's grasp.

Granville had handled himself well up to this point. Though, at times, he felt like he was having a full-on contact dance with a snorting Brahman bull. The potential for serious injury at the ham-hock hands of his sparring teammate was constantly evident and a dangerous threat that Granville never took lightly. George's power was his trump card in a loaded deck. In the close quarter struggle within the Gladiators' circle, speed and dexterity could be an elusive advantage until it wasn't.

...

This practice session was the final practice before the scheduled intra-district finals, a precursor to the state-wide National Federation of State High School Associations' (NFHS) sanctioned meet.

Once again, the gym's bleachers were filled with eager spectators.

Granville and George now faced each other across the Gladiators' circle in full gear, prepared to wrestle full-out.

George decided he would take control of this match from the start. He reached into the circle as he saw Granville give a head fake. His huge hand closed around the smaller boy's neck, pressing his head toward the mat. Granville stepped into the mat centre to spin out of the downward pressure, momentarily giving his back to George.

George expected this counter, a move that Granville had successfully used to avoid the hold in the past. This time, George was ready for him and caught Granville's waist before he could complete the spin.

Now holding him in a bear hug, George lifted the smaller opponent off the mat and began spinning clockwise, still holding Granville above the mat surface.

George dropped to one knee across Granville's left leg while throwing the boy to the same side. The crunching sound of Granville's left knee joint, trapped under George's downward pressure combined with the powerful sideward throw, echoed by Granville's shrill, agonized scream, filled and reverberated throughout the gym.

George, glancing up at the high bleacher perch, where he knew BJ was holding court while closely watching the proceedings, was very pleased to see the quick thumbs-up signal of a job well done. *Gotcha, lil' fuckin' bitch! Won't be skating with my Molliah any fuckin' time soon!*

Coach Sheer's eagle-eyed vision, following George's brief unwarranted refocus up into the crowd, also perceived the gangster's universal signal of approval, clear evidence that what had transpired in the match was not an accident. *Damn! How could I have missed that?*

High atop the bleachers on his usual perch among his ever-present crew, Black Jesus grinned, trying hard not to reveal the deep belly laugh that threatened to burst out at the sweet sound of his vengeance realized.

Hearing the resonating scream and cry bouncing from surface to surface around the sprawling gym was true music to his ears for Black Jesus. As he watched with tightly held glee, the coach rushed to the broken wrestler sprawling in a tight knot, and wrapped a bandage around the damaged knee, lower leg at an unnatural angle to the upper thigh.

Feeling no need to mask his gloat while moving amongst his crew, he crowed in his low guttural growl, "Good job, George, gym full of witnesses and no one can fault you for the 'accident' in the heat of the match. You just fell to your knee in the takedown. You took him down permanently.

"Couldn't have done it better myself. Still, a broken back or neck would have been icing on the cake."

Part 4: "Is It Just Lust All Dressed Up?"

Granville passed out from the shock of the searing pain, to awaken briefly in the ambulance. He couldn't see his leg that was elevated and pointing in the wrong direction below what should have been his knee. The next return to conscious reality greeted him in post-op reception ward.

He tried to see his leg that was suspended from a frame above his post-op gurney. He could not feel anything below his hip on that side.

Turning his head to the side, he saw the back of a nurse about three feet away, standing at a waist-high cabinet and countertop that extended the length of the side of the room from wall to wall. She was facing the large window that opened into an adjacent room behind a sliding glass partition.

Next to her was a doctor standing shoulder to shoulder with her. His hand was stroking and gently yet incessantly massaging her buttocks through her uniform. Moving from one cheek to the other, while slowly pressing her uniform skirt into the cleft between her buttocks as his hand passed over the deep, tight valley between her plump cheeks, causing her to slightly clench the invading appendages.

All the while, the nurse did not move away, try to avoid, or stop the hand. She seemed to slightly shift her weight from foot to foot to provide or restrict access by the clawing, fawning touch.

Granville felt very groggy and was not sure whether he was dreaming or perhaps fantasizing, until she spoke. "Please, Doctor, not now, not here! I'll be on my dinner break in a couple of hours. We can meet then, Paul, please. Paul, stop!" The hand froze in its invasive position, but did not withdraw, at the nurse's insistent tone.

The nurse stiffened as the doctor said in a very officious tone, "Fine, in my office. I'll be waiting. I'm the department head, my favourable employment recommendation will certainly assure your posting in the hospital post probation. Remember, any indiscretion on your part will not be tolerated. I strongly suggest that you be prompt," and left.

Drug-induced sleep claimed Granville once more and he never saw the nurse or Dr. Paul again during his remaining stay in Cook County General.

Granville did not reawaken until after nightfall. The room was midnight dark. The only light was provided by a small desk lamp that illuminated a Black nurse reading what looked like a magazine. Her pleasant, round features and dark chocolate complexion reminded him of Pilar, one of the nursing students he had met at their University of Illinois sorority house when he was shining shoes for extra spending money.

He couldn't be sure what was the focus of the nurse's attention

He was suddenly fully aware that he was very thirsty and needed to pee very badly. He tried to get her attention, only to discover that his voice was no more than the whisper of a bone-dry throat. Looking for a call bell, he managed to find it pinned to the underside of his pillow.

Pressing repeatedly seemed to get the woman's attention, though she did not respond right away. Perhaps delaying just long enough to finish the last paragraph of the article she was reading before answering the bell's call.

"Well, hello, sleepy head, nice of you to rejoin the living. Is there anything I can get you?" said the nurse in a deep, bell-like tone.

Again, Granville tried to speak without success, so he pantomimed: water, thirsty.

"Oh, you're thirsty, no problem. I can fix that."

She left briefly to return with a small pitcher of water and a plastic glass with a few ice cubes. The drink felt so good that he almost forgot his other pressing matter. When he could speak, he croaked a soft whisper, "I need to pee really bad. I can't move."

The nurse instinctively checked Granville's sheet at his crotch area, looking for the telltale urine stain, and saw a long protrusion outlined by the slightly elevated tentpole shape of the draped sheet.

She had to stifle the urge to draw back the sheet for a closer look.

Surprised and somewhat taken aback, she couldn't resist staring at the size of it on such a small boy.

Thankful for the low light and noticing that the boy was more interested in emptying the water glass than watching her expression, she replied, "Right, I'll get you a urinal. Be right back."

In the hallway, her mind began to race. *This, I've got to see. The question is, how? It can't be that long. What was his father, a horse?*

"Feel a little better?" she asked, in her best bedside manner, upon her return.

"Yeah, but I still need to go! But I can't move with my leg, it's immobilized." His anxiety was becoming more evident with the mounting urgency of each passing moment.

"Let's see what we can do about that." Her lighthearted, calm, professional clarity was certain to impart her confidence upon the boy, assuring him that he was in the best of hands.

"Okay."

The nurse, standing on the side of the bed opposite the injured knee, reached for the top of the sheet and pulled it down past the hem of Granville's hospital gown. "Open your thighs and pull your leg up so you can lift your bum enough for me to slip the bedpan into place."

"Sure, how's that?" Granville, thankful for his upper body strength, abdominal curled to lift his hips as high as possible before the pain bit hard, racing through both hips and up his lower back, pausing as a blazing knot nestled between his shoulder blades, causing him to freeze while holding his breath so as not to cry out.

"Good, now hold that position," encouraged the attractive young nurse.

So much easier said than done, thought Granville.

As soon as the urinal was in place, Granville lowered himself to the bedpan and guided his stiff, piss-hard penis into the urinal's mouth. With a long, soft sigh of release and relief— "Ahhh, sooo good"—the tension drained away from his demeanour and a big grin of gratitude spread across his beautiful, youthful countenance.

"Thank you, so very much."

"My pleasure." Granville had no idea how pleasurable it was for the nurse to have seen for herself the length and girth of the boy's taut erection. *Yep, your father must have been a horse, a real stallion. I think I would have envied your mother, and your girlfriend. Easy, girl, don't get ahead of yourself.*

"By the way, my name's Serene." Disaster averted, her demeanour became more cordial toward the young boy. She was struck by how the boy appeared, so much younger than the birthdate on his chart.

"Hi, Serene, I'm Granville."

"Yes, I know it's on your chart."

"Right, of course."

"How did you get injured? It must have been serious to have required reconstruction."

"Wrestling, at school; I'm on the varsity wrestling team, the Gladiators. I was working with George, the team's heavyweight, on takedowns to help him improve his reflex trigger speed. I made a mistake, and he got behind me in a bear hug, then spun around before dropping to the mat, his knee landing on mine as he threw me down sideways, tearing my knee joint."

"Ouch. I see . . ." *A wrestler? Only the last thing I would have expected to have befallen this handsome young man-child; a bicycle accident, perhaps a fall from a tall tree, falling down a flight of stairs playing chase games . . .*

Instead, you're a high school varsity team wrestler? My, my, what other interesting surprises might I find between your sheets?

"Do you know how long I'll be in here?"

"It was a spiral fracture. Apparently, the repair was a complicated job; I think you'll be here for some days for observation."

"Do you think my wrestling days are done?"

"Sadly, I believe so. That knee will take a long time to regain its strength and your flexibility will never be the same again. The added stress of wrestling is out of reach for you now. The knee will no longer support that level of intense athleticism. Eventually, though, you will be able to run and jump once more.

"All of that will take time, though, lots of time, hard work and above all patience. Your high school years will be primordial history; you will be older, wiser, indeed better for it."

Burning tears welled up in Granville's eyes unbidden, bitter, hot lava rivulets streamed down his cheeks for the sport he loved, forsaken. Quiet sobs shook his shoulders as he cried, a soul-deep pain much worse than the injury wracked his body in waves until he was silent.

Serene waited patiently at his bedside until the tears subsided, reaching out to hold his shoulder. "It's hard, damn hard, and hurts like hell when a dream dies; but you're strong, Granville, stronger than the accident that sent you here. I'm here for you and I'll do all I can to help you through this. Now, you should rest, try to get some sleep. That's the best thing you can do to start your healing. Would you like anything for pain, might help you relax into sleep?"

"Yes, please?"

"The doctor has prescribed a sleep aid and something for pain. Be right back," Serene abruptly spun on her heels, in the direction of the exit.

Granville watched her rolling hips as she hurried from his bedside into the lighted hall toward the nurses' station. He unconsciously gave similar attention to the soft bounce of her ample breasts as she approached his bedside.

"Here you go."

Serene waited for Granville to take the pills and wash them down. "You just close those big, beautiful baby-brown eyes and have some sweet dreams. I'm here if you need anything." She then bent down and kissed him softly on this forehead, then more fully on his trembling full lips, and in a whisper so soft it was felt more than heard, "I'm here for you, Granville."

"Gran, my family calls me Gran."

God, girl! I think I'm in love; or is it just plain lust all dressed up?

"Goodnight, Gran."

"Good morning, Gran! How's my young Gladiator doing today? Did you sleep well?"

"Yes, thanks for last night. I really appreciate all you did and said. Thank you for being there."

"You are so very welcome, big man. You are a very big man to me. I know grown men who couldn't deal with what you are going through without getting lost in their bitterness and self-pity. The courage that you have shown in the brief time we have known each other is some-thing that is so very special."

"Thank you, Serene. I like your name; I like what it means. Do people sometimes call you 'Serenity' as a nickname?"

"Sometimes. My family uses it to tease me when I'm not being very serene."

"Ha, ha, ha," Granville laughed, a deep, rolling belly chuckle, until he choked on his phlegm at the inner recesses of his throat. "I'll call you Serene, it's special, you seem like a tranquil person. It suits you. I promise not to call you Serenity if you don't call me Granny. I consider that nick-name an abuse. I'm not anybody's little ol' granny.

"Thank you. Gran. My shift will be ending soon. I would like to clean up your area before I go. You have been wearing your post-op finest since you arrived late to the ward. Let's get you cleaned up. Just in case your mother might be visiting you today."

"Mom, great!" The thought of his mother's imminent visit instantly lightened Granville's mood considerably. Though at the same time it troubled him, a feeling of having let her down. Laying here with a wrecked knee, his future in grave doubt as a result of doing something she didn't really approve of. *I've come a long way down a fool's road to wind up in this bed. Damn! I've really fucked myself this time.*

Serene brought towels and two washbasins and helped give Granville a sponge bath. She was careful to appear nonchalant as she sponged his injured leg up to and including his groin area and buttocks that he couldn't reach. The sight of his soft penis was not a disappointment.

Stay calm, girl, you're not sixteen any longer and it's nothing you haven't seen before. Well, maybe a bit more than the usual, is all. He's just a kid!

Granville seemed oblivious to her interest in him and, more importantly, comfortable with her intimate touch as she helped him out of his post-op gown and replaced it with a pajama top and bottoms that had buttons in the legs to facilitate access to his injury.

All the while her thoughts were engrossed in a deliberate yet delicate self-criticism. *He trusts me, no tension, no strange vibe whatsoever. Of course not. I'm a professional with seven years of advanced education. I'm his nurse, not a stalking lecher. Serene! Be present, be real! Do not blow it! Really?*

Honestly, truth be told, I'd love to do just that!

"There you go," said Serene, giving the folded corner edge of the top bedsheet a final, sharp, wrinkle-smoothing tug. Yet her self-reproach continued. *That-a-girl, job well done. No harm, no foul to his trust in me or in myself, disaster avoided.* "Feel better, Gran?"

"Oh, yeah, smell better too," said Gran in a relieved tone, with open admiration for the young nurse's deft touch and professional manner.

"True enough. Well, I'm off, it's time for the shift change. I'll see you again tonight."

"Cool! See you then, Serene."

"Till then, say hello to your mother for me."

Part 5: Truth Visits the Ward

Ines had been worried sick since she had left his side after the operation. Granville had been deep in his post-op drug-sleep while she waited in the reception area for news of his condition.

The thought of her beautiful boy-child surviving so many fights and various vicious attacks through the years, to be crippled by a wrestling accident at a school-sanctioned sporting event, seemed the ultimate tragically cruel irony. She had cried bitter, long pent-up tears of soul-deep frustrated regret: Would this have happened if she had kept him at Saint Philips? Why did she agree to his joining the Gladiators? What was the point if he might be disabled as a result of it?

Nonetheless, it had happened, and there was nothing more to do about what was the heartbreaking reality of it than to love him through this with every fibre of her being.

She had hardly slept since he had been admitted. Her parental guilt was the hardest cross to bear. It reverberated in her soul all the way back to the "revenge affair" with their next-door neighbour, his father, which had led to his birth, when things like this happened: falling off the high diving board, fighting the racial bigotry of "blockbusting" warfare, enduring the ever-present subsequent fear of the Black gangs' prey for sport, his beautiful visage being forever scarred in a gangster street fight on her very doorstep. She hungered to better protect her little warrior from the pitfalls of their life that felt like a quagmire quicksand pit amidst a vast minefield: slow life draining suffocation interspersed between deadly explosions.

Now, once again at his bedside, he seemed so peaceful and at ease, though his features would briefly contort into a pained expression, his whole body would stiffen, and a low moan would ripple through him in his fretful slumber before relaxing once more. Softly, in the deep hush of her presence, his eyes fluttered open.

"Morning, son."

His eyes! They looked so tired.

"Hi, Mom."

"How are you feeling? Much pain? You sleep okay?"

"Yeah, Mom, pain's not too bad. Slept." Suddenly the hushed sound of her son choking on his barely restrained, rage-born tears filled the room, which had become deathly quiet. After what seemed to be an eternity, through his bitter sadness, in a croaked voice no louder than an angry whisper, he cried, "This really sucks, Mom! I don't believe it was an accident. That bastard, George, knew what he was doing. He didn't have to throw me during that takedown. He was just pissed off because he couldn't beat me. I am way too fast for him."

"I know, son. You're probably right. He didn't have to hurt you. Still, there isn't any way to prove it; and we both know that if we do report him, he will claim it wasn't intentional. The coach shouldn't have paired you with a wrestler so much bigger and stronger than you in the first place."

"Yeah, Big George 'Bullshit' Bellows, the blowhard, definitely more brawn than brains."

"I talked with the principal and your homeroom teacher; they said not to worry about your assignments. I really like Ms. Houston, she seems to have taken a great interest in you, says that the entire classroom was at the meet cheering you on and send their regards."

"Yeah, I saw and heard 'em. It was cool having my own cheering section chanting, 'Go, Granville, go!' Maybe that's what pissed 'Bullshit' Bellows off. He fuckin' hates sharing the spotlight."

"Gran, your language," Ines reminded him in a tone so clear yet soft, overflowing with empathy for her fallen warrior.

"Sorry, Mom, I mean no disrespect. This situation's maddening!"

"Hello, Granville, Ms. Andrea."

All conversation ceased as Coach Sheer entered the small cubicle that passed for Granville's area on the ward. Neither knew how long he had been standing at the entrance to the larger room or if he had overheard the conversation about George Bellows. Ines secretly wished that he had.

"I just came by to see how you were and to let you know personally that I saw that takedown for what it was. Bellows tried to cover that throw after he dropped his knee on your leg, but I saw all of it. I have coached wrestlers from elementary through collegiate for twenty years, longer than I care to admit. I know a faked illegal takedown and throw when I see one.

"You were right, George denied it as well, from hell to high heaven that it was an accident and not intentional. I didn't buy any of it.

"Ms. Andrea, you were also correct that I shouldn't have paired Granville with him in terms of the weight and power difference. Also, if I had known of George's affiliation with a certain gangster, Black Jesus, I would have never had him on the team to begin with.

"That all came out in George's long tirade in my office, when he received the judgment of his suspensions.

"Apparently, Black Jesus put him up to it as a way of wreaking revenge upon you, Granville, for getting the best of Black Jesus in a gang fight, one on one. You also managed to steal George's supposed girlfriend."

"Astra. She was my skate partner at the YMCA, and a friend," said Granville, twinging at the pained memory of his lost love and their humiliation in the park.

"You're welcome back on the team as soon as you feel you're able. Bellows has been suspended from the team for the remainder of the school year and from school for four weeks. Evidently, he didn't appreciate that, and just quit school altogether.

"Granville, you certainly have a way of racking up some powerful enemies in the community," continued Coach Sheer.

"He has always been a lightning rod for trouble. I believe that path was set before he was born," Ines replied with a tired smile

"Never a dull moment?" inquired Sheer, a wry smile flicking across his expression.

"Ever since I was seven months pregnant with him, when his father died, he's been raising a fuss."

"Thank you, Coach. I really appreciate it," said Granville, somewhat surprised that he hadn't lost his place on the team, at least not just yet.

"Yes, thank you, Coach Sheer. I apologize for my remarks," said Ines, echoing her son's gratitude.

"Don't mention it; they were justified. I just don't run my teams that way, never have. You are very welcome.

"Granville, I'll be seeing you on the mat. Take your time, heal well. You have a bright future ahead of you in the Gladiators' circle when you're ready." *Son it doesn't look good, few come back from your injury. Still no point in pouring cold water on your hope for recovery. You're one hell of a fighter, a true Gladiator, we see how you do when push comes to shove. We'll see when it's time to cross that bridge over this troubled water.*

"Sure thing. Coach, I'll be there with bells on!" Granville's expression lit up the room with his beaming, glowing, toothy smile.

Quiet, hopeful tears glistened as they meandered their well-worn rivulets over Ines's full cheeks to cascade a waterfall, sprinkling the collar of her green-gold patterned silk blouse. Lost in a mother's heartfelt joy, she hardly noticed them as she kissed her son's forehead and admonished him to get some rest. "I must get to work; I'll come again tomorrow. I love you, son."

Then she followed Coach Sheer out the room while he held the door.

Nurse Serene, who had come into the ward to retrieve a misplaced chart from another patient who shared Granville's room, managed to pause, examining the chart long enough to overhear most of the conversation around Granville's bedside.

She was very pleased to hear some of the backstory behind Granville's "accident." *The boy's a lightning rod for trouble from before birth; no wonder he seems so different and interesting, worth getting to know him better*, she thought as she exited into the hall on her way to the nurses' station for the end-of-shift staff rotation meeting.

Molliah had sat in a chair near the nurses' station, waiting for Granville's mother and coach to finish their visit. Ward policy, limiting the number of visitors allowed on a post-op ward at one time, meant she had to wait her turn.

Her mother had dropped her off on the way to work and would be back to retrieve her during her lunch hour. In the meantime, she waited.

Eventually, the door opened, and the others walked out.

"Hello, Ms. Andrea, Coach Sheer."

"Hello, Molliah, how nice of you to come check on our wounded warrior."

"Happy to, ma'am. It's all over school about what happened to Gran. My mother dropped me off so I could visit while she was at work. She'll pick me up on her lunch break."

"How nice of her and thoughtful of you, to take time off to see how he's doing."

"Coach Sheer, will he be able to wrestle anymore?"

"He'll have to heal, and the knee will have to be rehabilitated, then we'll see. We want him on the team. It would be a great loss for him as well as for the team. He's a valued member, and we will do the best we can to support him in whatever happens from here."

"Thanks, Coach."

"Molliah, please give him a big kiss for me."

"I will Ms. Andrea."

Molliah watched them walk to the elevator. What could she say to Granville that would cheer him up? She walked to the doorway that had been traversed by Ms. Andrea and Coach Sheer, to see the boy she loved lying flat on his back, staring out the window beside his bed. As she approached, she could discern the tears tracing rivulets down his cheeks to pool on the pillow beneath his head.

"Well, if it isn't the life of the party. Hi, Gran," she said in cheerful a tone as she could manage.

Granville turned to face her, wiping his tears off his pajama sleeve, and smiled through them as she neared his bed.

Seeing him putting on a brave front nearly broke her heart. "Baby, I'm sorry to see you this way. I'm sure you—we—will get through this together. All will be well on the other side.

"I spoke with Coach Sheer and your mother as they left. She sent you this," she said. Bending down, she planted a big, full-lipped kiss on him, pressing her tongue through his mouth to meet his, intwined in a love dance that only young lovers could appreciate.

Parting slowly to see his lips and his eyes were smiling broadly, she heard him whisper, "I love you, Molly."

Her heart soared as tears of joy began a happy slide over and down both of her cheeks, "I love you, Gran." She'd found a truth shared between them that would enrich both their lives in the difficult times ahead.

Sitting on the edge of his bed, she shared Coach Sheer's news and the school gossip about his match. Granville was eager to hear all sides, and versions, some of which spanned the range from strange to hilarious. They laughed often and deeply throughout their time together.

When Molliah's mother arrived, she greeted Granville fondly, while reminding Molly that it was a school day and her "home-sick" day had to come to an end.

"Goodbye, Gran; if you're still here on the weekend we'll come and visit then."

"See you one way or another, Molly. Goodbye, Mrs. Stevenson."

"Good evening, Gran; how was your day?"

"Hi, Serene. It was a good day, had a great visit with Mom, Coach Sheer, my girlfriend Molliah, and her mother."

"Good news about the accident?"

"Yeah, George Bellows, the guy that injured me, was suspended for the rest of the year from the team and four weeks from school, so he decided to quit school altogether. Coach Sheer saw the illegal takedown and throw and knew that George did it on purpose. Black Jesus, the Vice Lords gang leader, put him up to it."

"Do you know this Black Jesus?"

"Yeah, I've fought his gangsters many times. I also fought him with his gang once and broke his collar bone."

"Do you have a gang?"

"No, but they've been hunting me for years."

"Why?"

"Cops labeled me a Supreme Gangster one night because my family was one of the first Black families in the neighbourhood. I fought the white gangs alone until they moved, then I refused to move, join, or die, defying the Black gangs formed from the Black families that moved in. I still fight all the gangsters for my right to be left alone. I have become the Supreme Gangster."

"So cute to be so tough."

"Goes with the territory."

"The territory being your own, what you're willing to defend, your freedom, your home."

"Exactly! Fighting gangs is not something I have ever wanted to do. My world has been more or less ruled by them, Black and white. They rule by fear."

"Aren't you afraid of them? There's so many and you're fighting alone."

"Actually, I'm scared shitless when I'm being chased, and before the fight starts. Once the battle is on, I'm calm. Determined not to let them destroy my life like they have for so many others. It's do or die, here and now, come hell or high water!"

Part 6: The Witching Hour

The witching hour. Granville rolled over onto his belly and hips to resettle in his sleep, as if his swelling cock had sought the warm caress of his belly and mattress, suddenly throbbed, becoming a being with a mind of its own. He groaned.

Molliah was naked, shimmering in a liquid nightgown of glistening sweat, her back swayed to the music. Her taut buttocks slid side-to-side over his engorged organ with sensual abandon. Cock trapped in the cleft of her half-moon globes of rhythmic loveliness, he pressed his head against her tailbone's pointed firmness, relishing the smouldering contact.

Granville's hips matched her sway while rocking forward, back, a slight up-thrust, enhancing the touch, stoking the enveloping heat. Molliah arched her back, pressing hard against his throbbing penis. Her head turned to his ear to nibble his lobe with a breathy moan.

Granville's left hand grasped her hip while the right hand cupped, caressed, and massaged the firm fullness of her right breast, occasionally tweaking her rock-hard nipple. Simultaneously his left hand would slide over her lower belly, dividing her pubic curls' topiary, seeking her moist, virginal apex and clitoris hidden within.

Rolling his feather-light fingertip touch over the ball in near-perfect unison with his long index finger's stroking deep within the folds of her vagina's recesses, accenting each rock-roll and thrust.

Granville's deep-throated purr was tiger-like in his growing urgency, a soul-deep hunger for ever more, wanting the fire to burn deeper and deeper forever.

The earth became molten beneath as they flowed, suspended above a river of white-hot churning lava, to pass through a frigid, icy waterfall roaring in their ears, bathing in steam-cloud thickness, yet soothing coolness warmth immersing, falling, tumbling through sky-blue light, sunset-red echoes in their eyes; soaring arms and legs entwined, pressed lips, breasts crushed upon chest, searing tongues searching the caverns of their mouths, flying, climbing higher still.

Granville startled awake to the piss-urge near breaking, a burning bladder warning; sheet already showing signs of slight leakage, sweat-soaked and clinging.

"Damn, fuck. where's that fucking call button?"

Midnight. Nurse Serene was reading her magazine. It had been a quiet night to this point, and she was somewhere between enjoying the peacefulness and boredom when Granville's help light dinged on at the nurses' station. She felt a soft sigh of release, both from the tedium and the relief that an opportunity to talk to the darling boy, which had filled her thoughts all evening, was upon her.

Thought he'd never call for his soon-to-be favourite nurse. Great, now I don't have to "accidentally" wake him for a little one-on-one. Serene, you're such a bad girl.

Quickly, silently, she approached his bedside. "Can I help you, Gran? Trouble sleeping, pain?"

"Yes, no. Urinal?"

A quick glance confirmed the urgency. She opened the bedside cabinet, retrieving the long-neck inclined jar, to place it between his thighs as he guided his swollen member into its mouth. She waited patiently as he relieved himself.

"These sheets need changing." Without waiting for a reply, she went to the bedding pantry in the centre of the ward and returned with two sheets, a light blanket, and a clean pair of pajama bottoms.

"Here you go. Let's get out of the damp bottoms, then we'll change your sheets while we're at it."

"Okay. I've made a bit of a mess, I'm afraid."

"Think nothing of it. I've seen and cleaned much worse."

"I guess you have."

Serene carefully stripped the pajama bottoms and rolled up the sheets on one half of the bed. After recovering that half, she removed the remaining sheets that Granville was lying on.

Once the cover sheet was spread, she smoothed the fresh sheets underneath him, then began sliding his pajamas underneath and over his legs and crotch. While working blind, under the cover sheet, smoothing the bunched cloth between his legs, she gently grasped his penis and pulled it aside.

Granville stiffened. Serene paused. Still holding his soft penis, she began gently, softly massage his post-wet-dream penis. Almost immediately, it began to swell and extend.

Watching his expression carefully, saying nothing, she continued to stimulate the growing, hardening cock. *Serene, what the hell are you doing? This is your job you're fucking with. Let it go! Shit! It's hot, so firm, so thick.*

Damn! I can't, have to feel it! Please? Oh, please be okay! So long! So hard!
"Are you . . .? Is this . . . okay?" *Please, forgive me if it isn't!*
"Yesss."

Fearful of his reaction, she rolled the top sheet down, revealing his fully erect penis. His cock looked like an extra appendage in relation to his body. His balls were large and even in this state of exaltation, did not particularly hug the base of his shaft very tightly. *Still lots more room to grow. Son, you are so well endowed. Indeed! How do you keep it all in your pants?*

Holding his penis firmly upright, Serene slowly began stroking up-'n'-down. No longer maintaining the pretense of massage, she began to masturbate the boy.

Fighting the urge to take it in her mouth, while maintaining the motion, she grasped the stem with both hands side-by-side leaving only the head above her double fist. *I wonder, could I get it all in? Oh well, in for a penny, in for a pound.* She lowered her head to the pulsing crown, and slowly let her mouth replace one hand, then the second before her gag reflex halted descent.

"Ahh, ahh, yesss, Serene!"

Serene's mouth filled with the salty, sticky fluid as Granville came in thick, pulsing globs of seminal fluid and sperm. She swallowed it all, the licked her full lips, before kissing him full on his open mouth. Her thick tongue caressing his, withdrawing only to catch her breath. *Glorious youth! Won't need a lunch break.*

"Gran, this has to be our little secret, okay?"

"Okay, I won't tell anyone. Thank you, Serene. I'm tired. Good night."

"Good night, Gran."

...

Nurse Serene's visits to Granville's bedside became a nightly occurrence during his remaining stay on the ward. Though she was less aggressive than in her initial violation of healthcare patient protocols, perhaps concerned about possible discovery. There was also the possibility that Granville might reject her inappropriate advances, which may have cooled her ardour somewhat.

Yet despite those concerns, her sensual touch, her demeanour, and the probing questions as to the nature of his sexual experience with girls his age implied that she was available for sexual gratification if he so desired.

Granville was racked with the conflicting desire for her continued sensual, sexual touch, and nagging guilt about that desire. The hunger for sex was seldom far from the surface of his thoughts.

Was it the need to prove to himself again and again that he wasn't gay after occasionally succumbing to his cousin DJ's incessant urging for sexual favours? "Come on, cous, ask Ines if you can come over to watch the game. We can have some fun. I'll make it worth your while . . ."

[[Author's Aside]]

Granville had discovered that even here in the hospital recovering from a life-changing injury, all relationships–casual, romantic, familiar, professional caregiver–could become sexualized.

The adults in his world, whom he depended upon for care and guidance, had obliterated the concept of personal boundaries, exemplified by appropriate behaviour.

Thus, any situation, any activity, at any time, could devolve into a sexual experience. Where was the line? Where was the defined expectation that did respect familiar roles, when familiar adults and others insisted on redefining life through the kaleidoscopic prism of opportunistic lust?

His pretty face, full lips, tight ass, big cock, were objects to be admired only so their use might be made available. His parts all meant more to those adults around him than he did as a person. He resented and sometimes despised them for it.

Yet, he could not, would not, deny his complicity. None of it made sense.

Part 7: "Going Home?"

"So, you're going home tomorrow." Bittersweet waves of relief to see him leave cascaded through—professional pride in his recovery, guilt-tinged regret about barriers breached, not regretting a moment of any of it, and her belief in the bond formed between them.

"Yeah, Serene, it's been a week. I'm feeling better and missing home, school, my friends." Granville felt uncomfortable in this awkward place, giddy nervous excitement, the new lust/love experience, while feeling the strange, stomach-churning uncertainty of where to go from here. *Now what!*

"Missing your girlfriend?" Serene felt the weight of what she was suggesting and its consequences, yet the desire to see him again became more important than the risk.

"Yeah, I haven't seen her since last weekend." His love, Molliah's smiling eyes flashed, sparked a hot, guilt-edged sense of betrayal now lurking behind his eyes. His smile hardened.

"After you leave, do you think you'll miss me?" *There, boy, need I say more?*

"Yes, I've only seen you here. You're not a part of my life at home." *Here it comes. Please, let this be well. I want this, and I'm scared shitless!"*

Maybe we can fix that." Staring deep into Granville's eyes, reading his response, watching the boy's expressions ripple-play across his youthful features, was like watching a beautiful blossom unfold. His rooted openness spoke of his confidence, and she liked what it said to her heart.

"What do you have in mind?" He smiled broadly at the invitation, becoming more curious, intrigued by the possibilities.

"Well, I could give you my home number; you could call when you want. Then we could arrange a time to get together." Heart thumping loud in her ears, her words seemed to bounce with the beat.

"I'll be on crutches for a while, and I don't have any way of getting around on my own."

"Where do you live?" *Honey, I'm not going to let a little thing like transport get in the way. This is logistics.*

"Harrison Street and Kedzie Avenue, next to the expressway."

"That's not more than twenty, thirty minutes from my place. I have an apartment in the Michigan Towers Condominiums down on the riverfront near the lake. I could pick you up, maybe have you over for lunch on my day off."

"Sounds like a plan, I'm good; I'd have to get Mom's permission, especially because of the injury. She would want to know where I'm going, and with whom."

"Tell her the truth: a friend you met in the hospital invited you over for lunch and a matinee movie."

"So we would be watching a movie at your place. What kind of movie?"

"I'll be honest with you, young man, there'll be erotic films, hot and juicy, like our time together is going to be. There will be the kind of movies your mother wouldn't approve of, and we'll be doing the kind of things your girlfriend wouldn't want to hear about. Are you interested?"

There it was; the familiar heat started in his loins and rose to his face. There was no subterfuge, no subtlety, just clarity and honesty. He admired her for it. He craved the experience and liked that this beautiful Black woman wanted him. He couldn't deny that he wanted her. "Yes, I'm interested."

"You've been with older women, haven't you?"

"Yes, I have, mostly within my family."

"Does your mother know about that?"

"No, she doesn't."

"So, you know how to keep a secret."

"Yeah, seems like my life is becoming filled with everyone's secrets."

"Would you like to share any with me?"

"No, it's something only I can deal with. I will say that sometimes I feel like having sex is the only thing that people want to do with me. Men, boys, women, girls, sooner or later, the offer of sex is there; so is the need to keep secrets."

"So, I'm just another woman lusting for your body. I apologize for my imposition."

"I'm sorry. I'm not complaining about you, Serene. I like you. You're funny and I want to have fun with you. You have been good to me, and I'm not talking about the sex. I just want to feel that you want to spend time with me, not just to have sex with me. Is that okay?"

"You're wise beyond your years. I have never had any man complain about the chance to have sex with me, period. Though, I have felt the way that you do, when I've been approached by men wanting to hit on me for a quickie or an affair; happens a lot within these halls, including the need to keep harmful secrets. So, I understand how you feel."

"Do you know a Dr. Paul?"

"You mean Dr. Paul Flensing. Why?"

"I don't know his last name, but when I woke in the post-op, he was trying to feel up the bum of the nurse. They were standing with their backs to me, and his hands were trying to pull up the hem of her uniform. I watched for a while before I fell back asleep."

"Yeah, that's Flensing, all right. He's a real horn dog when he's not being an asshole, or both. He thinks that every nurse in the fucking hospital is his to harass."

"So, can we still have that movie date, as friends?"

You're only seventeen, gifted in more ways than one, and beautiful; it's assumed that any boy your age would be more than grateful for the opportunity to have multiple sexual encounters, particularly with an older woman.

"Gran, I would be happy to spend some quality time with you, as friends. If anything more develops between us, that will be strictly by mutual consent, including any secrets," said Serene, happy to begin as friends. The boy's mature attitude reflected clearly how much his mother had taught him about the true path to a woman's mind, spirit, and heart. She was thoroughly impressed with the teenager and his mother.

"Great! It's a date."

"May I kiss a friend to seal the real deal?" asked Serene, reaching out to softly touch and stroke Granville's cheek, marvelling at his soft skin, then sliding her thumb along the fulness of his lips. Her lips replaced her thumb, gently pressing, then slightly opening to allow her tongue tip to flitter along the soft, moist valley between Granville's breathless, welcoming mounds, where tip to tip they said hello. *This is so good, more please!*

...

Part 8: "Great . . . It's a Date!"

Serene's condominium was on one of the uppermost floors, located in the east tower of the twin-towered Marina Towers, 300 North State Street. The circular towers were Chicago landmarks. An innovative solution to high-rise ingenuity: cozy interior kitchen in warm colours, utility area, river-stone tiled bath 'n' shower bathroom, bright white dining room, living room, private shaded bedroom, curved balcony with spectacular one hundred and eighty degree views of the Chicago skyline, Chicago River, and Lake Michigan.

Serene's condo was compact, stylish, multi-faceted, and very comfortable.

Granville made himself at ease as he carefully flopped into the centre of her deep-cushioned living room couch, facing the view, and was impressed as he savoured the image of the city from a brand-new perspective.

Feasting his eyes on the view, his world suddenly expanded. It was a brand-new city, a different place. In all the grim and grind that he knew too well, there was beauty in this metropolis on this brilliant, sun-drenched day.

The balcony was his favourite part of the apartment. Feeling the occasional brisk breeze was refreshing, and the air itself was devoid of the greasy, smoggy city street stench.

Sitting next to Serene in the living room, arms intertwined, he almost forgot the discomfort of his cast nestled into an adjoining large ottoman.

Serene felt his relaxed mood and appreciated his banter as they shared life stories. She enjoyed Granville's storytelling, his clarity of speech and the expressive way he talked with his hands. The boy was a wealth of information about so many varied topics. "I do believe there's an encyclopedia hidden somehow between those big ears."

Their movie date turned out to be just that. The romantic comedy, *Cinderfella with Jerry Lewis and Judith Anderson,* that they watched was perfect for the occasion.

They laughed their way throughout and shared deep, intense kisses at its conclusion.

Serene turned out to be a great cook and a gracious hostess. She was loving without being overly attentive, giving Granville space to be expressive toward her without expectation of more than he was willing give. Acutely aware of his comfort zone, she treated him the way she would've liked to be treated in a similar situation.

Granville's response was also affectionate. He found that he enjoyed her gentle touch, her unassuming presence. Their kisses were mutually warm and heartfelt. The last being goodbye as she dropped him at his doorstep, with a promise to meet again.

As she returned his farewell wave at his door, and drove away, she thought, *This is crazy! I am in love with this young boy; old woman, however this ends, you're definitely along for the ride. You know this to be true.*"

Climbing the steep flight of stairs to his apartment was a slow, arduous, oh-so-careful process with several stops, gripping the banister to re-establish his balance as he tottered on a step, nearly falling backwards.

To his relief, his wrestling reflexes and improved upper body strength were very evident. The necessary pauses became moments for reflection.

Really loved being with her, just being together, no sex, no secrets, so nice; true to her word, felt so good to be just a friend. Didn't betray Molly's trust. Don't have to lie to Mom if she asks.

Serene's hot, a fine woman, felt wonderful to be held and to hold her, true enough; maybe some time, we might go further. No rush, no need, nothing to prove; that's just fine by me.

Ines had watched that parting kiss. She saw Serene help her son from the rear seat of the car, probably seated there so he would have more room for his full-length leg cast and crutches.

The affection between them was obvious. They parted more like lovers than friends despite the age difference. That didn't bother her; she trusted her son and felt that every young boy would have his teenage crush, sooner or later. She knew he could handle himself.

The woman, she knew to be the nurse from the hospital who had attended him. Her interest in him also was not a surprise. Gran's innate attraction was palpable; women noticed, no matter their age.

She greeted him with a warm hug, a kiss on both of his smooth cheeks, sans questions, and his favourite dinner meal: hog maws, chitlins, corn on the cob, collard greens, and sweet cornbread.

CHAPTER SEVEN:
"Grit and Guts in the Big Village"

· · · · ·

SPRING BREAK HAD come and gone. The end of the school year was on the horizon. Granville's knee had recovered to the point that he could walk with a cane and a slowly disappearing limp. He attended all the wrestling competitions to support his team. Yet he had begun to accept that he would not be returning to the Gladiators' combat ring. The knee was just too sensitive to any lateral stress; his speed and flexibility had been lost.

Thus, the weakness was a constant source of vulnerability that prevented any real possibility of regaining his speed, strength, and dexterity.

"How's it feel, Granville?" asked Coach Sheer, after watching his recovering Gladiator go through his paces in a sparring match, against a freshman. The reduced trigger speed and tendency to favour the knee was obvious to the trained eye. It was going to be a long road back; still, the boy's experience, strategy, and gamesmanship made him a threat not to be taken lightly. "Stiff and clumsy, really slows me down. There's more discomfort than pain. When I move, I automatically shift to minimize any pressure on that side. I try to trust it, yet I instinctively move to compensate for the weakness.

"Take a break, boys. Cool down, do your warm-down stretch regimen," said Coach Sheer to all the assembled wrestlers, in his usual upbeat tone.

"Granville, I need to talk with you in my office."

The coach and prodigy walked to the coach's office adjacent to the gym's main entrance in silence. Granville sensed that this talk required privacy, and probably would be about his progress since he had returned to the Gladiator's circle. In his heart, he dreaded this talk.

"Granville, your participation with the Gladiator summer camp has been invaluable, especially with the new recruits that look up to you as a role model and mentor.

"There's no easy way to say this or to hear it. I think we're at an impasse with your recovery and retraining for the next season. I don't believe your knee will be able to stand up to competition next year without risking further injury."

"But Coach!" Granville's heart seemed to burst within his chest upon hearing the dreaded pronouncement. The acute pain filled his consciousness.

Coach Sheer, seeing Granville's pained expression, continued to explain the reasoning behind his inevitable decision. "It's good, true enough, and by the season's start-up it may be eighty percent to ninety percent, which is very good considering the nature of the injury and reconstruction. I, and the team, need you to be one hundred percent by the first intra-squad meet and beyond."

Granville, recognizing in Sheer's decisive tone that which rendered further discussion or objection pointless, was overwhelmed by the realization of a stolen dream and drowning in the bitter taste of hope's failure. He wept caustic, acrimonious tears of rage. "It's just not fuckin' fair, Coach!"

"No, it isn't and never will be. That's the truth of it, yet your welfare is more important and must take priority over personal ambition. You were one of our best wrestlers. I'm here for you. The team owes you a debt of gratitude."

Throughout Granville's attendance at John Marshall High School, Coach Sheer was always very supportive and remained a good friend and mentor on the staff.

Art class was the last period on Granville's school schedule four days a week. He liked that it gave him a respite from the more onerous subjects. He welcomed the opportunity to be creative. Thus, he applied himself wholeheartedly.

Though he recognized that many of his classmates considered it slack-off time. They were there in name only and paid little attention to instruction and less commitment to the process. Their work, if and when completed and submitted, was often far below par for their age and grade level.

Validera stood out in the crowd. Her unique personage was what struck Granville when he met her in art class. She seemed to be set apart from the general hubbub of the other classmates, who spent their time planning after-school hook-ups for most of the period.

Validera was dark-roast coffee-cream-coloured Black, and beautiful.

She wore her hair in a close-cropped, natural, almost boyish cut that framed the sharp-featured, ivory-white brilliance that was her smile. She smiled often, softening her visage with a disarming effect that prompted a return in kind. Her pleasant demeanour and calm assurance was contagious, putting everyone around her at ease. Clearly at home in a crowd, yet not defined by those around her, "groupthink" was not her way; independence exuded from her every pore.

Validera, like Granville, tended to work alone.

Mr. Vandross was a sculptor by craft and trade. He was a professional artist, and as such, pursued his passion unreservedly. He taught the same way, especially when creating sculptural art.

The teacher would introduce the latest project during the first fifteen minutes. After that, the students were free to organize and prepare whatever materials would be needed for the assignment.

His end of term projects were challenging and multidisciplinary in their planning, development, and completion.

This year's senior project was a combination of visual art and sculpture: sketch and paint the image or scene, then develop a two- or three-dimensional diorama of the scene with the painted image as the setting's backdrop.

The students were encouraged to work in pairs.

...

Granville began working on sketch of a scene depicting a T-rex and a Stegosaurus facing each other over a large nest of Stegosaurus eggs with flight of large leather-winged Pterodactyls overhead and an erupting volcano spewing lava in the background—thus combining in one setting his favourite historical reptilian species, which he had studied at length on his own and knew a great deal about.

Validera, seated across from him and watching his initial rough sketches take form, liked what she saw and thought, *That would be more interesting than drawing cars, houses, or street scenes, as most of the teams are doing.*

"Would you like to work together?" asked Validera.

He paused mid-stroke and looked up, meeting her bright hazel-green eyes. "Sure, what would you like to do?"

"Looks like you know a lot about the anatomy of dinosaurs. Still, I'd like to draw the background with the Pterodactyls. You could work on statues of the others."

"I was thinking that I would form them out of Silly Putty then cover with tissue dipped in glue and paint in the details. I have a three-dimensional see-through erupting cut-away volcano, attached to an ant farm board, that I built for a science fair in elementary school. It won a prize. We could incorporate it into the diorama as part of the backdrop and save a lot of time and effort."

"Great idea. We could build everything around it to scale. It will fit perfectly into my landscape painting."

"Right, the volcano is about two feet tall, so our diorama will be about thirty inches tall, including the sky."

"Sounds like a manageable height, say, two feet wide and sixteen inches deep, overall, so thirty by twenty-four by sixteen inches sound right to you . . .?"

"Perfect! It's going to be awesome."

"Validera, I've been meaning to ask you: It's an unusual name, what does it mean?"

"Well, roughly, it means grit and guts."

"Cool! I like that. Granville is French, it means big city."

"Nice! So, it's grit and guts in the big city."

"A winning combination, irresistible force meets immovable object."

"Something like that."

Granville looked upon Validera as a kindred spirit. A strong woman that could be a friend. She reminded him of Emma, of Astra, each girl was a friend, even best friend, that he had grown to love. Working with her, sharing their talents, sitting across from each other, it became obvious that their styles were similar and complementary.

She was quite impressed when he brought his volcano to class on the following Monday. He had spent the weekend refurbishing the ant farm chambers throughout that led from the base, draining and cleaning the queen's chamber that had been filled with dish soap, white vinegar, warm water, and food colouring; the channels that eventually reached the surface, where there were small exits for the ants, needed to be cleansed. In between the chambers, the space filled with multi-coloured strata sand to represent the layers of Earth's crust remained intact.

The drilled holes into the cone sides, through which the inserted clear plastic tubing connected to the chambers in the ant farm at different levels, were visible, though the clogged plastic tubing had been replaced.

"I'll refill the empty queen's chamber with the mixture. When I'm ready for the eruption, I'll add baking soda wrapped in tissue . . . voilà.

"The lava will erupt throughout the ant farm chambers, including the clear tubing leading to the sides of the volcano, not to mention the main opening in the cone's bowl at the top. Because it's part of an art project instead of science exhibit, the area strata won't be needing labelling and identification."

By the week's final sessions, Validera's painting of the detailed back-drop sketch was developing quite well. She had an excellent eye for appropriate setting. Granville's sculptures, using one of the volumes of encyclopedias that he brought from home as a guide, now also in paint mode, looked equally authentic.

"What do you think about the colour of the sky?"

"The erupting volcano would be spewing dark clouds of hydrogen sulfide gas, which would collect and react with the moisture in the atmosphere, creating acid rain and probably cumulonimbus cloud pillars that will also spark thunderstorms with lightning and thunder. Thus, it would be a very violent, storm-laden sky. Better add more reds, violets, and purples with just streaks of dark blue."

"Needs bit more cloud-to-cloud lightning strikes?"

"Yeah. What do you think of the T-Rex?"

"Body's good, head could be more distinct, coarse-coloured, more an extension of the dark reddish colouring of the neck blending into the lower jaw, toothier."

Their classmates, noticing the evident quality of their project, redoubled their efforts to enhance their own.

Mr. Vandross also took note when Validera and Granville asked to return to their art piece after school hours to apply finishing touches to the drying surfaces.

Their friendship had rapidly deepened during their collaboration. As they walked toward their respective lockers, Validera inquired, "Do you have a girlfriend?"

"Yeah, her name's Molliah. Why?"

"Oh, I'm just curious about the other girls in your life. Does she attend John Marshall? I would really like to meet this girl that you care so much for."

"No, George Westinghouse College Prep." He had wistful aspirations for life, far from the rigours of John Marshall, in a better place where being with his love would be an everyday occurrence.

"GW College Prep? So she's planning on post-secondary," said Validera, somewhat impressed.

"She's pretty smart and ambitious," replied Granville, pride in Molliah rich in his tone.

"How about you?" inquired Validera, not bothering to conceal her curiosity concerning Granville's fate and future.

"Once upon a time, I dreamed of being a pilot, which became unrealistic. An accident in a public community pool led to vision issues. Then, after Saint Philips, I had planned on training for the priesthood in the seminary, the Jesuits."

"That's a Catholic order, isn't?"

"Yeah, the priesthood order tasked with defending the faith. I've decided that celibacy couldn't be all they professed it to be. I wanted a life that included women in a more meaningful way. Now, I'm unsure of what's next in my life. I want to attend university. Though I haven't decided on a course of study. There's plenty of time to cross that bridge when I reach the need to decide."

"Pilot to priest, quite the span. Never met an aspiring priest before, let 'lone a Black priest. I've never met a boy so deeply immersed in a religion that he dreamed of devoting his life to worshipping God, shunning women, living outside normal society. I understand that it would be difficult figuring out where to go from there."

"Perhaps I'll be a writer, a poet, or an artist. I do love creating art, literary and visual. Poets create visual images in the mind using words, the best of both worlds. Then again, I'm from a musical family, so there's that option as well."

"Watching your work ethic, your attitude, I'd say that you're well on your way. My grandma used to say, 'If you like the music, get up and dance.' At first, I didn't know what she meant, so she explained that it meant be true to yourself, what you feel, what you believe, and live by it if that's what you want to do."

Feeling this easy with Granville, Validera was reminded again how hopeful she was that this relationship could somehow grow into more than simply classmates. Deep within, she could not deny her smouldering envy of the other girls in his life, especially his girlfriend, Molliah.

"I love to dance, but I don't get the opportunity very often, so I used to do my dancing on skates. That's how I met Molliah. She and Astra were my skate partners. They're best friends that I met at the YMCA before it closed. Astra was a skate guard when we became skate partners. After she stopped coming to the rink, Molliah and I became partners; now she's my girlfriend.

"Thanks for the compliment! Whatever I do, however I do it, I will create the means to escape this ghetto, one way or another."

"You don't like living around Black people?" Puzzlement framed her expression. His revelation cast her upon the rock and shale of an alien, perhaps hostile, terrain. Suddenly, she felt an unfamiliar lack of confidence, fearful to chance her fate; this guileless venture within his tainted, violent world seemingly devoid of light.

"Val, I fought the white bigots in this neighbourhood to make room for Black people to live here without harassment. Now, I'm hunted by the Black bigots. Our racially obsessed society is culturally cannibalistic. It's a pervasive, poisonous environment that destroys dreams while frustrating any hope of building and living a better life."

"Whew, I think I struck a nerve! You've given this a lot of thought."

"Yes, you did, an unbridled nerve; it's a worn-out train of thought. I've been riding it as long as I can remember. The world may be Black, white, brown, red, or yellow; racism all boils down to the same violent bigotry, just a different colour."

"I've never had the opportunity of living anywhere else. My world has always been Black. Sure, I deal with white people, like we all have. I've never lived among them, so Black on Black gang violence is the only 'cannibalistic culture' that has been a problem for others, not for me.

"The only harassment I've had to confront has been jealousy, envy, fear, stupidity, in overblown male egos, chased by fools vying for my attention. They come in all shapes, sizes, colours, and cultures."

"Have you ever heard of 'Bad-Ass Black Bitches'? They're an all-female gang on the South side. My cousin belongs to them. If you value your health, you wouldn't want to be crossing BBB's hood and wind up in the wrong place at the wrong time. They're trouble for all outsiders, for boys, especially young pretty boys, so you'd better watch your ass if you're ever in their 'hood."

"Is that what passes as a compliment?" quipped Granville, smirking.

"Takes one to know one. Mirror doesn't lie. Take a good look sometime, pretty boy." Teasing, looking Granville straight in the eyes, watching the play of his expression carefully for the false bravado, the know-it-all macho conceit, the desperate arrogance, an inability to appreciate a girl's joke, that she eventually found in other boys. Whom she had rejected as not being worthy of her time. Granville passed her litmus test, dud detector. It was clear why he had been found so interesting by others before her.

One thing, though: he really did like to talk about himself. Still, she thought he just might be worth keeping.

"That's what I mean; I'm tired of all the 'inbred' violence, the rationales, the excuses that support it. People need to find better things do with their time, rather than stalking and destroying strangers for 'trespassing' in a public area that belongs to everyone."

"Speaking of that, we should get out of here before the VP locks us in," said Validera, glancing at the big clock on the classroom wall.

"We better get going. Of course, we walk the same way. I'll walk with you till I pass my street," said Granville, enjoying their conversation and happy to continue growing their surprising friendship.

"Cool, partner," said Validera, sensing that there was something special developing between them. Knowing that Granville had a girlfriend, a smart, ambitious, probably beautiful girl whom he obviously cared deeply for, intrigued her. His assumed unavailability for romantic involvement only served to increase his inherent attractiveness. Though she felt he had no clue as to how much she had grown to want more than friendship with him. It was clear to her that he was different, a "good guy going places" and she envisioned going there with him.

The walk toward the expressway and across the bridge was quiet, unlike their sometimes-animated discussions in the classroom and hall that seemed safe and noncommittal. The shared public walk seemed more like couple time and a new experience outside their mutual comfort zone.

"You asked me earlier if I had a girlfriend, and I've told you much about her, about us, but you've never said whether or not you have a boyfriend." Needing to understand what she truly expected of him, feeling that there was something she was hiding. Sensing that he may have said more than he should.

"I'm not really interested . . ." Validera began.

"Is it having a boyfriend, or is it boys altogether, that holds no real interest for you?" interrupted Granville, finishing her thought with a question.

"Has it been that obvious? The jury's still out; perhaps the latter."

"Now, I'm curious. Let me know when you figure that one out. This is my corner. My building is just a few doors down, above the storefront church."

"Granville, I have a ways yet to go. Would your mom mind if I used your bathroom?"

"Sure, she's still at work and my brothers are probably watching TV at Uncle Prince and Aunt Leena's place in the back. I have a key, so I can let us in, it'll be no problem."

"Thanks, nature is definitely calling."

"Resistance is futile and will not be denied . . ." chimed in Granville.

Granville and Validera hurried to his door and up the stairs to his apartment, entering quickly, "Here you go, you can leave your books here."

"Thanks, I won't be long."

"No rush, you're not on the clock."

Granville decided to have his favourite quick treat, a cold glass of milk. He had just finished pouring a second glass for his impromptu house guest.

Upon hearing the door to the bathroom open and close, he turned, holding the chilled glass, to face a completely nude Validera. "I, uh—Val!"

Validera: five feet, six inches; broad back, powerful shoulders, above-wide lats; pert coffee-cup breasts, large areole nipples atop well-developed pecs; glistening abs clearly defined, tapering to her small waist; boyish hips, long well-muscled thighs and calves. A runner's physique, ultra-athletic from her head to her toes. An ambiguous beauty that lived somewhere between handsome girl and beautiful boy. She could be either or both depending on how she dressed. Now, before him, she was very much undressed. Granville was mesmerized.

"I thought now is as good a time as any to figure that out, the former or the latter." Her full lips smiled in a sultry come-hither look of daring certainty.

Granville was dumbfounded, in utter shock, seeing all of her there, open, waiting. His mouth refused to work. Her beauty was arresting, yet the situation was impossible.

Slowly, she approached. "Resistance is futile, and I will not be denied." Then she took the offered glass of fresh milk, taking a long drink as she watched his eyes devouring her sudden nakedness. Placing the glass on the table beside him, she stepped in close and kissed his slightly open mouth, her tongue tracing and stroking his.

Validera was correct, nature had been calling, resistance was futile, and she wasn't about to be denied.

Granville's bed was the sweat-soaked overheated setting that cradled Val's quest, the answer to her quandary, yet still not discounting girls. Yes, she liked boys, perhaps, certainly this boy in particular.

Gran and Val had barely consummated their lust-fest and said their farewells before Ines returned after work, tired and strained by having to fend off yet another attempted harassment involving her bigoted shift boss.

Part 1: "Superwoman Coming at Ya!"

The super was still trying desperately to make her "pay" at every opportunity for the last incident where, wielding her razor-sharp rock hammer, she had spurned his ham-hocked, disgusting attempt at sexual intimidation; thus embarrassing his over-inflated ego, pencil-dick, drug addicted, alcoholic groveling cowardice, which was witnessed by most of the evening crew.

The man's featureless hate of Ines had poisoned the workplace to the extent that some of the other men on her crew were completely engrossed in feeding his simmering rage to win brownie points in an obvious attempt to curry favour for future considerations; or cowed to silence for fear of reprisal if their opposition to the hate-mongering might make themselves a target as "Nigger-lovers."

...

"Hi, Mom, you worked some overtime?" *She's so tired.*

"Yes, Gran, there was another DOA on the afternoon shift. Damn! That crew of closet alcoholics and dopers are such a corrupt bunch of wasted humanity. Where are the boys?"

Once more, Ines had that feeling of running on empty. Needing to once more perform for the same bastard who was doing all he could to run her into the ground, because she wouldn't allow him to abuse her. Knowing he would fire her if he weren't so hungry for her body. What he couldn't have, he would dominate or destroy. Her destruction was imminent, and she knew it was only a matter of time before it'd be one or the other.

"They're still at Great-Uncle Prince's."

"Go fetch them, will you? I want to get our dinner on the go. I'll have to go back in later to supervise the revamp of a group of exec sleeper coaches, which means I'll be cleaning toilets, draining, and flushing sump tanks till dawn. Gran, you'll be on duty with your brothers. I'll tell Uncle Prince, so they'll be your backup, if needed."

"I should be back in time to make your breakfast. Thank God for Saturday, my day off, from this hell!"

Ines loaded her cart, double-checking its contents. She really hated to have to leave a job to retrieve a supply item that was accidentally left in her shed halfway across the yard, a terrible waste of her time and energy. She carefully wrapped her sump hose diagonally across her body and began the trek, pushing her cart across the yard toward the waiting VIP sleeper coaches.

The first two coaches were relatively clean; the third and last was used by a sports team and their fans. All the cars were filthy throughout. *Figures that the last would be the worst, what a bunch of shit this is. Did they really have to drink until they either threw up in the aisle or pissed in their seats or both? The toilets, could they have been so drunk and stoned that their shit somehow missed the bowl and graced the floor? Shitting in the sink? What the fuck is that about!*

Ines cleaned for three hours, grinding her way through the reeking filth. She swore that she would complain loud and long to Mr. D'trinaire about the condition of the coach, given there were areas of carpet, window drapes, and walls that were irrevocably damaged and would have to be refurbished with paint. Some carpeting would have to be replaced altogether.

Leaving the last of that horrid mess, Ines was a bit less attentive to her surroundings. Walking in an exhausted haze, she paid little attention to the cart's unexpected jostling, as if it had come upon some large bits of debris scattered on the walkway. She gave the heavy cart an extra shove meant to clear whatever was the obstacle. The cart bounced and jerked again, rolling free, and she stumbled on the slightly upturned edge of a large manhole cover. Her next unintended footfall landed, with her full weight and that of the cart's wheels, on the opposite side of the cover, tipping it partially open underneath her.

Ines, her work boots slipping on the wet, somewhat greasy surface, fell through the opening, banging her knees, hips, buttocks, and upper back on the top of the manhole cover as she passed.

The sump pump was bolted on the lower shelf of Ines's work cart. The over-large cart, and the sump hose wrapped around her upper torso with one end bolted to the pump's outlet valve, prevented Ines from falling completely through—thus, suspending her below the opening and above the train shop floor thirty feet beneath her dangling feet.

Desperately she clung to the extended sump hose, hanging from the cart's lower shelf through the uprights and the partially closed cover lid, now above her head.

The hard impact with the lid and abrupt jerk, as the free section of the coiled hose reached its limit, squeezed Ines's abdomen and lungs, inhibiting her breath. She managed to croak out a plea for help that expanded to a scream as breath returned. "HELP! HELP MEEEE!"

The trainyard rotunda is a very noisy environment. Idling locomotives periodically blowing steam, reverse warning bells of heavy equipment on the move, loud machines and men of all shapes and sizes adding to a cacophony of withering noise. Most men wore sound-dampening earmuffs to protect against the defining industrial racket.

Through all of it came this piercing, lifesaving, roaring scream for assistance. Ines's life and death hung by a thread. Most didn't hear it; and those that did, didn't recognize it for what it was.

Ines, with a slipping grip, holding up her bodyweight, heavy coveralls and boots plus the added weight of the fifteen-foot sump hose coil, knew that if she didn't do something to save herself, there'd be no saving to be done.

"FUCK! Now what?" *Check the cart, looks like it's well stuck, wedged in the opening too wide to come through. Test it, give a good jerk. Check the hose, still secure to the pump, bolted to the cart good. Check that cart, last time.*

Make like a monkey, shimmy, shimmy, down, down, hand over hand! "Shit!" *Hose's too short, too far to drop! Lord! Wings would be handy. Damn! Looks like the cavalry's arrived and getting organized.* "I . . . I got this!"

Carl the lug-jockey was just finishing his break in the pit under the rail tracks of Engine No. 9, tossing down his last gulp of espresso black coffee, laced with Johnny Walker Black, from his thermos. He had just moved the cup away from his upturned face when the first boot hit him square between his eyes, nearly breaking his nose. He never saw it coming.

Big John the engineer was taking a long-awaited major crap inside the little screened off toilet cubicle and was peering down into the muck bucket to check the quality of his contribution, as was his habit, while he buckled his coveralls, when the second boot hit him square on his sweet-spot at the base of his skull. Lights out, he toppled headfirst into the muck and had to be hauled out. He got an unexpected extreme close-up view of all of it that he would never forget nor be allowed to live down. A legendary story to be embellished with each telling in the railyard.

The super had watched her approach the manhole cover. He had personally set the trap. It had taken just a bit of wedging in just the right place when she reported for the evening short shift. Having assigned everyone's schedules himself, it was easy to isolate her to that section of the yard.

He knew all too well that she would be pushing that fucking heavy cart. The last coach would be her worst by far and she would bust her balls to get it done in a reasonable time.

She would have to cross that manhole to get to her workstation before checking out. He smiled to himself when he witnessed his revenge take shape, figuring somebody would have to pick up her broken body and clean up the mess on the train shop floor below. Wouldn't be his problem or responsibility, just an unfortunate accident in the yard. *Shit happens! It also rolls downhill! And I just buried your uppity Black ass in it!*

His ears perked up at the sudden sound of silence. Its sudden onset was deafening to ears accustomed to the raging roar of the shop's mega-decibel assault.

Then he heard the cheering . . .

"Whoo! Whoo! Goddamn! I don't believe it! SHIT! She's gonna make it? That's one serious little bitch. What happened up there?"

Suddenly there was a tight knot of men gathered around the cart still wedged partially in the manhole. They were jostling each other to peer through a small opening around the skewed cover and cart. The super barked orders: "Clear a space! Anchor that cart! Open it up!" Peering into the opening, a ring of rail workers around him, he stared into fierce, fear-less eyes retreating away, yet never wavering.

From below, somebody heard her cries and took charge, shouting orders. "Hey, she's stuck! Short hose. Get those tarps; double up. Everybody, grab a corner or an edge! Pull it tight! Lift to shoulders! Get it level! OH! KAY! INES! We're ready when you are!"

Ines scrutinized the activity and organization forming beneath her— trust them with her life, or risk dying while trying? Which one? It'd have to be now or never!

"Take good look, fellas! Superwoman's coming at ya!"

The dumbfounded super had hurried over and cleared a space to see Ines releasing her grip on the hose, falling, facing upwards.

Seeing the look on that fat fucking hog-face was almost worth this, thought Ines, falling, mid-flight for the last fifteen or twenty feet above the tracks, into a folded heavy tarp held by a dozen men. Then to be hoisted onto the shoulders of two men and paraded around the yard like a hero to applause and cheers, while a couple of eager beavers broke off from the crowd to search for her boots.

Part 2: "I'm Pregnant . . ."

The knock on the door was soft, tenuous, as if the knocker was hoping not to be noticed or answered. Granville would not have heard it if he had not been passing by after having a pee. Nonetheless, he did answer the knock, which changed his life forever.

"Hello, Val, where have you been? I've missed you in class. I was afraid that you had dropped out."

"I know. I haven't dropped out, but it may be difficult to finish . . ."

"What's the problem?" Granville, suddenly regretting asking a question to which his intuition already knew the answer, listened calmly to his fate, redefined before his eyes

"I'm pregnant."

It was only then that Granville looked down toward her belly, expecting to see the evident protrusion. Seeing a slight though noticeable change, his gaze returned to her troubled expression. He felt a growing disquiet, desperation, a blooming, jagged knot forming in his gut. The acrid taste of fear filled his throat, constricting his breath in its choking gauntlet.

He had witnessed scenes like this encounter involving Levi and Laura, leading to their redirection and ultimate loss of freedom.

Their experience was now his to accept or deny. His heart flipped a coin, two sides of the same sad cry of obligation. A compulsion to an imposed duty laced with self-revulsion and regret, the reek of dying, decaying dreams and aspirations. What if the child was not his? Yet how could he prove otherwise, and who would listen or believe? Certainly not his mother. She knew this song and dance all too well: "*You fucked her; you marry her!*" A deep, quiet, dishonoured sigh concealed his surrender.

"Please come in. Mom is not home yet; but she should be arriving soon." *Welcome to my hell on earth, another dance, anyone? A sad, sad waltz through a minefield, blindfolded.*

"We need to talk."

"Of course, I don't need to ask the obvious question." *I need to hide . . .*

"No, you don't, thank you. I'll answer it anyway. It's been seven weeks." *Facing down my mad, furious, avenging harpy mother . . .*

286

"Yeah, I gathered that, otherwise you would not be here. You know, we got an A+ on our art project, Prehistoric Playground, Fight for Life. Mr. Vandross really liked the art as well as the title. He thought it was iconic, ironic and a very creative blending of media."

"Sounds like you and I, our blending of mediums, all right."

"Right, our grit and guts in the big city."

"Make that the big city inside my grit and guts." *Getting crowded . . .*

"Of course, we're playing with words only to avoid the elephant between us."

"Mom thinks, I may have twins." *Double dose of disaster . . . shit 'n' shinola!*

"Whew, that's a big elephant. This is really scary."

"Tell me about it. I'm terrified! I'm too young to be raising a child. I'm not ready for any of this." *And I'm damn sure not ready!*

"I was worried about you; now I'm worried about both of us."

"Are you going to help?" *To make 'em is to raise 'em . . .*

No more cues were necessary. Granville pulled her into his arms for a long, deep kiss, feeling the slightly increased swell of her breasts, their hips merging, sparked a memory, relighting the smouldering embers of a fire within his loins. Neither wished for the embrace to end.

"Yes, I will do all I can to help you through this."

"I'm going to have the babies, you're the father . . ."

"I know. I understand that's what you believe. I do have some doubt that I am the father. Still, I will support you."

"Are you calling me a liar?" *What the . . . fuck?*

"I mean that you may not know for certain, and I am the one you would like to be the father." *I'm no coward; it's too damn convenient. Parent trap?*

"I'm not lying!" shouted Validera, her anger becoming palpable between them.

"I didn't say you were. I repeat, I'll support you in this because there's no way to prove otherwise. Val, I like you very much, and I just may be responsible for this pregnancy. So, you know that graduation's only a few weeks away . . ."

"We've met with the principal and because of my high marks last term, I'll have to repeat my incompletes, all except art, where I got an A+ and excellent report, thanks to you on our final project. So, I'll be able to graduate from summer school."

"That's really good to hear, you'll graduate before your due date."

"Thankfully, yes. Hopefully my morning sickness will have subsided by the start of summer school."

"Last week I received my draft notice. I must report for registration and a physical to get my lottery number. I probably won't be drafted anytime soon. I still must register to prove that I am alive and physically, psychologically, intellectually fit, available for the draft when it comes."

"After that they could call you at any time."

"After graduation, depending on my number. True, I could be drafted before the twins come. The way the war is going, the military is clearing the streets of every able-bodied Black man that is not deaf, dumb, or blind. Not too choosey at all, when it comes to cannon fodder."

"So, we both have life-changing news."

"It seems to be the time in our lives when everything is changing fast and will continue to."

"This is what we've been preparing for all our lives."

"Ready or not, we are here."

"Where exactly is the 'here' that you two are 'ready or not' for?" demanded Ines, from the open doorway.

The surprise was palpable on the faces of Validera and Granville. The naked truth hung thick between them. Avoidance was not an option or an issue. The situation was not to be denied.

Ines needed no mere convivial greeting: a thinly veiled, failed attempt to dispel the tension between her son and his friend, to recognize that lightning had once more struck her family. *Oh, no Gran; not you!*

"Hi, Mom!" Granville heard the hoarse plea, saw his mom, icebound by the irony, the pain of his lost childhood, his unwanted adulthood forced upon her once more, yet could not respond.

"Hello, Ms. Andrea." Stubborn resolve cloaked in soft shame flickered across Validera's expression.

"Hello, Validera, good to finally meet you. I watched Granville's project with you take shape. It looked to be a very interesting mixed-media project. It had been a bonus seeing the science portrayed in an artistic and dynamic way, even being able to incorporate his award-winning science sculpture. The project deserved the excellent grade that it and both of you received."

Stay calm, you're the adult here. Damn it! Act like it, thought Ines.

Ines was standing just inside the doorway, carrying her work coat and lunchbox, and showing a dark purple bruise on her right temple. She moved across the room to the table with a noticeable limp. Pu down her belongings as if she was shrugging the weight of a lifetime off her shoulders. Looking desperately tired, she graced them both with a tired smile.

Granville could see something was very wrong with his mother, though instinctively, he would have peppered her with a dozen questions as to the cause of her state if they were alone. With Val's presence, he sensed it would be prudent to be patient. She would reveal all when she was ready, not before.

"Mom, would you like anything? I made some fresh lemonade earlier, it should be cold now."

"Yes, Gran, that would be great."

Granville quickly fetched three tall goblets out of the pantry and filled his mother's glass as well as one for Val and himself. Ines took a long, slow drink, nearly emptying the goblet. "Ahh, so very good. Thanks, son." She looked at her son and his friend with fresh eyes and decided to tell her tale. "Would you like to hear a story?"

"Sure, Mom."

"Yes, ma'am."

Ines emptied her glass and held it for Granville to refill, took another drink, cleared her throat, and began to regale them with the backstory of the day's incident at the railyard.

When she finished her elaborate retelling, complete with insightful gestures and comical facial expressions, both teenagers were stomach-churning grossed out and doubled over in fits of side-splitting laughter, in equal measure, at "Superwoman coming at ya!"

Ines gave them time to regain their teenage composure before she decided to quench her curiosity about Val's presence in her home. She had already noticed the fullness, as well as the girl's quiet discomfort. The physical signs were easy to discern to a mother's eye. She was awaiting confirmation, of perhaps her worst nightmare and fear, which might be sitting at her kitchen table smiling back at her.

"Val, Gran, who's going to tell me why we are having this special time together? Val, I like you. As I said before, I'm proud of the professional-quality artwork you and Gran have accomplished together. I believe you both have real talent, and knowing how to work well together is more than half the struggle on the road to becoming a success at any art.

"Still, I'm a mother and I know a pregnant girl when I see one. No offence intended. Could you tell me why you're here today?"

"Ms. Andrea, I'm sorry, but the truth is . . ."

"We made love here in my room before you came home from work," Granville blurted out, interrupting Validera, as if the need to express his role in their indiscretion and betrayal of his mother's trust overwhelmed his deep guilt.

"I'm pregnant."

"How far along are you?" she asked, ignoring her son's abrupt confession, while being aware that he said they "made love," not "had sex." *Evidently, they're not just friends.*

"About seven weeks."

"What does your mother say about it?"

"She's very unhappy and pissed off with both of us"

"So am I, and horridly disappointed with you, Gran!"

"I'm sorry, Mom, and disappointed in myself. I'm here for Val and the babies when they come."

"They? Babies?" *Oh, shit, shit! You gotta be kidding me! Breathe . . .*

"My mom thinks they'll be twins." *He's not the only one disappointed!*

"You kids have taken a giant step toward adulthood. As you were saying, 'ready or not,' parenthood is a lifetime commitment. Yes, you can continue your education, graduate, and with familiar support, perhaps go even further. Yet from this date, further care of this new life you both created is job one, period."

"Yes, ma'am."

"Gran, being there for Val will likely mean finding a job after graduation. University may still be a possibility for either of you with the help of student loans. From now on, the quality of your life will depend upon your planning and ability to follow through.

"Teenage parenting is likely to be hell on earth, mostly because everything you encounter is structured to ensure failure. Society generally is not kind to those starting this path at such a young age. Been there, done that.

"I will do what I can to help but even with that assistance, the burden is on your shoulders, not mine or your mother's, Val. When push comes to shove and you want out; feeling that you can't do it anymore, remember that your mothers have felt those same feelings of defeat and desperation. If we had quit, you wouldn't be here today, to listen to these words of wisdom. 'This, too, will pass, always,' will become your mantra, your saving grace."

Granville and Validera, reaching across the table to hold hands, looked at each other with reaffirming, hopeful expressions, while unconsciously recognizing the soul-deep fear of their mutual future that belied that silent promise.

The slamming of the hallway's back door and subsequent humble-bubble along the hall heralded the arrival of David and Joseph, returning from their game of street-ball hockey in the laneway behind the house with their friends.

"Hi, Mom." Twin voices spoke in unison.

"Hello, boys."

"Hi, Gran." Once again, twin chimes.

"Hi, Dave, Jo."

"Hi, hey, are you Val, from his art class?" Thrice, without forethought.

"Hello, David, Joseph. Yeah."

"Mom, we're going to watch some TV. *Amos and Andy,* okay?" Speaking in unison was often their tendency when speaking together.

They should have been twins. Two peas in a pod, like minds, think alike, especially like us, Val, where fools seldom differ, thought Granville.

Part 3: "What If . . .?"

"Mom, I've been thinking about the pregnancy. What if I'm not the father of Val's twins?"

"That is perhaps a distinct possibility, but then why would she tell such a lie, knowing what it would mean to your future and hers going forward?"

"That's what bothers me. What if she knew that she was likely pregnant by someone else at the time? What if she seduced a preferred partner to secure me in a 'parent trap' after deciding that I was better 'father material' for the babies? What if the true father, the one who got her pregnant before she met me, had refused to accept responsibility or support her?"

"Gran, are you just trying to dodge your responsibility?"

"Val and I had been working together on the project as classmates. There was never any romantic sexual energy or interest between us, none! Then she seduces me."

"You didn't initiate the sex?"

"No! When she asked to use our bathroom, I thought it was a perfectly appropriate request to make of a friend walking and talking on the way home. Then she came out naked and walked toward me to hug, kiss, and caress me in an intense embrace. I was blindsided, did not see that coming. I lost it, Mom! The next thing I knew, we were in my bed having sex."

"Perhaps you did not feel any desire for her sexually, doesn't mean she didn't feel that way toward you, and simply used the opportunity to fulfill her wish to have sex with you."

"Then shows up on our doorstep pregnant? The timing is just too convenient."

"Be that as it may, the proof of the pudding is growing in her belly. Now it's your responsibility to accept your role in all of this and do the right thing with her, for those babies. Gran, you now have a family of your own to care for. You don't have to marry her right away."

"I don't want to marry Val or anyone else."

"Your preferences mean little when compared to the needs of your unborn children. Once they arrive, all bets are off. Their needs are all that matter, and you had better be prepared to be there for them. In important matters such this, I taught you better than to dodge your responsibilities. Marrying her is the right thing to do."

"Like Levi and Laura did, right out of high school? When Levi, Joshua, and Man aren't arguing and fighting with Bea, Marcy, and Laura, they're out gambling, chasing, and bedding other women. Both Bea and Marcy have their own lovers, not their husbands. Laura's just growing old before her time, struggling alone under the burden of her kids, too young, too many, too soon. Marriage sucks, Mom!"

"Yes, marriage is not the issue. It's accepting your responsibility."

"Like you did, being married with two kids yet having an affair with my dad, a married man with kids? He was your neighbour living one house over from you, right behind your house on the other side of the alley. His back door practically faced yours. He truly was your 'backdoor man,' taking advantage of the easy access. Is that how you honoured your commitment, accepted your responsibility? I am your love-child, remember. I am the living proof of your betrayal, or was it revenge?

"Marriage meant no more to you than it does to them. Yet you want me to join that sad, angry existence; it's a ticket to misery and dishonesty, a life of lies. Doing the right thing is the wrong thing for me. No, ma'am! I will NOT do it! No matter what you say! No, Mom! NO FUCKING WAY!"

Suddenly, Granville was bounced off the kitchen wall he had been standing in front of and found himself sliding down that smooth wallpaper with a lit fire burning an acute pain within his sternum, where a deep, fist-shaped bruise was forming in the centre of his chest next to his heart.

The recollection of the pain and humiliation inflicted by "Tank" Fraser that mournful day at the park flashed through his consciousness, as he fought to regain his breath.

Looking up at his mother's eyes of rage glaring and blazing down at him, he was shocked at the horror of the realization that his beloved mother could be angry enough to strike him with her fist. Through the burning well of tears gathering in his blurred vision, he watched the rage fade to dismay at what she had done, then fear of whether he was badly hurt, and finally sorrow at how it all had come to this explosive conclusion.

Through salty rivulets sliding over each cheek, he saw her turn away just as her hard-held-tear-dam broke through walls of self-reproach to flow freely.

Ines sat hard in the kitchen table chair, loudly striking the tabletop with a closed fist, underscoring a quiet curse of exasperation, before collapsing in a tearful shudder that racked her entire body, partially stifling a bitter groan-growl through clenched teeth.

She had instinctively struck her Gran, her love-child, with intent to do bodily harm, regrettably aware that by reacting to Gran's tirade, she may have invariably scapegoated him for the recent workplace sabotage that she had barely survived. *Not bad for a Superwoman*, thought Ines, yet frustrated with the knowledge that the bastard super who had set the trap would never experience the justice he deserved.

Many years would pass before she would be able to forgive herself for that loss of temper and lapse of control.

After a time of quiet timelessness, Granville finally was able to move to his knees before using the tabletop and adjacent chair to pull himself to his feet, facing Ines, her elbows resting on the table, head cradled between her palms, an epitaph of stillness set in stone.

"Gran, you made a mistake. Levi, Laura, and I, we all made the same mistake, one way or another. It all happened on my watch. I am the one responsible, the buck stops with me. What you have said is only the truth of what has become the sad reality within our family. Blunt as a sledgehammer blow, its power to hurt cuts deep as only the bitter truth can.

"For all of it, I am truly sorry. Going forward, I will do all I can to make it up to you. Gran, understand this, I am your mother. You will never disrespect or curse me again!"

"Yes, ma'am. I'm sorry, Mom."

He sat across from her, his hand outstretched toward the meaning of life in his world, silently hoping for forgiveness and reconnection. Slowly, her soft, comforting touch met his across that gulf that only the love of a mother for her child could captivate, ensnare, and delight in an instant.

...

Part 4: "Serene . . . Please Be My Sanctuary?"

"Mom, I was wondering if it would be okay to visit Serene. She called while you were at work, and we talked for a while. Kinda like what we did before. You know, dinner and a movie." Granville had pondered how to approach his mother to request more time with yet another woman in his life, let alone an older woman as friend. He knew that her first question would be about to the purpose of the visit.

"Does that include sex?"

"Mom! Really, Mom!" He was not disappointed. His response was a challenge that he hoped would not be met with too much resistance.

"I trust you, Gran. I know the nurse is a mature woman and if you did have sex with her, I'm sure that she'd take precautions to not get pregnant or create any other issues as a result of whatever you did with her."

"Mom, I have no intention of having sex with Serene, though I know that she probably would like to make love. That may be what she has in mind."

"Exactly!" Ines interrupted. "She is a very attractive woman, Gran. She could have any man that she desired. Still, she calls you, a seventeen-year-old boy, wanting another date. Serene wants you, period. Who knows, she may have convinced herself that she is in love with you. You have that effect on women. For your own good and my peace of mind, it's time that you accept that is how you can affect people."

"Mom, I know some women seem to look at me as a sex object. I'm not, and I refuse to be treated that way. I like Serene, she's fun to be with. Besides, Molly is my girlfriend, and I'm not having sex with her."

"Please keep it that way. Molliah's a very different kettle of fish altogether, as you have discovered with Validera. Young girls aren't always careful or prepared."

"That's a lesson I'll be learning the rest of my life and paying for it," Granville acknowledged with bitter regret that would not be denied.

"Unfortunately, that's the bitter truth," Ines acquiesced, reflecting once more on her missteps.

"So, I can go?" He asked, needing her approval, yet keenly aware that he would obey her wishes if she chose to deny his request.

"Yes, Gran you can go; don't stay out too late." *Lord, son, please don't make me regret this decision.*

"Great, Mom, I won't be too late." Granville's infamous last words, heavily laced with good intentions.

When Serene hadn't heard from him after their wonderful, yet brief, time together, she felt that was probably a result of teenage indecisiveness or thoughtlessness. Yet she couldn't stop thinking about him. She had argued with herself for weeks, months, before deciding to call him to see how he was doing.

I'm just going to see if everything is going well with him. No expectations, no pressure. It's reasonable for friends to check up on each other. If his mother answers, all the better, we'll chat. I'll use the opportunity to speak with her, letting her get to know something about me. Hopefully, I'll present less of a threat to her family, to her son. After all, I am his friend and I do love him. I would never do him harm. Like any port in a storm is a welcome destination, any rationalization would do in this storm of hunger for his presence in her life.

Serene picked him up at four p.m. They had decided on an early evening dinner to make the most of the day. She noticed right away that he was moving without a noticeable limp or discomfort. It had been months since their last date. He once again looked strong, as she had imagined him in her thoughts and fantasies.

They were sitting together, holding hands on her deep-cushioned living room couch, facing the view with the sliding doors open to the patio. He was once again impressed as he savoured the image of the brilliant, cloud-streaked, red-orange evening sunset over Lake Michigan.

"Well, handsome, it's great see you again."

"Hi, beautiful, sorry that I hadn't been in touch for so long."

"It's okay, Gran, we live in very different worlds. I'm at the hospital; you're busy getting well while finishing up your senior year."

"Yeah, I'll be graduating soon. Hard to believe when I think about it, four more weeks and my life begins a new direction. Feeling wistful and apprehensive."

"And what direction might that be?" Serene couldn't help but wonder if that direction would somehow include their relationship in some fashion.

"I wish I had an answer to that question. I have focussed so much on the process of getting through, I really don't know what to do next. I received my registration notice. I'm thinking about volunteering for the draft."

"Gran, you can't be thinking about going off to war?" Serene's stomach knotted in a fierce spasm of anxiety. "Why, why throw away this young life I've learned to love? Why, Gran, why?"

"Yes, I am. I know it seems insane, yet it's what my fate calls me to do. I know that I will survive. I just can't explain why. I must take this dreaded path through hell's half acre to be who and what I will become. This is not the first tragedy I have danced with. Shit, it won't be my last. Still, I just know that I must do this."

"Why would you want to do that? You can't be serious!" Her ears heard his words, words she could not accept or process. Anger bubbled and roiled beneath her fresh-edged fear. She knew suddenly why he had agreed to the date; not to spend a romantic evening engendering their love. *He's here to say goodbye, to let me down easy.* Her heart sank with the weight of the swirling certainty.

"Things have changed since I saw you last." *Tragic changes that cannot be denied. I thought I could make a success of living here, that through my education I could create a way out. That ship has been sunk by my hand. My direction is clear. I'm focused on how and where I must be, now or never if I'm ever to survive.*

"Must be drastic to prompt you to even entertain such a drastic change of direction. Does your mother know what you're considering?"

"No, she doesn't. I haven't shared this with my family. The reason I wanted to see you is that I thought that I could talk with you about this and get your advice. I just had to talk with someone about this who is not a part of my family. I need you to be my friend. I know you really care for me."

"I am your friend, and yes, I love you, young man. I have had to admit that to myself, despite our age difference. Loving you may be wrong in the eyes of others. I don't care what anyone thinks about what I feel for you. I love you as a woman loves a man, and I am your friend, no matter what you do."

"This will be a test. Are you ready or not? This is bigger than me. It's bigger than both of us, and it's hard to say as well as harder to hear."

"Try me. Be truthful, always, as I'm with you. That's all I require of you.

"Okay, please bear with me. About two months ago, I had sex with a friend from my art class. We got to know each other while we worked on a class project. We worked hard and developed a project that gave us both an A+ for the project and an A for the final subject grade. We started spending many after-school hours on it. We had sex. I say that because she did seduce me. I hadn't any inclination to have sex with her. I saw her as a friend and enjoyed our friendship. I had never been with a girl before; in that regard, I was a virgin. I gave of myself in an unthinkable situation in my home when we were alone. Her name is Validera, and she is about seven weeks pregnant.

"I know that my mom forced Levi to marry Beatrice when she got pregnant while he was in his senior year. She also insisted that Man marry Laura when she got pregnant by him. She was sixteen.

"Validera, whom she does like, shared the news of her pregnancy a couple weeks ago. Mom hasn't tried to persuade me to 'do the right thing' yet, but I'm sure she will soon insist that I follow suit, as did my older brother and sister.

"I am not ready nor interested in this 'shotgun wedding' family tradition. I'm not sure I can resist Mom's pressure to do just that.

"I fear that if I marry Val, 'do the right thing,' it may be right for her, right for our child. Yet, it would be the worst for me. I'd be trapped here in a lovelorn imitation of life in marriage, like all the others, including my mother.

"I like Val very much as a friend. I don't love her, nor do I want to have sex with her again. She was the first girl I have ever had sex with outside of my family."

"Not with your girlfriend?"

"No, Molliah and I have never made love, not for lack of desire. She's not on the pill and doesn't want to risk pregnancy, and neither do I."

"She's a virgin?" *We come so easy to you, yet you respect us, all of us. God, I love your mother.*

"Yes, her mother is a legal secretary in a big firm downtown. Molliah wants to be a lawyer. I love that about her and totally support her ambition. She is determined to have a different life.

"I've spent all my life fighting the violent, oppressive, self- destructive environment that I've lived in. I had my first knock-down, drag-out fight with a bully, Big Buck, a third-grader twice my size in grade one, over a girl he liked who liked me; and I've been fighting them ever since.

"I'm known as the Supreme Gangster, a street moniker that the cops gave me, because I'm not a gang member, yet I fight the gangs alone. I refuse to move away, join them, or die in the fight.

"Remember, we met as a result of an assault by 'Blowhard' George Bellows that was arranged by Black Jesus, the leader of the Vice Lords. The attack was his revenge for my breaking his collar bone during a gang fight. I'm still fighting that gang and the Roman Saints. Before any of them, I was fighting the white gangs. One day, I will lose the fight and they will kill me.

"My Uncle Jake owned a gas station on the corner of our block. He and Aunt Sara worked for thirty years to make their business the best Black-owned business on the near West side. They were a family success story and doing well. The Italian Mafia decided that controlling their station would be a key to establishing dominance in the neighbourhood, but Uncle Jake, my hero, wouldn't sell. So, first they harassed them, the business, and their customers, until they ruined the business, chased away their clientele. When he still wouldn't sell to them, they blew up the station, burning him alive as he tried to save it.

"My only fervent wish is to somehow escape this place. I yearn for a better place in which to live a better life.

"This ghetto is a dream destroyer, a soul killer. I thought being a priest would be my escape through a life within the Catholic faith. Being a pilot would lead me to an exciting, challenging life amidst the clouds, far and away from the maddening crowds of dead-end lifestyles.

"Because of an accident when I was eleven at the Garfield Park Community Pool, I lost my 20/20 sight and my dream of flight. Still, the military can give me training that I can use to build a future in a similar field, help Val with the baby expenses while I'm in training, as well as during my active service. I will be able to attend university when I complete my active duty, as a reservist using the G.I. Bill."

"You know there's a war on; the draft may send you to Vietnam to fight and perhaps die in the jungle."

"As a volunteer, I can get my choice of training, if I qualify. The war is a reality, the eighty-ton elephant sitting on my future. Serene, I've learned, through it all, that I'm a very difficult little guy to kill."

"An easy little guy to love."

Granville blushed; his face became a crimson shade of shyness. Serene was reminded of his youth, his innocence, belied by his youthful experiences, especially the abuse, which hadn't yet tarnished this shy, courageous love-child. Her heart swelled, as she loved him even more for it. Once again, she hungered to be with him, deep inside her.

"Gran, you've mentioned having sex with the women in your family before. I have a difficult question. Have you had sex with boys?"

"Not boys. A man, my second cousin, began raping me when I was thirteen, I think. He is constantly persuading, cajoling, bribing, trying to manipulate me to have sex with him. Thinks he's in love with me. His touch makes my skin crawl, still I've done it with him a few times. I don't know why. I know I'm not gay!

"I love him as my cousin, he has saved my life in a gang fight. If he had not been driving by and seen the fight and come to my aid by joining, I would not have survived. He also got me my first real well-paying job. I always feel like I owe him.

"I hate what he does to me, when I just want to be with him as family."

"I see, so young to be abused in such a manner. He's a grown man and a sexual predator, a master manipulator. You don't stand a chance against him. Does your mother know?"

"Difficult question number two? No, she doesn't. I haven't found the courage to tell her. She needs Dyak Jihad, her cousin. Sometimes, his support is important to her, and I'm afraid of what she'll think of me."

"You're her son; she'll love you and kick him the hell out before she reports him to the police!"

"Incest and infidelity are alive and well in my family; many others would be implicated by DJ. It would tear my family apart."

"Gran, you are far too young to have to shoulder such a heavy burden within your family. I understand how you have such an aversion to keeping secrets."

"The weight of it all is crushing the life out of me."

"Gran, you were sixteen and badly injured when we met, and I was given the opportunity to care for you. We have had some of the most pleasant and meaningful time to get to know each other since that time; better than I have ever had with any man. Now you are seventeen, soon to be eighteen, and contemplating a direction that may expose you to the hell of a war from which you may not return. I long to be with you as a woman loves a man, while I have this opportunity that may never come again. No matter what we do together, now or in the future, I will love you. You're safe with me."

"I know, that's why I love you. Serene, you're my sanctuary."

Serene leaned in toward him slowly, her full lips meeting his in their fullness, a firm softness that enveloped both mouths in hungry abandon.

The heat was instantaneous. Serene pulled him to her, enveloping mouth extended down the length of her body as she used her size to enclose Granville, wrapping his entirety in her long arms and legs. Her soft yet firm pubis straddled his hip, pressing and pulling in the same sensual motion, burning an electrical point of contact with his hip and penis trapped under her inner thigh, firing Granville's mind; exhaling unconsciously, he swooned into her.

Granville's cock began to pulse against her thigh. Feeling the pulse, Serene gently rubbed the hardening shaft and Granville groaned deep down his throat. Their tongue dance intensified. Serene moaned into the kiss, pressing breasts into his chest, hard nipples doing a dance of their own against his.

Their hands began to discover all the places where curiosity had wondered—what it would have been like to touch one another there? Chest- and breast-stroking, swimming in desire and love's celebration.

Serene pressed her young lover down to the plush couch cushions, never losing the full body contact in the process. Clothes, soon becoming a perceived obstacle to the ardent lovers, began to rapidly disappear. Their haste was breathtaking yet non-deterring in their overriding need for physical closeness.

Restraint was no longer an option. Quickly changing to positions of easy access, release was all that mattered as lips and mouths kissed, licked, and sucked cock and clitoris in unison. There, Serene climbed through the first realization of her long-held fantasies to her first eruption.

On the other side of that mountain, she climbed onto the tall peak within her grasp to ride slow and easy, no rush now; white hot embers flared once more.

Granville's balls began to ache as he was pressed deep into the couch cushions by her weight. Stroking and lightly slapping her buttocks, scratching his nails deftly across her lower back, he felt like a horse being ridden while prodding the rider upon him. Serene rode the embers smouldering deep in her vagina as she stretched to swallow his girth, devouring him whole, feeling the eloquent pressure on the mouth of her uterus. An altogether new sensation radiated through her. "Ugh, God damn, size so matters!"

At that moment, suddenly noticing the cool city breeze upon his sweaty body, he turned to see the city lights twinkling on the river mouth leading to the lakefront harbour, realizing that they were in full view of anyone with binoculars or balcony telescope to witness.

Shock sparked a deep belly laugh that bounced her up upon the saddle, catching her attention. Serene, following his gaze and making an evident discovery of her own, joined him in the full, throaty laughter, and the careening, screaming, mutual climax that soon followed.

"YES! Oh, Gran, yes!"

"SERENE! Yesssss!"

...

They were dressed once more, sipping sweet Zinfandel wine in light crystal goblets when the phone rang. "Hello, Serene, I'd like to speak with my son."

"Hello, Ms. Andrea, of course, he's right here . . ." Handing the phone to Granville, Serene felt that Ms. Andrea's conversation with her son would be the proof in the pudding: be it poisonous, intolerable, criminal, credible, or somehow acceptable, given the sexual nature of their relationship. She was so aware that her future was literally in this woman's hands, rightfully so.

"Gran, it's getting late. When can I expect you home?" Ines prayed that he would say, "Mom, she'll drop me off in about an hour or so." Instead, she heard the pronouncement of his independence: too calm, too clear, too self-assured, far too soon.

"Mom, I want to stay the night," said Granville, his tone soft as silk over velvet, practically purred in her ear.

"A new girlfriend?" Her pinched tone belied her sense of betrayal.

"A friend, Mom, a friend, that I need to spend some time with. Molliah is my girlfriend. Mom, it would mean a lot to me. Like the night you had me stay with Bea, as a favour to her. This is like that."

"All right, Gran. This is the way it must be. Tomorrow is my day off. When you are ready to come home, call me and I'll pick you up. I want to meet her again and see her home. We can have brunch together, say around noon."

"She's not working either, so that will be fine, Mom. I really appreciate you're trusting me. I feel safe here." Gratitude, unquiet burst sparkled in his voice, like fireflies lighting the night.

"I do trust you, son. Put Serene on." *Love-child, the hard time of loving you has just begun, letting go. Damn, too soon!*

"Yes, Ms. Andrea?" Serene's mind was anything but serene, bouncing off the walls of her guilt at barriers broken, trust betrayed of the woman she respected more than any other, yet praying that she could forgive the trespass, upon her life and that of her child.

"It's Ines. I'll expect a call around elevenish for brunch at your place at noon, does that work for you?"

"Yes, Ines, that will be fine. Thank you for this time with Gran."

"Serene, please understand, this is hard for me, but my son has always made me stretch outside my comfort zone and sometimes my sanity to love him well, and I've never regretted it; I've grown by it. Anyone who loves him will feel the stretch. Be careful what you wish for."

"I do feel that pull, it's like gravity. I will never betray his welfare or abuse your confidence."

"I trust Gran, and now, I must trust you; so, I'll join you for brunch at twelve tomorrow." Ines's calm, well-measured self-confidence—no-nonsense, mother lioness with claws sheathed for now—meant business.

"Ines, I really appreciate your trust; brunch at noon it is." Serene replaced the phone in its cradle, yet her feet were dancing on marshmallow clouds of relief and quiet joy floating through an azure blue sky. Cautious acceptance, most certainly. She could live with that, loving this boy and his mother.

"How's your appetite, Gran?"

"I'm feeling bit hungry."

"How does pizza sound to you?"

"Sounds great. I believe we've played hard to create the perfect fun food for a fun time, for sure."

"Are you a poet?"

"I will be. I love playing with words and phrases, subtly altering meanings; language can be fun. To be a poet, I'm going to get a bit more living under my belt to have something to say in my poetry."

"I think you already have more living than I would have expected for anyone your age, and you're just getting started."

"Comes with being a lightning rod for trouble."

"That's what I mean. You were giving your mother fits at seven months . . ."

"When my father died."

"Of course, you were there, felt it as she did, no filter."

"That's how I knew of death well before life. Still, I hung on for a month or so and helped her get through it by calming her, giving her a reason to carry on.

"She once lectured my big brother, Levi, about it, after we had a big fight. She told him the story. I overheard them talking when they thought I was asleep, later that night."

"I believe it. As she said, you stretch those who love you. That can be hard. I believe loving you is a stretch, and I feel it. How we are together has certainly never been within my comfort zone. Nonetheless, here I am."

Part 5: "Brunch at Noon . . . It Is"

Ines was impressed with Serene's building. Though she knew that these twin towers held offices as well as apartments, she had sometimes wondered how it would be to live this high up and so close to the river and the lake, yet well above the hustle and bustle of the downtown traffic.

The elevator doors opened immediately upon pressing the button. The ride was almost devoid of the feeling of motion as the floor numbers flashed. When she reached Serene's floor, she paused in the hall to admire the view from the observation platform. *Nice view, to say the least; easy to see how Gran was so impressed by all this. It was a done deal for this woman, as a friend, before he even opened the door to her apartment. I'll bet my pension that it's also furnished to impress and astound my impressionable young man. I must give it to him, he's always had great taste in everything, especially in women.*

"Hello, Ines, please come in."

"Nice place, Serene. I'm impressed, and I don't impress easily."

"Hi, Mom. Thanks for coming."

"This is not my first rodeo, in this regard. Levi and Laura broke ground along this prickly path. Gran, you have disregarded the path altogether to set a new direction, wholly your own. No surprise there."

"So how do buckwheat blueberry waffles, bacon, and eggs strike you, Ines? I'm being adventurous. Seemed suitable for this meal in such a high-risk situation."

"Serene, I like the way you've acknowledged the elephant in the room. I sense that there is more to this conversation than what will be on our plates. I would like to the deal with what is the true purpose of this meeting before we go any further."

"Ines, I agree. Gran does have some important news to share with the most important woman in his world; the meal can wait, so I will say no more."

"Now you're just trying to butter me up. Your diplomacy is appreciated. You best let him speak for himself."

"Mom, I asked to spend the night with Serene because I needed to talk with someone whom I trusted and respected, and her opinion, I could trust. I had to discuss things that I couldn't talk to you about."

"Okay, so it wasn't just sex?"

"Serene didn't seduce me, Mom. We did make love.

Ines's involuntary angry glance at Serene was not missed by her or Granville, who continued, not losing a beat, "I needed to know what it felt like when I'm not being used by someone, sometimes against my will. So, it was mutual between us.

"I have been sexually abused by DJ for more than two years. He raped me that day you had to be taken to the hospital by ambulance because of your bleeding peptic ulcer, and you left him in charge of us. He's always trying to manipulate me into being his 'female' sex partner. I love him for the things he has done to help us. I hate what he does to me."

"Oh, Gran, why didn't you tell?"

"I do hate it! But sometimes I liked it. Mom, I was ashamed. I know it's wrong, sometimes I felt like I was just paying him back. He was always quick to remind me how much he had done for you, me, our family. He saved my life once."

"I remember. BUT he had no right to turn his 'generosity' into an IOU that you had to pay for with your body! I'm going to charge him his ball, for that fucking IOU! Just wait till I see that bastard!" The lioness was fully provoked, claws out, craving blood, revenge, and justice!

She continued, "He called this morning asking to take you to that brand-new roller rink that just opened: the Dr. Martin Luther King Jr. Park. Said you'd probably enjoy it. Just another bribe and excuse for access to rape and abuse you?"

"Yes, ma'am." Quiet now, enough said, filled the room with reverence, born of hard times endured, shame lived as a way of life.

"FUCKKKK!"

Serene watched Ines's rage as she abruptly bounced out of her cushioned recliner to angrily pace the small living room, murmuring death threats and curses, a furious visage; a loose demon in the room, bouncing, roiling through the space, craving a victim. She was relieved when that white-hot Black maternal demon did not alight on her as it flashed by.

Fuck, I see the power here, the source that makes all this worthwhile, no secrets, no more. Mother as Superwoman breathing fire! thought Serene.

"Mom, I'm sorry for not telling you sooner!" Granville blurted, shame no longer contained, breathing the sweet air of freedom that only truth revealed can provide.

"Gran, you have nothing to be sorry for. Baby, I'm sorry for not noticing sooner. I was distracted and so relieved that you had regular quality time with what I thought was solid male attention within the family, not passing through like all the others. I should have seen it myself. We will get through this together."

"Mom, I have been doing a lot of pondering about what has been happening in my life. I feel that my choices are limited at best.

"With Val's pregnancy, expecting twins no less, perhaps it is time for a change. I don't want to marry Val. I like her a lot, but I'm also not convinced the child is mine. I'm just not ready to commit my life to a woman that I do not love.*

"Plus, I know that if I do, I will never escape the ghetto we live in. The same ghetto that killed Uncle Jake. That is, if I can survive the endless hunting. I'm so sick of being prey. Eventually, they will kill me, Mom!"

"Only over my dead body, Gran, that will never happen."

"Mom, you can only protect me if you're there, which will be unlikely when that awful day comes. It'll be the gang against me; no back-up, no escape. I'll fight until the end. I'll be out-numbered, as is always the case, only this time, it will be the end.

"Lastly, Mom, I have decided to enlist in the military. The draft is a certainty because of the war. If I wait to be drafted, I won't be able to choose what field I wish to serve in. Enlisting gives me that option to choose the field, if I qualify, to get the training I want. My income can go to Val to help with the twins from the start. I won't need it. After active duty, as a reservist, I can attend university on the G.I. Bill."

"You want to go off to war?"

"No! This is not something I want to do; it's what I am willing to do, the lesser of several evils. I'm going to get drafted as soon as I turn eighteen. It's happening all around us. The registration centre was full of draftees, almost all of them were eighteen and Black. The handwriting is on the proverbial wall and my name will be there. I want to make it work for me, rather than against me."

The tears of acute frustration welled up in Ines's eyes, hot and near blinding. All her efforts throughout his life suddenly seemed pointless and foolish. She had never wavered from her dedication to his welfare, yet he was willing to risk his precious life in a faraway jungle consumed by war.

Yes, it was true, the impending draft couldn't be avoided; once the call came, there'd be nothing to be done. Still, to volunteer in hopes of something positive out of the opportunity did speak to the wisdom that she had worked so hard to instill in her love child. That, she could not deny or find fault in. His reasoning, his courage of conviction was undeniable.

Once more she must stretch to love her man-child, so much more a man, a child no more.

"Gran, I love you. I understand. I don't have to agree. You're your own man now, and the path you've chosen, I know you'll walk with honour. For that, I'm so very proud of you, young man."

"Thanks, Mom, for understanding, as you always have. I'll make you proud of me."

"One thing that has bothered me for a while, since we are clearing the air of secrets between us. The night you spent with Bea, you said, was like this . . . Did you have sex with her as well?"

"She seduced me while I slept"

"Shit! Anyone else?"

"Her again, with Marcia, the next morning."

"Also had sex with you?"

"Yes, Mom, they knew about DJ. They're all perverse predators that take advantage wherever and whenever possible."

"Has it happened with them since then?"

"No, Mom, I've avoided them ever since. I'm sorry, Mom, for letting you down. I'll make it up to you."

"You already have. Son o' mine, no more secrets?"

"No more secrets, Mom."

"Serene, I think I'm more than ready for waffles, bacon, and eggs. Feel like I just ran a minute mile through twenty hurdles, a long jump, and the pole vault. I'm ready for the Olympics, with an appetite to match."

"Sure thing, Ines, coming right up," she said, giving Ines and Granville her proudest, brightest smile.

Part 6: "Molliah . . . Fond Farewell . . ."

"Hello, Molly, my love." Fear made his throat dry, tight.

Knowing that he had betrayed her trust with Serene was just one of the hard truths he must share with her. Owning up to what he had done, the decisions he'd made, was the hardest aspect of talking his walk. She would likely leave him today. He knew parting would break both their hearts.

"Hi, Gran, how have you been? I feel a little strange having to ask that question of my boyfriend." Molliah was not used to boys disappearing, especially if she showed any interest in them whatsoever, yet Gran, the boy she loved, had done just that. Her heart said, *Listen for truth in his words, his heart still beats for you.* Still, she was pissed!

"Yes, I know I have been distant lately. I'm sorry for vanishing on you, Molly." Into the dragon's maw. Full-blown anxiety was clear in his eyes as they met her raging expression, fiery eyes burning his.

"Good of you to acknowledge it. So what's going on? Have you stopped caring about us?" *Let's get this over with and be done with it.*

"Molly, I still love you. I have been dealing with some very difficult truths about my life and myself. What I'm going to share with you will be very hard on your heart to hear. It will be no less difficult for me to say."

"Do you want to break up with me?" Breath held in calm resolve for whatever came.

"No, but you may want to end our relationship when I finish." *Yet I still love you and will love you, no matter how this ends, Molliah.*

"Please, just spit it out. Let me decide what, if anything, I wish to do or not." *Damn, your tone is killing me.*

"I had sex with my classmate about two months ago. She's pregnant and believes that I am the father." *Something I'm not at all sure of.*

"Are you?" *Don't you dare lie.*

"I don't know. My mother believes her, and at this point, her point of view's all that matters." *She really doesn't give a damn about us, except that I must pay for my play . . . period!*

"I guess that is the truth of it. I don't matter to you?" *The truth . . . Gran!*

"You matter the world to me. Mom pressured my brother and sister into shotgun weddings when Levi's girlfriend Beatrice became pregnant, and when Laura was pregnant with Man's baby.

"I know she is going to try to do the same with me, declaring that I must do the 'right thing' by Validera." *Sooner rather than later, come hell or high water.*

"Validera, is that her name? Do you love her?" *No lie . . . Mr. Andrea!*

"Yes. No. I like her as a friend." *Damn, clear as mud over quicksand!*

"So how did this baby happen between you?" *Be careful. I want all of it.*

"We had been working on an art project together for about three weeks. Sometimes we worked after school because the project was complicated and we both wanted to get an A on it, which would probably mean an A for the course.

"We were walking home together, just talking. She asked if I had a girlfriend, so I told her about you. As we reached my street, which is on the way to her neighbourhood, she then asked if she could use the bathroom in my apartment, since her place was quite a distance further. I thought nothing of it and said that would not be a problem.

"When we went into my place, Mom wasn't home. As you know, I'm latch-key. Val went into the bathroom, and after a while, came out naked!

"I was shocked! Didn't know what to do! Then she walked into me. Was instantly hard. I was so horny! I guess all those nights I went home with a bad case of blue balls after wanting you, making out with you, all that pent-up sexual frustration and hunger got the best of me."

Spare me the details. "So, you're saying she seduced you. Don't you dare try to put that on me, Gran"

"Molly, I'm not trying to excuse my behaviour. I fucked up big time and take responsibility for what I have done." *I'm not a coward.*

"So, what are you going to do about it?" *No bullshit, please.*

"I will not marry Val, yet I must fulfill the responsibility for my role in this mess. The children must be supported. I must do my part." *As best I can.*

"Children!" *Oh shit!*

"Her mother thinks it may be twins." *One or two the consequences remain the same. In for a penny, in for a pound.*

"Mess? This certainly is truly fucked up, Gran!" *God, man, and I love you!*

"Yes. To answer your question, I'm thinking of being proactive in terms of the draft." *More mud in the water, quicksand closer!*

"What do you mean by that?" *Now what?*

"I'm planning to volunteer for the military instead of risking being drafted. When I went down to register for the draft, the registration centre was full of drafted eighteen-year-olds. Almost all of them were Black. The handwriting is on the wall. The army is cleaning out the ghetto of young men like me for 'cannon fodder' in that fucking war in Vietnam. If I volunteer, I can qualify for the type of training I want and possibly avoid the war altogether."

"So, you've sired a set of twins with another girl and are now planning to leave me and go off to war to support them. Do I have all that about right?"

"Maybe. Yes, and no. I'm also very aware that if I don't leave this ghetto, the gangbangers will eventually kill me, as they have been trying to do for years. I'm sick of being hunted. This place doesn't feel like home any longer. It's more like a prison of poverty and the hate is dragging me down as the hate grows within me, choking off my dreams of a better life. I've got to get out!" *Babies or no, I've got to go!*

"The prospect of fighting in the jungles of Vietnam is just another war in another jungle, not much of a deterrent compared to the perpetual guerrilla warfare in this concrete and brick jungle I've been fighting my entire life." *War has been my life, my karma . . .*

"I love you, Molliah, as I love life. From the beginning, I've supported your direction and ambitions. As you must go your own way, so must I seek the truth of my fate, whatever that may be. I can't hide from it, nor can I change it. It's bigger than both of us." *Do you see? Please?*

"I understand. Your fate has always been that of outlier, warrior. And I love you, as well. Perhaps our paths will cross again if the fates allow. Now, I know we must go our separate ways." Clear resignation, thick in her tone, the sound of letting go. The tears, so many tears, would come later.

"Actually, I'm envious of Validera, for she is bearing the connection to you that I was hoping to have one day. Yet, it is what it is; I cannot deny my sense of direction any more than you can. Didn't really believe we would have been able to sustain our relationship through law school, though I felt we were more than worth the effort.

"Your honesty, integrity, and courage are three of the reasons I sought you out as a partner in the first place. Thank you for being clear with me. I wish you well over there. Please contact me when you come home. I'm sure that you will make it through. Farewell, Granville."

"I will. I promise. Fare thee well, Molliah."

Their parting bittersweet, long-held embrace and kiss was as deep and meaningful as was their first, lingering in their hearts long after their longing for each other no longer danced in their dreams.

...

Validera's Phoenix was born with her twin sister Phaedra to an absentee father. Phoenix, the smallest twin, died three weeks later.

Parent trap refugee . . . doing the right thing's not for the other. Chasing a dream of freedom in government-issue gear.

Validera's mother knew he would never return.

Whether he lived or died in the war . . . He was gone forever. An aching poisoned pit inside . . . owned.

-"I Am an Honourable Man" (Excerpt) . . . by Granville Johnson

...

Epilogue:
To Dance

· · · · ·

GRANVILLE'S BAGS WERE packed and stored in the luggage rack above his seat. He wasn't carrying much: sentimental keepsakes; family photos; letters from Mom, Laura, Serene, and Molliah; several changes of shirts, pants, t-shirts, underwear, socks; a jacket; his dress shoes; his treasured Converse All-Star gym shoes; and some spending money to tide him over.

Orders designating his first assignment—United States Army Basic Training, Fort Polk, Louisiana—were in his light jacket pocket, burning in its finality. Alone among many recruited young men wishing this choice away.

...

Train's throb, a pitter-patter drumbeat on his heart . . .
Quiet, fearful tears, streaking reflection, mirrors his anxiety . . . speak of
loss amidst discovery's trust, flashing through coach's opaque dust.
So much fear, so much hope, dream's remembrance released as
improvable mountains yet to climb. Goodbye, good riddance to paths
well-trod. Wonder in the wander through forest dark, sun-drenched
sky fills the mind. Live the choice chosen when none other had risen
to save the life after all has given, to the best of you yet to be driven to
the madness of war. Kill for country paints a hero to some, yet a being
monstrous alien.
Home forsaken, universe awakens, forever more . . . to dance.

BACKSTORY II

THE Many Lives
OF Granville Johnson

Warning: Violence, Graphic Sex, Rape, Racism.

Printed in the USA
CPSIA information can be obtained
at www.ICGtesting.com
JSHW011020120224
57163JS00010B/26

9 781039 184114